ELEVATING EQUITY

Advice for Navigating
CHALLENGING CONVERSATIONS
in Early Childhood Programs

Angela Searcy, EdD

www.gryphonhouse.com

Copyright

© 2023 Angela Searcy

Published by Gryphon House, Inc.
P. O. Box 10, Lewisville, NC 27023
800.638.0928; 877.638.7576 [fax]
Visit us on the web at www.gryphonhouse.com.

All rights reserved. No part of this publication may be reproduced or transmitted in any form or by any means, electronic or technical, including photocopy, recording, or any information storage or retrieval system, without prior written permission of the publisher. Printed in the United States. Every effort has been made to locate copyright and permission information.

Cover images used under license from Shutterstock.com. Image on page 131 courtesy of Lena Searcy; other interior images courtesy of the author.

Library of Congress Control Number: 2022947537

Bulk Purchase

Gryphon House books are available for special premiums and sales promotions as well as for fund-raising use. Special editions or book excerpts also can be created to specifications. For details, call 800.638.0928.

Disclaimer

Gryphon House, Inc., cannot be held responsible for damage, mishap, or injury incurred during the use of or because of activities in this book. Appropriate and reasonable caution and adult supervision of children involved in activities and corresponding to the age and capability of each child involved are recommended at all times. Do not leave children unattended at any time. Observe safety and caution at all times.

Dedication

This book is dedicated to my family. The reason I am an author today is because my mother, Mathrell Nelson, called my teachers to make sure I did my homework and because my father, Freeman Nelson, Jr., laughed out loud when I told him my stories as a preschooler.

This book is also dedicated to all the children and educators of the world and to anyone who elevates equity.

Table of Contents

Acknowledgments vii

Introduction 1

Chapter 1: Labeling, Bias, and Empathy. 7

Chapter 2: What Young Children Understand about Differences and Equity 37

Chapter 3: What This Means for Early Childhood Educators 59

Chapter 4: Equity and Families of Young Children. 113

Chapter 5: Understanding Historical Trauma 153

Chapter 6: Elevating Equity with Your Staff 175

Chapter 7: Pushing Past Conflict with Adults. 205

References and Recommended Reading. 239

Index 271

Acknowledgments

A higher power wrote this book, and I am grateful to glorify Him! I want to thank my husband, Reginald B. Searcy, Jr., for your love, support, and ideas such as the "kids' bill of rights." I want to thank our children, Daniel, Maya, Lena, and Zaria Searcy, who hold me accountable to elevate equity every day. Lena and Zaria, thank you both for your art contributions. Thank you to my sister Lisa Wilkerson for always keeping good quotes of inspiration coming. A special thanks to my friends at Erikson Institute, Kaplan Early Learning Company, and Gryphon House who started me on this journey. A special thanks to Stephanie Roselli and Jennifer Lewis for believing in me and giving me this great opportunity! Thank you to Jacob's Electronic Data Recovery and Repair in Oak Forest, Illinois, for recovering my manuscript when I broke my flash drive not once but twice, and to Tamara Kaldor who suggested the idea! Thank you to all my cousins on my Facebook side for your contributions. Thank you to Jane Elliott, Dr. Barbara Beale Spencer, Dr. Bruce Perry, and the teachers and families who contributed their stories to this book.

I wrote this book for my ancestors, who weren't allowed to.

Introduction

I started my career as a preschool teacher in 1990 in the yellow room. Who better than a former preschool teacher who grew up constantly navigating statements like "You're not my friend" and "You can't come to my party" to write about equity?

I continued my exploration of equity during my doctoral studies, and my dissertation on behavior provided alternatives to exclusionary discipline to ensure equity and inclusion for young children. That research grew into my first book, *Push Past It! A Positive Approach to Challenging Classroom Behaviors*, which provides a laundry list of steps for dealing with challenging behaviors in young children. The first steps include sorting out personal feelings and identifying any implicit bias. In that book, I introduce research showing that high levels of emotional support result in positive changes in child behaviors. After my doctorate, my action-based research project for my infant and early childhood mental-health certificate explored the efficacy of tools created in *Push Past It!* that focus in mindfulness and empathic responses when intense challenging classroom behaviors occur. My research fits within a body of scientific literature demonstrating the power of positivity.

Since then, I have developed "What Is Said in the Teachers' Lounge," a tool to help educators identify bias. In this book, I use the same positive approach as I sharpen my focus and broaden my audience on typically divisive social topics. Often topics of race, language, gender, class, immigration status, sexual orientation, religion, or ability are framed as "difficult" or "uncomfortable." While this perspective acknowledges the feelings of discomfort these conversations might evoke in adults, it might inadvertently miss the opportunity to acknowledge the discomfort, frustration, confusion, or awkwardness that silence on these topics might evoke in children or adults.

> **I am not calling anyone out. I am calling you in, with love.**

Okay, before we dive in, I want you to keep in mind that this book is a gathering place for all of us to learn together. Yes, when I appear on a morning news show, the commentator will call me an "expert" on child development or equity. And yes, I have been working in the field of education since I was a nap-time teacher. I moved on from teaching to experiences as a child developmental specialist, pediatric neurodevelopmental therapist, educational consultant, and researcher. But I am not going to sit here and pretend I am some sort of vessel of wisdom who knows everything there is to know about equity and who is now going to teach it to you. I may sound smart, but to be honest, I can't even remember all my passwords.

CULTURAL HUMILITY IS...

- **active, ongoing engagement in a lifelong process.** For example, engagement happens every month at your equity affinity group at work.

- **continuous self-reflection and critique.** For example, using journaling to reflect on your experiences around equity or having an equity committee to reflect on the policies at your business.

- **acknowledgment of power imbalances.** For example, "I am this person's boss, and even if I consider them my workplace BFF, I have to admit there is a power imbalance when I lead a staff meeting."

- **a modest view of oneself and respect for others.** For example, saying, "I could be wrong."

What This Book Is About

This book is grounded in the principles of cultural humility. Originally developed by medical doctors Melanie Tervalon and Jann Murray-García (1998), *cultural humility* is defined as follows:

> [It] is best defined not by a discrete endpoint but as a commitment and active engagement in a lifelong process that individuals enter into on an ongoing basis. It is a process that requires humility as individuals continually engage in self-reflection and self-critique as lifelong learners and reflective practitioners. It is a process that requires humility in how [we] bring into check… power imbalances… And it is a process that requires humility to develop and maintain mutually respectful and dynamic partnerships… (Tervalon and Murray-Garcia, 1998; Chávez, 2012).

When it comes to cultural competency, social worker and educator Ruth Dean (2001) argues we are constantly learning about culture because it is continually changing. Dean asserts that our differences, beliefs, and biases are inevitably active. In other words, equity is an ongoing conversation that is always evolving. Just like my hairstyles and fashion choices, the limit on those changes does not exist. A study by researcher Kiara Sanchez and colleagues (2021) found that having these discussions may lay the foundation for making relationships between friends and colleagues stronger. Another study by Jocelyn Glazier and colleagues (2000) even showed that once participants started talking about a topic such as culture, they wanted to keep talking about it and continued to have literacy circles on the topic after a course on the subject had ended.

On the opposite end of the spectrum, call-out culture can potentially create resentment and embarrassment instead of engagement in conversations that could lead to learning. The Urban Dictionary defines *call-out culture* as "a group of people, especially on social media, who ridicule others for real or perceived words or actions that go against their beliefs." Drawing attention to a problem is one facet of activism. And not having difficult conversations does not mean there is no discomfort; it only means no one is talking about it. It is also important to acknowledge that the reason we often avoid these conversations is because we care so much about others and don't want to make a misstep. However, author Cheryl Richardson once said, "If you avoid conflict to keep the peace, you start a war inside yourself." No matter where you are in the discussion, when we elevate equity, the discussion is always a safe space in which we practice humility and don't silence anyone or call anyone out. Instead, as professor and activist Loretta J. Ross (2021) suggests, we call people in, with love, to learning.

This book is based on the premise that no matter how many times someone encounters the topic of equity, they have the opportunity to expand their competency. Throughout the book, I offer exercises to encourage reflection and discussion. My reflective questions are as much for my learning as yours. I supply tools to help you elevate equity in your home, at school, with the children and families you serve, and with your colleagues.

How to Use This Book

This book provides evidenced-based strategies for elevating equity and navigating challenging conversations that occur in early childhood programing. Chapter 1 helps us to understand more about ourselves and makes a case for why it is important to elevate equity. Chapters 2 and 3 discuss what very young children know about equity and what this means for early childhood educators. Chapter 4 addresses issues of equity and the families of young children. Chapter 5 looks at historical trauma and how to respond as educators to children and families. Chapters 6 addresses equity and the professional environment, and the last chapter helps us to understand how to deal with conflict at work when it arises.

When researching for this book, I was surprised to discover that conflict is a part of the human condition, and even in the best of circumstances, it is inevitable. So, instead of "burning that bridge when we come to it"—a saying attributed to German writer Johann Wolfgang von Goethe and set to music by American artist Jimmy Buffet (1984)—this book gives professionals the skills that help them elevate equity and turn conflict in to collaboration. Each chapter provides reflective questions and activities for a book study, training, or consultation. My goal is to help improve relationships among the adults who work on behalf of young children. To elevate equity for children, we must first elevate ourselves. Equity is not something we just talk about but is something that must be experienced and executed intentionally every day. As a result, the following chapters also provide concrete tools that help bring equity into action and flip the script on conflict.

This book also builds on information from my previous book *Push Past It! A Positive Approach to Challenging Classroom Behaviors* (2019). You can find it by using this QR code:

My author page on the Gryphon House website includes worksheets and other useful information from that book that will help you elevate equity. You can find them using this QR code:

Together, we will learn, reflect, and grow. This is a lifelong process. American psychologist Jerome Bruner suggested that learning is one continuous, ongoing spiral. If you prefer to learn life lessons from rock and roll, a saying attributed to singer Maynard James Keenan stated, "A circle is the reflection of eternity. It has no beginning and it has no end—and if you put several circles over each other, then you get a spiral." My hope is to keep that spiral going.

CHAPTER 1

Labeling, Bias, and Empathy

"Colorblindness"

I remember my first-grade teacher saying, "I don't see color." I thought, "Well, if we aren't supposed to see it, and I am the only girl in this classroom that has it, having color must not be a good thing." As a result, at six years old, I began to feel shame about my color. I had the thing we were not supposed see or talk about. And since my teacher said good character was measured by not seeing color, I began to actively suppress anything associated with it. The good character of other children was also measured by how much they were able to actively ignore it. I got the message that I could talk about race only with my family or other people of color. But I was the only Black girl in my class until fourth grade, so this took a lot of effort on my part. At times, I felt lonely and isolated. It was alluded to that I should be grateful the school was so kind to ignore my imperfection. My family told me that, in the past, a Black girl going to a white school had led to violence. I felt I would be ungrateful to complain because people had died for me to have this opportunity. But I still felt sad at times because I couldn't share large parts of who I was as a person.

Right or wrong, I also never told anyone when other children said racist things to me, because all the adults in my school had made it clear race should be ignored. I still remember feeling very alone because it also didn't seem socially acceptable to share any burdens or fears I felt. I was raised in a largely white, upper-middle-class community, and looking back, I guess I thought it was a measure of kindness for me to not make anyone else feel uncomfortable. I took on the task of adjusting myself to make adults and children feel comfortable. I remember feeling great fear that my family would not be welcome in places due to our race and the fact that my father was in a wheelchair. I felt a burden that I could never share with the majority of my friends from school.

Years later, I was inspired by the death of George Floyd to start having conversations about race and equity with people outside of my community of people of color—for the first time in my life. It seemed that that moment, occurring during a global pandemic, grabbed everyone's attention and resulted in people seeking conversations about race and equity. My family and I have lived in a majority-white neighborhood for the last fifteen years, and the summer of 2020 was the first time my very close friend and neighbor Jodie asked me what it was like living someplace that has so few Black people. I didn't end up sharing any of our challenges in our community, but her comment made me feel seen and cared for, and it deepened our friendship.

One of my best friends from high school, Kathy, and I also had our first conversation about race that same summer. We have been friends since we were fourteen. When I told her how I felt about the term *colorblind*, she said something that surprised me: "Ang, if I had known you felt this way, I would have supported you." She went on to share a similar situation about a friend who was gay. She said she wished I would have shared this part of my life with her. There was a whole context surrounding why I hadn't shared any of this with Kathy and which I now realize had nothing to do with her. Because adults and children had always seemed uncomfortable when I mentioned race, I learned by what *wasn't* said not to bring up the subject. Now, I understand how not talking about race diminished our relationship. I wish I had taken a chance on sharing, and Kathy wonders if she could have done more to make me feel safe enough to do so. Don't worry—we are still life-long friends. (We even rehabbed a house together!) But I learned a valuable lesson: If your friend never talks about all parts of their identity, do they feel safe sharing everything with you?

If you live by the seemingly harmless mantra, "I don't see color," consider what Dr. Bernice King, daughter of Dr. Martin Luther King, Jr., shared about the term *colorblind* in an interview with the host of *The Tonight Show*, Jimmy Fallon: "People are always saying Dr. King was for a colorblind America, and nothing could be further from the truth… He was basically explaining that, no, there's a beauty in who I am as a Black person, but I should not be judged by those standards. It's not that you don't see my race. You see my race. You acknowledge my race. And you accept everything I bring along with that" (King, 2020).

In her TEDx Talk "Color Blind or Color Brave?" finance executive Mellody Hobson (2014) acknowledges that even though talking about race can be "the conversational equivalent of touching the third rail," she thinks it is "time for us to be comfortable with the uncomfortable conversation about race." She elaborates, "We cannot afford to be color blind. We have to be color brave. We have to be willing—as teachers and parents and entrepreneurs and scientists—we have to be willing to have proactive conversations about race with honesty and understanding and courage, not because it's the right thing to do, but because it's the smart thing to do, because… all… will be better with greater diversity."

Turns out talking about all aspects of children's identities might actually be the secret to ending inequity. Researchers Sarah Gaither, Samantha Fan, and Katherine Kinzler (2020), set out to explore just that idea. They looked at a diverse set of school-age children. Those who were reminded of their multiple social identities (sons, daughters, readers, friends, and so on) were more likely to show advanced problem-solving. For children, something as simple as thinking about their identities from multiple perspectives could potentially decrease rigid thinking and increase the open-mindedness needed for equity. The book *The Development of the Social Self*, edited by Bennett and Sani (2004), discusses that having a positive view of one's identity is important for children's healthy development. Researchers Ana Marcelo and Tuppett Yates (2019) found having a positive identity can be a protective factor that lowers the impact of adverse experiences for children who are part of groups marginalized by the dominant society. Another study showed self-identification and knowledge of one's ethnicity is related to positive functioning at home and at school (Serrano-Villar and Calzada, 2016). If you still aren't convinced that talking about children's social identities is important, another study by Andrei Cimpian and colleagues (2012) found that when children mistakenly believe their performance is due to an uncontrollable part of their identity and internalize stereotypes such as "Boys are good at this game," it can negatively affect their performance.

The colorblind approach could shut down conversations that children of color might have around a salient part of their identity and could distort the reality for white children who want to know about their friends and support them. Moreover, clinical and community psychologist Riana Anderson states that adults talking about their own experiences and improving racial-socialization competency could help prevent negative psychological outcomes in children (Anderson, Saleem, and Huguley, 2019). "Some educators [and families] believe that it is noble to avoid looking directly at race, arguing that if we do not introduce youth to the concept, they will maintain a naturally unbiased stance toward others. However… evidence suggests that the real damage occurs when we choose not to talk to our students explicitly about race and racism (Hughes et al., 2006)."

Silence Is Not Always Peace

Even though many of us have been raised to believe "… ignoring race is… a graceful, even generous… gesture" (Morrison, 1992), American poet and National Youth Poet Laureate Amanda Gorman reminds us in her poem "The Hill We Climb" that silence does not mean peace, and injustice is occurring whether we discuss it or not. We cannot fight injustice with more injustice through silence or inaction. Dr. Martin Luther King, Jr., told us in his book *Strength to Love* (1963), "Darkness cannot drive out darkness; only light can do that. Hate cannot drive out hate; only love can do that." This book offers some tools to apply those principles. Keep in mind that injustice is interconnected, and if we are all acting in a spirit that elevates equity, we are elevating not only ourselves but society. We all have a shared experience of oppression, and if your friend is not sharing their experiences around this topic, then I hate to break it to you, but you don't know your friend. We are all sending messages each day about equity—whether we are conscious of it or not.

My Story

> As I tell my story, I want to write down all the feelings you are experiencing as you read. This isn't a debate, so you don't need to choose a side or pour any energy into deciding who is right or wrong. Instead, focus on what you are feeling and the intensity of those feelings. Keep in mind all feelings are welcome—including ones that contradict mine. This isn't an "I believe _____ and therefore you should" kind of book. Each of my stories is meant to lovingly call everyone into learning and help you to reflect on your own story.

Let's go back in time to the fall of 1981, when Rick Springfield was topping the charts with a song about Jessie's girl, and there was a new show on TV called *Dynasty*. We had just moved into our new house, and I was excited to have one of my friends from school over. I don't remember who that friend was, but I do remember more than forty years later that her parents never found our house. Keep in mind that GPS and cell phones didn't exist back in 1981, and I just remember sitting there waiting for what seemed like hours thinking about my friend's visit with anxiety. Unfortunately, she didn't make a visit to my house that evening. What I didn't know was this would be the first of many "lost" friends, not because our house was hard to find but because the adults driving already had an image of what the house of the only Black family on the block should look like. If they finally did find our home, they would always say, "Oh, we passed the house so many times." It was not lost on my nine-year-old intellect that Black people or anyone working at our house always found the house with no issue.

To shed further light on the situation, I was the only Black girl in my class until the fourth grade. (My classmates were mostly white and Asian.) I will never forget one of my friends telling me they thought I lived in the brown house with shutters or the green house without any landscaping, and how it never looked like we were home and had no furniture. I told my friend that was because that brown house with shutters was an empty house that was for sale and the green house was a new house still under

Chapter 1: Labeling, Bias, and Empathy | **11**

construction. How are you going to make my house a vacant house? How could I live in a home not fully constructed? How can you see an address and still not believe your own eyes when you see a beautiful house with well-manicured grass greener than Wrigley Field? (My parents loved our automatic sprinkler system).

My parents just laughed at how ridiculous that was, and I took their cue and joined them. Then my father would begin to tell a barrage of jokes about people and their assumptions. This put into place my coping mechanism going forward, and I began to use humor to think about how my race affected my friends' and their families' behavior: "Now you know my house isn't going the look like a project from the show *Good Times*, right? Your mother isn't the only one who reads *Better Homes and Gardens*!" The funny thing is, I never said these jokes out loud. The behavior of adults showed me that I could only share these humorous moments with other people of my race. Way before the age of nine, I had already internalized that it was impolite to talk about race among mixed groups. As a result, I learned to endure any upsetting feelings about race alone in silence until I felt better.

Psychiatrist Bruce Perry and colleagues (1995) describe how the temporary emotional states children experience can become enduring traits. Although Perry and his team look through the lens of trauma, this approach also gives great insight into how these states of mind become states of being and how injustice can endure generation after generation. (My story highlights an implicit-bias action, but my silence didn't draw attention to that action. As a result, my silence helped maintain it.)

> Now look at the words you wrote about my story. Are your words positive, negative, or a mix? Do you feel hot? frustrated? indifferent? How strong are your feelings? After reading my story, some of you might think, "Here we go again!" or "Aren't there two sides to every story?" You might think, "There could've been many reasons they couldn't find the house! Why is everyone so obsessed with race?" or even "What about when people of color…" Still, some might be having a "me too" reaction or even feelings of anger, sympathy, or sadness.

Whatever words you wrote down or feelings you experienced, that is what your brain and body *should* be doing. The intention of my story is not to cancel or call anyone out. I am not angry at anyone, and I'm still connected to all my childhood friends—even the ones who couldn't find my house—on social media. If you have had a similar experience to mine, you might be thinking about that. If your experience was different, you might be thinking about that.

The purpose of this story and this book is to get you thinking about equity and actions that might uplift equity. All experiences and ideas are welcome here. Different perspectives and stories are not in conflict with one another. We are often so preoccupied with picking a side that we forget equity is about listening to someone else and actively eliciting a variety of perspectives (Zhou, Majka, and Epley, 2017). Everyone on the same page makes for a short book of knowledge. Unless it is violent or hurtful, every idea has a space in our ongoing elevation of equity.

Empowering with Equity

Don't get me wrong. I do understand how these types of discussions can be awkward, painful, and even gut-wrenching, but characterizing our conversations only by their potential problems is a narrow discourse that can lead to what is termed in education a *deficit lens*. A deficit lens involves viewing a person, group, or topic primarily in terms of their perceived deficits, dysfunctions, problems, needs, or limitations. If you focus only on what's wrong with something, you aren't going beyond the surface far enough to understand how to make things right. It is important to use a strength-based lens when describing individuals or ideas to discover the potential problems along with the potential possibilities. I want to get you excited about equity!

A deficit lens can conjure up feelings of sympathy, which involves viewing an idea through your own lens. Framing the topic this way also runs the risk of alienating those who might already feel marginalized by associating their identity with something negative and might provide yet another roadblock toward engaging in conversation. Empathy and a strengths-based lens, on the other hand, involve understanding the meaning behind an idea from the perspective of others.

Simply put, as a Black woman, it sometimes becomes tiresome that parts of my identity are being associated only with negativity, pain, or trauma. Historical injustices are one part of my experience. While these are important to understand, I also crave discussions about my identity that don't involve conflict or "big" feelings that require me to be courageous. I have a range of feelings around my identity that include joy, pain, fear, pride, and an abundance of love. I remember once having a discussion about race and being told to "go big or go home." I think they underestimated my ability to go home. Sometimes I like going home. And taking a long nap when I get there.

Unpleasant or Unprocessed and Unpracticed?

Discussions about identity aren't inherently unpleasant, but our feelings about these topics are often unprocessed, so the ability to navigate them is typically unpracticed. Anything unpracticed can feel uncomfortable. For example, you might not like playing the piano until you have had many opportunities to practice playing the piano. And for those of you among the "I don't need any practice—I already love everybody" crowd, Fred Rogers (2003) put it best: "Love isn't a state of perfect caring. It is an active noun like *struggle*. To love someone is to strive to accept that person exactly the way he or she is, right here and now." To accept a person, you must accept all parts of them, which will include great pain but also great joy.

Even though Mister Rogers offered a place to feel fully accepted, I would often call into question whether I wanted to introduce any type of "struggle" into my home, classroom, or workplace. And let's be honest: I don't know about you, but I already have a lot on my plate. As an educator, I am already counting down the days to summer break. As a wife, I just fired myself from cleaning my own house. (I didn't like my attitude.) And as a mother, who knew elementary-school math would be the hardest part of parenting? Now I need to save the world by empowering everyone with equity?

Instead, together we will think about equity in everyday moments, to make it manageable. For example, instead of devoting my energy toward evaluating whether a conversation is on one side or the other, I've decided to just have conversations and to put my best foot forward while embracing the spirit of equity. In my discussions about identity with educators, families, and friends, I've noticed that people sometimes back away or even worry about "uncomfortable conversations," but I've been hard pressed to find anyone who objects to equity. As a result, this book takes a positive approach to these topics by embracing differences, acknowledging how others might be at different levels of equity based on what they've got on their plate, the topic, and the time of day.

It encourages us all to elevate equity within small yet meaningful everyday interactions that we are already doing. Yes! Reclaiming your time.

The book meets you at whatever equity level you choose. I want you to realize how much you already know about the topic. (Remember the last time you wanted to revolt because you didn't get the biggest pizza slice?) I want to build the knowledge you already possess to the highest level.

This book might include ideas you don't agree with, and I am sure you have your own opinions on equity—and I respect that. So, do you mind if we just skip the "I agree or disagree part" and move right into the "seeking to understand" part? If it makes you feel more comfortable, focus on what you might gain from elevating equity. Try to understand that my ultimate goal is not to change your mind but to open your heart. I just want to make a connection to what you do believe.

Who Are You and What Do You Believe?

Let's engage in an exercise. Take out a piece of paper and a pen, pencil, or markers. Draw a home and your family. Include what is comfortable for you from the list below. The goal is to explore your identity in an inclusive way that allows you to reflect on your unique life circumstances. If a question is uncomfortable or triggering, skip it or adapt it to make it work for you. You are always in charge of how you will engage in the exercises in this book. Feel free to adapt or add to the list below.

- Who are the people who live in your home? Remember, family members are not always blood related. Think of the VIPs in your life! This is an inclusive view of family that is a compilation of the people who are important to you. Or make a list of the people you wish you had in your life.
- Next, label where your home is located. Where do you come from? You could write down your city, state, province, or country. You could write down your school or that you come from a spirit of peace. Think about your community and where it is located. If you wish, you can label where you are going instead of where you are from.

- On the mailbox, label all your identities: wife, husband, partner, father, mother, sister, teacher, Black, white, Latina, dog owner, hamster mom, and so on. Who are you? How do you identify?
- Next, at the foundation for your home list your strengths.
- Draw and label the foods cooking in the kitchen.
- What celebrations happen in your home?
- What books or magazines are in your home?
- What kinds of art do you display? How is your home decorated?
- What is on TV? What music is playing?
- At the top of the house, write down your values. For example, are you goal oriented? Or do you think taking each day as it comes is more important? Do you value healthy competition or collaboration? Make a list of things that are important in the way you live your life. What is significant to you? What motivates you?
- Now, on the back of your paper, list groups you are in.

Here is my example:

This clever art activity has a larger purpose of helping you create an identity chart. It is intended to help you consider the many factors that shape who you are as an individual. Identity charts help deepen our understanding of ourselves and, potentially, how we interact with those around us.

As I ask this of you, I am reminded of a famous quote by martial artist and philosopher in his own right Bruce Lee (1971): "You know what I want to think of myself? As a human being. Because… under the sky, under the heavens there is but one family." This powerful statement is true; however, Lee followed it with, "People are different." You don't need to choose between one idea or the other—both are true. This exercise is meant to

16 | Elevating Equity: Advice for Navigating Challenges in Early Childhood Programs

BRINGING EQUITY TO THE FAMILY TREE PROJECT

Families can have complex histories that include historical trauma such as slavery, the Holocaust, or internment camps. Families can have trauma such as death, divorce, incarceration, foster care, or adoption. When asking children or adults to explore their identity and family, it is important to be inclusive and trauma informed.

- Ask the students (pre-K and older) how they want to explore their families, and make a list of ways to make the activity inclusive of all types of families and experiences.

- Before creating a family tree project, ask families how they want to explore this topic or issues that might be sensitive by sending them a survey.

- Give many alternatives and options. For example, children could trace their family lineage or explore family traditions.

- Instead of asking for a picture of someone's family, offer a choice to share a photo or a drawing or a special object that represents their family.

- Let the person choose what to include in the project.

- Families don't have to be blood relations. *Family* includes the important people in a person's life. Consider a "people tree" instead of a "family tree."

- Older students can interview someone else about that person's family instead of their own.

- Students can research the family of someone they admire.

- Create a family tree of the family you wish you had or that of someone famous.

You can find more ideas at
https://www.boredteachers.com/post/family-tree-alternatives

deepen our understanding of ourselves and how we interact with those around us in the name of equity and inclusion. I realize that identity charts can evoke strong emotions. Keep the following in mind.

Your List Is a Fluid One

Fluidity means that how you identify yourself is always changing and evolving. Identity is complex, and discourse around it should allow for a nuanced discussion. For example, as a professional I was always trained to use the term "special needs" to describe someone with a disability. But the use of the label *disabled* keeps changing. In one study, researchers Erin Andrews and colleagues (2019) explored the rationale behind the #SaytheWord movement, a social-media call to embrace disability identity. They argue that erasing the word *disability* can have unintended, adverse consequences, such as the reduction or elimination of services. To know whether someone prefers the label of "special needs" or *disabled*, one must always ask.

No One Else Can Label You or Put You in a Group

I remember I once called myself skinny, and a woman "corrected" me and stated I was thin. Girl, I am skinny! No one else can tell you who you are or "fix" your label. In fact, research by Alan Galinsky and colleagues (2013) showed self-labeling and reappropriating what might be considered a negative label makes people feel more powerful. Research by Donna Talbot (2008) showed that self-made labels are empowering to the individuals who create them, and further study by Colleen Butler-Sweet (2011) showed stress doesn't occur from self-labeling. Stress occurs when individuals outside of you try to place a label on you.

No One Outside Your Group Can Label Your Group

Many times, a group of people will develop a label for themselves as a way of expressing the experiences they have in common. However, when those outside of that group begin using that label without understanding its origin, they can they can rob that label of its intent and power. You might be surprised to learn that I am very sensitive to labeling someone as having "white privilege" (McIntosh, 1989) or "white fragility" (DiAngelo, 2018). "White privilege" became part of our lexicon when Peggy McIntosh created the label to describe her experience as a white woman. "White fragility" is term coined by Robin DiAngelo to describe her experience when she talked to other white people about racism. These labels have garnered both praise and criticism. Some have described the terms as helpful, and some describe them as hurtful. Those are self-imposed labels that are accepted by some and not accepted by others, because not all people feel the same about them. As a Black woman, I can read about that experience and understand a definition, but I don't use the term because I am not white. I am cautious about labeling someone, especially when it comes to groups I am not a part of. As a woman of color, the phrase *People of Color* is a self-created label intended to put people first before color. However, Loretta Ross reminds us of the complexity of labels and "how people will begin to slot in the new terms for the old [ones] without thinking too much about how the new terms are different" (Grady, 2020). Jonathan Rosa, a sociocultural and linguistic anthropologist at Stanford, reminds us that People of Color, or POC, and BIPOC, which stands for Black, Indigenous, and People of Color, were meant to be terms of solidarity. However, those terms can lose their nuance when used indiscriminately and "can blur the differences between the two groups [they are] meant to center" (Grady, 2020).

Depending on the context and discussion, it can be useful to focus on inclusivity, a shared positionality, and how groups are connected. At other times, it can be more valuable to specifically name that a group individually and can even be confusing and even hurtful to lump very different types of people into one catchall label. I have a degree in English and agree with linguistics student deandre miles-hercules, who reminds us to understand the history and the different semantic valences of a particular term before using a word or label, to decide for yourself "the appropriateness of a use in a particular context" (Grady, 2020).

Ivory A. Toldson, a professor of counseling psychology at Howard University, provides a critique of the label "at risk" that is often used to describe groups. Toldson contends that, when accompanied with good data, the label "at risk" can useful to identify risk and protective factors, but using the word as an adjective is problematic. "If the phrase 'at-risk' must be used," he says, "it should be in a sentence such as: 'This' places students at risk for 'that.' If the 'this' and 'that' are not clearly defined, the 'at-risk' characterization is useless at best, and harmful at worst" (Toldson, 2019). Organizations such as the National Black Child Development Institute (NBCDI) challenge narratives that overemphasize limitations and deficits. Instead, they "celebrate the considerable strengths, assets, and resilience demonstrated by our children, families, and communities" (NBCDI, 2014). "When these variables are clearly defined, it better enables educators and others to come up with the solutions needed to reduce specific risk factors and improve outcomes" (Toldson, 2019).

> **LANGUAGE TO ELEVATE LABELS**
>
> An *adjective* is defined as a "word or phrase naming an attribute" (Quizlet, 2023). However, "at risk," *underrepresented*, *underserved*, and *marginalized* are conditions one is placed in by structural inequalities; these are not attributes. Language matters! In the chart below, I elevate equity by putting people first and labeling who is being affected, labeling the problem, and labeling what or who is causing the problem.
>
> | INSTEAD OF: | TRY: |
> |---|---|
> | *Marginalized* or *underserved* communities | "Communities whose needs are not prioritized by _____" or "Communities who are historically excluded from _____" |
> | *At-risk* students | "Students can be placed at risk for lower test scores due to _____" |
> | *Underrepresented* groups | "_____ group who are underrepresented due to inequitable hiring practices in _____ industry" |

Social Constructs and Access to Equity

A *social construct* is an idea that has been created and accepted by the people in a society. For example, economic class or workplace hierarchies are both social constructs. Psychologist Urie Bronfenbrenner (1979) was one of the first to consider how our development is influenced by everything around us—called Ecological Systems Theory. Psychologist Margaret Beale Spencer and colleagues (Spencer, Dupree, and Hartmann, 1997) expanded on Bronfenbrenner's idea and provided a framework called the Phenomenological Variant of Ecological Systems Theory. (Look, if you can say *Beyoncé*, you can say *phenomenological*. But if you are having any trouble, just do as I do and call it PVEST for short.) One component of PVEST is how protective factors and risk factors operate in tandem with one another. In a nutshell, the theory explains how each individual has a unique combination of characteristics at the biological, psychological, family, community, and cultural levels that could increase the likelihood of negative outcomes, as well as protective factors that could increase the probability of positive outcomes and reduce the impact of factors that place us at risk. Both Bronfenbrenner's theory and PVEST can give us some insight into our own access to equity and how to elevate others.

PVEST theory is so important to understanding equity that I decided to contact Dr. Spencer. It took one day to get a personal invitation to speak with her. After admiring each other's bookshelves, I asked her if she had any specific thoughts that early childhood educators and leaders should consider in terms of her work. She shared the following.

> PVEST provides a theory of human development—the what and the how. Do the things you [professionals working with young children] are already doing: reading books, telling stories, and having conversation around equity. Educators don't need to do a new activity. These are things they already do. Tell preschool teachers to not break children's spirits. Use their spirits and give language to empower them.

Dr. Spencer went on to share a story about her granddaughter, who is biracial, in an after-school program:

> Another child told her, "We have a new doll and you can't play with a white doll because that would mean you hate your family." After hearing this, her granddaughter put herself in the quiet area. Because Dr. Spencer had had conversations with her about her identity, her granddaughter had the wherewithal and tools to respond by saying, "First, I love my family, and you can't put your thoughts in my head. I will have a turn." She told her grandmother that her teacher was not far away, but hadn't responded.

We both wondered if her teacher had the words to respond. Dr. Spencer wants early childhood professionals to give children the words to protect their own hearts and make sure children are prepared, have words, and develop understanding with each other and their teachers. Educators should take advantage of these interactions to help children learn.

From a psychological perspective, Dr. Spencer went to on to clarify, "The white child was not motivated by racism. The child was motivated by thinking of a way to get more time with a new toy. She was egocentric, as all children are!" But Dr. Spencer describes egocentric behavior as normal and an opportunity to model truth and help children gain a good sense of self. If her granddaughter hadn't had the words to respond to this situation, she might have come away with a distorted view of herself, and the white child would have come away with a new way to get her needs met. The feedback from this exchange led to the white child gaining proper feedback and a new consciousness of right and wrong. The child of color gained an appropriate way to protect her sense of self, was affirmed by using her words, created boundaries with her friend, and made the friendship stronger.

According to Dr. Spencer, there is no better period for supporting identity and preparing young children to have comfortable seamless identity formation than in the early years. Extensive literature is available on identity formation and protective factors and how they contribute to resiliency. New Zealand researchers John Fenaughty and Niki Harré (2003) put it best when they described our lives as being on a seesaw, with a delicate balance between risk factors on one side and protective factors on the other. Both risk and protective factors determine our access to equity. To make this clearer, take a look at the following example.

> I weigh 150 pounds. My weight has changed little throughout my adult life and fluctuates between 120 and 150 pounds. This aspect of my identity *could* be a protective factor, based on a society's preference for thinness. Does my weight make it easier for me to find clothes? Yes. Are the people who model clothes typically my size? Yes. My weight reduces the likelihood of struggle for me in that regard in today's society. It provides me with more access to clothes and choices of clothes because designers tend to cater to my needs. I can move through the world with the expectation that my weight will be perceived in a positive manner. I use the word *could* because protective factors are not static, and this can change the outcome. For example, if you were to drop me off in a different century, my weight would not be a protective factor because greater body weights were considered the standard of beauty in earlier times and societies.
>
> Protective factors can be internal or external. Protective factors can be unearned. For example, I rarely exercise to maintain my weight. Protective

factors can also be earned: I worked hard to earn my three degrees and professional credentials.

On the other hand, a factor that could place me at risk for inequity is my gender. Could being a woman increase my risk for bias based on the social construct of sexism? Yes. Do women make less money than men for the same work in the workplace? Yes. My gender could mean my needs are more likely to be pushed to the margins. I do not have the expectation, for example, that my income needs will be met. The following chart helps us to understand how we can support each other in our acquisition of equity. The more protective factors you have, the more you can potentially provide more space to provide support as an ally. In the following chart, I've listed my characteristics and groups and how they could increase or reduce my access to equity.

In the graphic on page 24, you see my life on a set of scales. Keep in mind that risk and protective factors have a cumulative effect (Stevens-Watkins et al., 2014; Perry, Harp, and Oser, 2013). Not all risk and protective factors are created equal, and some factors can have greater impacts than others. For example, statistics show woman make 83 cents on the dollar as compared to men (U.S. Census Bureau, 2021). However, this inequality isn't equal. Did you know women's pay, compared to men's, can drop to as low as 58 cents on the dollar for Black women, 50 cents for Native American or Indigenous women, and 49 cents for Latinas? The National Partnership for Women and Families (2022) shares, "In Wyoming, for example, women are paid 65 cents for every dollar paid to men… while in Vermont women are paid 91 cents for every dollar paid to men." Ninety-seven percent of congressional districts in the United States "showed the median yearly pay for women who work all year, full time is less than the median yearly pay for men" (National Partnership for Women and Children, 2022). This gap in wages isn't unique to the United States. Around the globe, women on average earn 77 cents for each dollar a man earns (United Nations Population Fund, 2017). For example, another report by the International Trade Union Confederation (n.d.) shows women in Japan and South Korea on average earn 30 percent less than men, and in Azerbaijan and Benin, the gender wage gap is greater than 40 percent for the same number of hours.

It is clear that women face inequities in pay, but that amount can vary based on unique characteristics of each woman, such as her age, race, ability, and location. For example, according to data from the U.S. Census Bureau, people who identify as having a

Characteristics	My Groups	Society's response could *increase* my likelihood of access to equity and/or inclusion	Society's response could *reduce* my likelihood of access to equity and/or inclusion
Gender	Woman		x
Race	Black		x
Socio-Economic Status	Middle Class	x	
Education	Three Degrees	x	
Parental Status	Mother		x
Appearance	5'7" and 150 pounds	x	
Appearance	Dark, curly hair		x
Sexual Orientation/Marital Status	Heterosexual/Wife	x	
Physical Ability	Lazy eye		x
Handedness	Right-handed	x	
Intellectual Ability	Average IQ	x	
Intellectual Ability	ADD/dyscalculia (undiagnosed)		x
Language(s)	English	x	
Immigration Status	U.S. citizen	x	
Profession	Teacher	x	
Country of Origin	Descendant of enslaved people		x
Religion	Baptized as Baptist and confirmed Roman Catholic	x	
Age	51 at the time of this writing		x
Physical Health	Peanut allergy		x
Other			

ANGELA'S LIFE ON A BALANCE SCALE

Black
Woman
Dark, curly hair
Descendant of enslaved people
Mother
Lazy eye
Dyscalculia
50 years old
Peanut allergy

Heterosexual
3 college degrees
Average IQ
Christian
Middle class
English speaker
Tall and slim
Teacher

24 | Elevating Equity: Advice for Navigating Challenges in Early Childhood Programs

disability earn less money overall (Day and Taylor, 2019; U.S. Census Bureau, 2017) and experience persistent poverty at a higher rate than people who do not identify as having a disability (U.S. Census Bureau, 2012). If a person with a disability is also a woman, you can see how she can be affected on many levels. We are all unique, multifaceted individuals with identities that others may not be aware of. The number, depth, and type of factors that could place a woman at risk vary, as do the unique protective factors she has. Women are not a monolith—no group is. There is no one woman who can represent all women. As a result, depending on each person's unique continuum of risk, women can be allies to other women where different societal constructs place them at more risk. Keep in mind that cultural constructs around who is accepted in society are not static. For example, in the twenty-first century, weighing 150 pounds with a height of 5 feet 7 inches is considered an ideal weight according to my body mass index. However, this factor might have placed me at risk in the fifteenth century.

Now that you have a better understanding of labels, take another look at your home drawing where have labeled yourself and the groups you are in.

- Think about how each of those characteristics contributes to your access to equity and inclusion.

- Consider whether each aspect of your identity *could* be a potential risk factor or protective factor in society, based on current social constructs. Create a list of each.

- Next, look at your list of risk factors and your list of protective factors.

Creating Access for Others

Your social identities that are associated with protective factors put you in a position to protect the equity of those who might be placed at risk. Protective factors deputize us to be diversity detectives. You could help curb any potential imbalance. Creating an equitable world requires a conscious effort of those with protective factors to protect the equity of all. Here's an example to make this a little clearer.

> I am right-handed. I should question why desks are fitted for me and not those who are left-handed. Why should I care when I am not left-handed? Why would this be my issue? Because left-handers make up

only 10 to 12 percent of the population (BBC, 2022; Searing, 2019). The left-handed person is already burdened with trying to find stores that sell scissors and baseball gloves that fit. As someone who is right-handed, I have more space to assist. This way, we all share the burden together and support one another. You might be thinking, "Hey, Angela, there is a Lefty Store! Problem solved. You're welcome!" But if every store isn't, or doesn't have, a place for lefties, there is a problem with the equity. Equity should never be place you must search for. To be equitable, every place should fit the needs of everybody.

If being left-handed can lead to an extra burden, then I want you to consider risk factors that could impact your health, income, places you can live, or places and resources that are accessible to you. Protective factors place us in a position of power—not the same type of power as being the line leader in kindergarten or jumping up high enough to reach a door frame, mind you, but power nonetheless. You may have heard the adage "With great power comes great responsibility." This responsibility entails constantly asking ourselves during our day-to-day experiences, "How can I protect equity? What are the potential unmet needs of others?" Equity is about engaging in solidarity with those who do not share your protective factor. That way, we all have the confidence in knowing someone is out there protecting us against potential factors that make us vulnerable. Margaret Spencer (2006) contends, "All humans are vulnerable… exposure both to risks and protective factors is part of the human experience." The more we protect others, the more others protect us. Each time we speak out to make someone's life better, we become better as individuals and a society. Dr. Martin Luther King, Jr., said, "Injustice anywhere is a threat to justice everywhere. We are caught in an inescapable network of mutuality, tied in a single garment of destiny."

Why You Are Not Your Bias

As you look at your drawing, I am sure you didn't place a label of *biased* anywhere on your house. It is a label that is usually not embraced and typically has negative connotations. In my overzealous attempts to end injustice I will admit that I have been guilty of using *biased* to label people. My previous book *Push Past It! A Positive Approach to Challenging Behaviors* has an entire section devoted to bias in chapter 2. In the past, I have stated that a person can be biased because our brains are wired for bias but that it is irresponsible to stay biased. But over the years I have learned that I should label only the food in my refrigerator—not people.

You are not your bias. You are so much more than that. We can't reduce bias by reducing people to the behaviors they might display at a given moment in their lives. However, just because you aren't your bias doesn't mean your interactions can't ever contain bias.

Now wait! Before you put this book down and start grabbing the TV remote, did you ever consider that somewhere out there (not sure where) is a person who has a bias toward exercise? If you think bias is only bad, you might be displaying a negativity bias against bias!

Some People Have a Bias in Favor of Vegetables: Why Bias Gets a Bad Rap!

Bias is not inherently good or bad. *Bias* is defined as "being against one thing, person, or group in favor of another" (University of California, San Francisco, 2023). When our biases lead to good outcomes, such as a healthy lifestyle, they can be helpful. On the other hand, if you run only because someone is chasing you, know that your potentially harmful bias against exercise might eventually catch up to you. (And when I say *you*, I mean *me*.) But seriously, biases can do the most harm when they inform the decisions of people in positions of power. If you are thinking, "Whew! That isn't me. I have no power, Angela. I was never even picked to be the line leader in kindergarten," I get it. You might not feel powerful, but keep in mind that everyone has protective factors that provide us with power.

Can a fish see water? Since a fish is constantly looking at water, its brain doesn't actively notice it. To conserve energy, our brains also naturally filter out stimuli that occur constantly. As a result, because bias is so integrated into our brains and bodies, it can be hard to spot. Neuroscience research shows our brains are designed for survival, and bias is our automatic default. It takes conscious effort to elevate your mind beyond survival to a higher level of living. The good news is that learning more about bias can help us recognize maladaptive bias when it occurs.

Even after reading that last couple of paragraphs, I understand that insisting our behaviors can have bias can feel like the equivalent of someone saying we all have cooties. So here is a warning: in the next few paragraphs, I am going to share some research with you about bias. But keep in mind you can either continue reading or skip ahead to the section titled "You Can't Elevate Equity by Making People Feel Bad." I will let you decide. So, if you're up to it, let's take a look at bias and how it might be affecting our elevation toward equity and healthy outcomes.

Research on Bias

Germany is known not just for delicious bread and beer but also for understanding bias. Scientists there conducted a study in which they could actually see bias in the brain. Neuroscientists Laetitia Grabot and Christoph Kayser (2020) measured the electrical activity in different parts of the brain in adults while they made decisions. The researchers noticed that when the adults were making decisions, alpha waves appear. When those alpha waves were weaker, the participants were resisting bias, but when those waves were strong, participants' brains were surrendering to bias. The authors of this study remind us, "The brain is a biased organ, frequently generating systematically distorted perceptions of the world, leading each of us to evolve in our own subjective reality."

Remember my story from earlier about my friends and their inability to find my home based on their assumptions? Research shows my friends were not exhibiting serious personal flaws but were exhibiting the normal stumbling blocks that occur when our brains make decisions. Bias is not a moral failing but a human adaptation that helped our species survive predators by simplifying information so our brains could make quick, automatic associations and decisions. Yup, your brain is constantly creating its own thirty-second movie trailers based on prior information and experiences to help you think about what you might be getting into when it comes to people and situations.

Another study in the United States highlights how our brains develop expectations from our prior experiences of what something should be and how we use that information to guide our judgment and decision making. Hansem Sohn and colleagues (2019) studied how our brains encode our beliefs and how those beliefs influence our behaviors. Turns out prior experiences affect the strength of connections between neurons in the brain. The power of these connections determines how messages in the brain act upon one another.

These are not isolated studies. You may be surprised to learn that there is a body of research that demonstrates how we rely on oversimplified information to make choices, overestimate the accuracy of those choices, and make errors called *cognitive biases* regularly. For example, Jonathan Baron, Professor Emeritus of Psychology at the University of Pennsylvania, wrote a book called *Thinking and Deciding* (2006) in which he identifies fifty-three types of cognitive biases. Researcher Rüdiger F. Pohl (2017) edited a book on bias and how it affects our everyday lives. And researcher Craig Carter and colleagues (Carter, Kaufman, and Michel, 2007) have created an entire taxonomy classifying decision-making biases. Wait, is that you snoring? It was when I started talking about taxonomies, wasn't it? Well, I think you get the point that bias isn't bad; it is a sign that you are a healthy human being with a brain that is working as it should be.

In short, I found that research shows everyone has an unconscious tendency toward bias, called *implicit bias*, that typically runs counter to a person's own belief system. Stating that all of our actions can be prone to bias is not an attack on your moral character. Bias is not a category people fit into but a continuum along which all our actions fall.

> We all have biases. For example, I have a positive bias for love stories but a bias against *Caillou*. If you are not aware, *Caillou* was a popular children's TV show. But for me, the only good thing that came from 2020 was that PBS Kids cancelled the show!* Where does your bias about *Caillou* fall?

> I dislike *Caillou* and am glad his reign of terror is over.
>
> I dislike *Caillou* (he whines a lot) but I could tolerate the show because my kids liked it.
>
> I mildly disliked *Caillou*.
>
> What is *Caillou* again?
>
> I liked *Caillou*.
>
> I loved *Caillou*! What's your problem? It is just a kids' show. Grow up!

We can't ascribe neutrality to a part of us that isn't inherently neutral. Our goal is not to never display bias (which is—spoiler alert—biologically impossible); instead it is our responsibility to recognize bias when it occurs, consider our degree of expression, and respond in a way that supports equity and inclusion.

---

*My editor tells me that *Caillou* has been picked up by another network. Yay.

You Can't Elevate Equity by Making People Feel Bad

If you're tired of reading about bias and are feeling like Samuel L. Jackson and want to double-dog dare me to say *bias* one more time, I can understand. We can't lift each other up by making people feel down on themselves. Here is why: shame triggers the need for self-protection and inhibits learning (Lanius, Paulsen, and Corrigan, 2014). If someone feels shame for having bias, instead of being able to listen and learn about that bias, the person will exhibit a physical stress response that has nothing to do with thinking and everything to do with feeling. They will feel a need to protect themselves and hide from danger. No amount of reasoning or facts will get through to that person.

The experience of shame is an automatic one that occurs in the limbic system, which is in charge of our emotional responses. That response will not involve cognition but triggers the pain system in the brain. Consequently, the desire to learn, evolve, and elevate cannot coincide with shame. They cancel each other out, much like the words "working vacation." Cultural humility should never involve humiliation. Professor, speaker, and author Brené Brown (2007) said it best: "Shame corrodes the very part of us that believes we are capable of change." You always have a choice. No one asked you to sign over your free will when you signed the receipt for this book purchase. You can choose to shame, but also know that once you make that choice, you have also made a choice to inhibit the elevation of equity.

Now after reading the previous section, if you are feeling some "Bah, humbug" vibes right now, I get it. Because guess what! There is actual science as to why we question science. For example, research by Garrett and Weeks (2013) found that corrections can cause people to be more resistant to factual information. Researchers Nyhan and colleagues (2014) found that when facts contradict long-held beliefs and threaten our identity or worldview (remember the homes we drew), we not only disregard that information but become distrustful of the source. This pattern repeated itself when Nyhan and colleagues (2020) found that fact checks did little to change people's attitudes or choices. If you think you have an open mind, you are right—we do!—and it is typically open only for the information that provides confirmation of what we already believe. For example, one study by Knobloch-Westerwick and Meng (2009) showed we spend more time reading information that aligns with our beliefs.

So, What Can You Do?

If this information has you wondering what helps us integrate new ideas, you might be happy to know that researchers LaCour and Green (2014) found that dialogue is what opens doors to change. They found twenty-minute—yes, I said twenty-minute—conversations that took place at people's doorsteps led to long-term shifts in thinking around typically divisive social issues. What made these interactions so powerful? The questioners established a rapport with the other person. They were consistently polite and respectful, engaged in active listening, and invited the residents to share their experiences. Those twenty-minute conversations involved the participants talking about their own lives and engaging in what educators and psychologists call *active processing*. In short, facts alone don't lead to learning; relationships do. And a big part of learning also involves integrating facts within your current thinking. People learn lessons for the long haul when reflective questions help them come to conclusions about themselves, not about someone else or a particular topic without any context. Overall, learning should be designed to point out our commonalities and connections. Connections are the only way we can learn from each other and explore new directions.

The Importance of Empathy

Brené Brown (2014) acknowledges that "empathy fuels connection… and empathetic responses challenge us to 'internalize the feelings of another.'" Empathy is a key component of equity. Brown outlines four key components of empathy:

- Taking a perspective
- Staying out of judgment
- Recognizing emotion in another person
- Communicating the understanding of another person's emotions

Turns out empathy is not just about being nice but is an evidence-supported instrument by which we can achieve equity and inclusion. Research by Batson and colleagues (1997) found empathy for an individual from a group can improve attitudes for an entire group. Researchers Eisenberg, Eggum, and Di Giunta (2010) found that empathy contributes to the quality of intergroup relationships. Diane Goodman (2000), an assistant professor of humanistic/multicultural education, describes empathy as one main source of motivation that must be present for people to support social justice. Once we understand the psychology behind what motivates someone to support equity, we can strategically engage individuals and institutions toward this goal.

In his podcast *Conversations with People That Hate Me*, Dylan Marron explores how to get these connecting conversations started. "[E]mpathy… is a key ingredient in getting these conversations off the ground, but it can feel very vulnerable to be empathizing with someone you profoundly disagree with. So, I established a helpful mantra for myself. Empathy is not endorsement…. Empathizing with someone you profoundly disagree with does not suddenly compromise your own deeply held beliefs and endorse theirs. It just means that I'm acknowledging the humanity of someone who was raised to think very differently from me (Marron, 2018)."

Some of you might be asking yourself, "Why sugarcoat things? If someone is wrong, they're wrong." I agree. I will not engage with someone if I feel my safety is in jeopardy, and I think identifying that something or someone is wrong or inequitable is a good first step. But that is not where we wash our hands of the problem and stop if we are working to elevate equity. According to an unattributed quote posted on Lori Deschene's Tiny Buddha website, "There are three solutions to every problem: accept it, change it, or leave it." And you always have a choice. But in the spirit of elevating equity, my choice is always to change it. If we stop with identifying what is wrong, then we can't help someone move toward a new idea that might be right. Elevating equity cannot exist without empathy. Elevating equity is about moving the needle forward with that goal in mind. I look at every interaction as an opportunity to elevate equity, and I have seen firsthand how powerful empathy can be.

I got a call after I presented my workshop "Elevating Equity" to a group of early childhood teachers. The organizer said it was her favorite workshop of the day. She paused and said, "You know, we were not raised that way. Black people had their part of town and we had ours. It was just how we were raised. That is what my mother told me. It took my children taking me aside and talking to me that changed me."

My book *Push Past It! A Positive Approach to Challenging Classroom Behavior* (2019) ends with this thought: "The ultimate goal… is to leave you with an increased ability to love, accept, get along with, and help children, their family members, and your colleagues. People are more than their worst moments. The next time someone describes a person as 'bad,' 'crazy,' or 'angry,' PUSH PAST that one-dimensional label and learn more about that person. The next time someone behaves badly, respond with curiosity and compassion, keeping in mind that behind every person's behavior is a complicated story as multifaceted as your own."

When you see someone who is in the wrong, you could be seeing someone on a path to learning. In his article "Why Being Wrong Is Good for You," author Robert A. Kenedy (n.d.) explains, "Research tells us that if we're only concerned about getting the right answer, we don't always learn the underlying concepts that help us truly understand whatever we're trying to figure out. Mistakes need to be seen not as a failure to learn, but as a guide to what still needs to be learned. As Thomas Edison said, 'I am not discouraged, because every wrong attempt discarded is another step forward.'"

Dylan Marron (2018) also acknowledges "that some people don't feel safe talking to their detractors, and others feel so marginalized that they justifiably don't feel that they have any empathy to give." So be engaged, but be cautious: I don't want you to be harmed by empathizing with someone who is threatening your safety.

Empathy can also be exhausting! Research by psychologists Anna Szuster and Maria Jarymowicz (2020) shows empathy is not automatically activated. Daryl Cameron and colleagues (2019) found empathy is for many of us (and when I say *us* I mean *me*) hard work that we would rather avoid. Moreover, researcher Karina Schumann (2014) found we are likely to avoid empathy when it is accompanied by negative emotions. Erika Weisz and colleagues (2020), as well as other researchers (for example, Chiao and Mathur, 2010), found we tend to empathize with those who are like us.

As a result, I want to treat each reader with respect, allow you to reflect on your own story, and, instead of trying to convince you of something you don't believe, move on to some shared values I think we all can agree on. To quote poet Alexander Pope (1711), "To err is human…." We should always strive to give one another grace when slip-ups occur and remember that our best teacher was our last mistake. What do you already do around about equity? Your best—I am sure you already do your best every day, and I hope I can help that best get even better.

If you are reading this book, I am proud of you! You have already made a conscious commitment to elevate equity. Elevating equity is not hard. In fact, if you can spell equity, you are already on the path to understanding my first tool to help guide you on a successful journey.

E: Equity is **evolving**. If you worry the world is getting "too sensitive," and if you are wondering when it will ever stop, keep in mind that the minute we stop changing, we have stopped evolving. One important element to cultural humility is being "flexible and humble enough to assess anew… cultural dimensions" (Study.com, 2022). Educators are held to an even higher standard of intellectual or academic *humility*, which is defined as "being open to other ideas, thoughts, and accomplishments (instead of pushing our) own ideas ahead of others' and …even belittle(ing) discoveries of those who disagree. True humility shows itself in holding up other opinions as having equal potential significance and correctness as your own." (Study.com, 2022).

Q: Equity is **questioning**. How do you know whether you should refer to someone as autistic or as a person who has autism? The only correct answer is to ask that person. No culture is a monolith. Culture is not static, and once you think you know all there is to know about a culture, you have put a ceiling on your knowledge that prevents you from knowing all there is to know about that culture.

U: Equity is seeking **understanding**. Instead of agreement or disagreement, the goal of any constructive conversation is to seek understanding. How do we better understand others? If you were going to say perspective taking, keep in mind that strategy has limitations. Research shows when we try to put ourselves "into someone else's shoes," we unfortunately make assumptions based on our own biases. Researchers Haotian Zhou and colleagues (2017) found that people were surprised they aren't always using the most effective strategies for understanding someone else. The researchers explain, "You're worse off going with your gut and trusting your intuition… We incorrectly presume that taking someone else's perspective will help us understand and improve interpersonal relationships." In other words, if you want to understand others better, avoid making assumptions. Remember the Q in *equity* and just ask them.

I: Equity is recognizing **individuality**. Seek to understand each person as a unique, nuanced individual with many cultural identities. Nigerian writer Chimamanda Adichie (2009) describes the effects that she defines as "the danger of the single story." She argues, "The single story creates stereotypes, and the problem with stereotypes is not that they are untrue, but that they are incomplete. They make one story become the only story." Having conversations with friends or acquaintances is a good first step to understanding each other. When we proclaim, "Well, I have a friend who says…," that friend or colleague offers a valuable perspective, but keep in mind that one single story about an experience or culture is not enough. In her TEDx University of Nevada talk, author Nilofer Merchant (n.d.) reminds us that we need to be cautious if we are seeing people "… by the group they belong to rather than as the singular person that they are. It is to see someone through a subjective lens rather than as the subject of their own story." Instead, she tells us to embrace onlyness. "Onlyness. Each of us, each of you, stand in a spot in the world only one stands in, and from that spot, your history, your experience, your visions, your hopes, everything that is you informs that perspective."

T: Equity is **treating** people as they wish to be treated. You probably know the Golden Rule: Treat others as *you* wish to be treated. I want to introduce you to the Platinum Rule. In their book by the same name, Tony Alessandra and Michael O'Connor (1995) ask us to treat others as *they* wish to be treated. The authors argue that dealing with others from our own perspective implies that we're all alike, that what *I* want and need is exactly what *you* want and need. Instead, they suggest "learning to understand other people—and handling them in a way that they tell you is best for them, not just for us."

Y: Equity is saying, "**Yes, and…**" This phrase suggests that each person should accept what another person has stated and then expand on that line of thinking without invalidating that person's expression or experience with words such as *but*.

❖ ❖ ❖

Now that you have an understanding of what I mean when I say *equity*, I hope this book will provide a conceptual framework for elevating those ideas. Believe it or not, you do not need expensive training or materials to do so. You already know the words and examples that will resonate with children, families, colleagues, and friends. Like a game of Minecraft or Candy Crush, this book outlines levels of engaging in equity. I remember someone saying a call to action around equity that states it is not good enough to be an observer. While I admire the sentiment, this doesn't acknowledge the learning process or the diverse ways people grow and absorb information. I am a walking contradiction, and I am constantly growing and changing. Sometimes the new me and the old me are at odds with one another. I am a work in progress, as is each of us, and this quality that makes us human shouldn't devalue any of our efforts toward equity, no matter how small! This is a space to learn, elevate, and evolve. Know that you as the reader are always in charge of your own learning, and you get to choose the level that is the most comfortable for you:

- Looking inward at ourselves
- Looking outward at the community, children, and families
- Listening for equity
- Learning about equity
- Leading activities or engaging in activism

I realize that the level you choose might change over time. This content is inclusive of all learning stages and understands that there is no one way to engage in equity, or else it would not be, by definition, equitable. Equity is not giving everyone the same thing; it's giving everyone what they need. This book will be safe space full of empathy and understanding, because without those two elements there is no equity.

Next, we delve into developmentally appropriate activities and what children know about equity. This will involve some hands-on activities, so go get your crayons. Come on, you can't have a chapter about children without crayons!

CHAPTER 2

What Young Children Understand about Differences and Equity

Teachers worry about scaring students if they directly bring up race, yet they still give students cafeteria food. Just kidding! But seriously, fires, tornados, and getting hit by a car are all scary, but we still include fire prevention, tornado drills, and road safety in early childhood programming. By the time I was five, my teachers had prepared me to respond calmly to a fire but had left me unprepared and terrified that something was wrong with my skin when another child told me I was dark because I had too much dirt on me. There is a clear message sent when we as educators and families discuss every other physical attribute except race or important parts of children's identities. When some aspects of our identities are discussed and others are not, it might send a silent message that these traits could be "bad" or that to discuss them is taboo rather than being openly acknowledged or celebrated. If we don't take time to educate young children about what they are hearing and seeing about equity, they could come up with their own inaccurate versions of what people's identities might mean. In the same way that children's television shows, movies, and literature tackle serious subjects such as homelessness, divorce, incarceration, and death, parents and educators should also support children in all aspects of their identity.

In 2006, Louise Derman-Sparks and Patricia Ramsey published a book called *What If All the Kids Are White? Anti-Bias Multicultural Education with Young Children and Families* (now in its second edition). The authors say the title is derived from one of the most frequently asked questions in their workshops on the topic of anti-bias education. They state, "It reflected an assumption that the absence of obvious racial diversity in their classrooms meant that young children were not forming ideas about being white or about People of Color. It also reflected a narrow definition of diversity, ignoring the many kinds of differences that exist even within racially homogeneous groups." For example, even within an all-Black setting, I would still need to understand all aspects of my identity, how to respect all attributes in others, and ways to support others around equity. I would also need to understand my own needs in terms of equity and how to identify inequity, as well as concrete actions I can take that support equity. Just because I am Black doesn't mean I somehow know everything to know about equity. I am sure that is true for everyone.

Often, families and educators don't mind talking about friends and fairness, but they worry that talking about subjects such as racism too early will result in a loss of innocence. Even though we strive to limit exposure to violent images or media, discussing how to respond to racial violence early on, for example, preserves children's innocence by equipping them with accurate information about physical attributes and gives them confidence to respond appropriately when inequity occurs. Not engaging in discussions about inequity can lead to fearful encounters that don't end inequity but instead might sustain it and increase the likelihood it will occur. As children grow older, it is important to recognize, point out, and describe how to act toward injustice. Discuss how people have fears for their own safety related to equity, and model speaking up for others who need help. Empower children to know they have an active role in making the world a better place.

Children might not notice attributes of anything at first until it is pointed out. And, just like discussing the physical attributes of animals helps children know and understand

> **Children notice differences before adults talk about differences.**

animals, or discussing the attributes of shapes builds a strong foundation for math, discussing race, gender, and equity in all areas of life builds a good foundation for understanding ourselves and others and being comfortable with all types of people. I have shared some ideas about equity for adults, but what about children? At what ages do children notice or even think about equity? How young is too young? What is the best age to start? The following sections will help you think about what children know about equity from the experts. Those experts include researchers, psychologists, educators, and you. Yes, you! Learning happens best when placed in context of your own ideas and experiences.

Infants, Toddlers, and Two-Year-Olds

> Close your eyes and think about infants, toddlers, or two-year-old children. Now, on a piece of paper, draw or create a collage that represents this age group. On the back of the paper, write down all the words you typically say when you encounter a baby, toddler, or two-year-old. If you don't interact with young children often, think about what you would or even could imagine yourself saying. You know that special singsong voice you use with when you interact with babies? Write any sounds you make or words you might say.

What do infants, toddlers, and two-year-olds know about the world around them? Research shows that babies as young as three months are already showing us what they are learning about equity. For example, at three months, babies show a preference for toys that adults would traditionally match to a child's gender (Campbell, Louisa, Haywood, and Crook, 2000). The same pattern showed up again when Brenda K. Todd and colleagues (2016) studied nine- to thirty-two-month-old babies, when Josh Boe and Rebecca Woods (2018) studied twelve-month-old babies, and again with two-year-olds in a study led by Gerianne Alexander and Janet Saenz (2012). A study by Marsha Weinraub and colleagues (1984) showed two-year-olds are already categorizing clothing by gender.

You may be thinking, "Wait. Angela, are you seriously suggesting there is sexism lurking inside our darling baby bundles of joy?" Of course not. What the research suggests is that babies are constantly studying us, noticing our similarities and differences, and making inferences based on how people respond to those characteristics. In short, just as my nine-month-old niece is noticing how shapes and colors are characterized, she is also picking up on the fact that her granny keeps handing her a pink toy and her cousin, who is a boy, a blue toy. Studies like these point out what babies notice and how early babies start to imitate us.

Another study showed babies at three months of age look at faces of their own race longer. If you are now wondering about these babies and their families, let's take a journey to a city known as Sheffield in the United Kingdom. There, in a 2005 study by David Kelly and colleagues, sixty-four full-term, healthy babies were shown thirty-two color images of male and female adult faces from four distinct ethnic groups—Caucasian, Middle Eastern, Asian, and African—projected onto a screen. When they were newborns, the babies showed no preference for any type of face. But when the experiment was performed again in three months, the babies spent more time looking at faces that matched their own race. Their families stated their babies had received little or no contact with people outside of their own ethnic group. I am not suggesting these little rascals were racist. Research shows that it is at about three months of age that a baby begins to recognize their mother's face. This research just implies that babies like looking longer at faces that look more like them. In the book *The First R: How Children Learn Race and Racism*, authors Debra Van Ausdale and Joe Feagin (2001) write, "Suggesting that children remain largely unaware of racial and ethnic matters until they are taught by adults denies their ability to absorb and manipulate the social world. This is akin to insisting that children cannot speak unless they are formally taught language by adults… infants mostly learn language by being spoken to, from the time they are born."

More recent studies from the University of Ohio and a study Anantha Singarajah and colleagues (2017) at the University of California also showed that eleven-month-old babies noticed race differences and had similar results.

I am by no means suggesting those precious little cherubs or their families were exhibiting any racial bias. UCLA professor Scott Johnson, a coauthor of the 2017 study, reminded us that the study results shouldn't be misinterpreted. This research shows only what babies looked at longer and how much they notice based on the communities they come from. If you think about it, this isn't so far-fetched. Have you ever witnessed a baby succumb to inconsolable sobs when encountering a person with a beard or a deep voice for the first time? If you have ever laughed at a YouTube video showing a baby's reaction to a family member's missing mustache or an extreme change in hair style, you already know how much babies notice about those around them.

More examples of what babies know and can do are highlighted in research by Grace Lee and Barbara Kisilevsky (2014), who discovered that babies prefer their mother's voice to that of their father. (No need to feel bad if you are a dad out there. By the time they are teenagers, your children will learn to prefer the voices of everyone else over those of both their parents.) And in research by Alan Slater and his team (1998), who found that babies look longer at what adults judge to be attractive faces. Erin Winkler, professor of African and African Diaspora studies at the University of Wisconsin–Milwaukee, asserts in her 2009 article "Children Are Not Color Blind: How Young Children Learn Race" that children as young as two years old use racial categories to reason about people's behaviors. And yet another study by researcher Athena Vouloumanos (2018) showed that by one year of age, babies can recognize that foreign languages communicate information even when they can't understand the language being spoken. Babies pay more attention to those that speak their own language, as demonstrated in a study by Katarina Begus and colleagues (2016). Does this mean babies are aware of gender identity or have bias against those who don't speak their same language? No. Taken all together, these studies show that babies are already noticing everything in the world around them.

What Babies, Toddlers, and Twos Know About Equity

I know two-year-olds have a reputation for being terrible, but you might be surprised to know they have a softer side. A study by Lara Aknin, J. Kiley Hamlin, and Elizabeth Dunn (2012) found this age group were happier giving than receiving. In the study, toddlers were introduced to a puppet and then given several treats. A researcher gave a treat to the puppet as each child watched. The researcher then pretended to find a treat and asked the child to give it to the puppet. Finally, the researcher asked the child to give one of his own treats to the puppet. The children were happy to give a "found" treat to the puppet and even happier when giving up one of their own treats.

Researchers Marco Schmidt and Jessica Sommerville (2011) found babies as young as fifteen months of age were able to notice the difference between equal and unequal portions of food shared by a researcher with two adults. (This study makes sense as I think about my own children as toddlers when it came to mealtimes.) The babies even preferred adult volunteers who divided toys up evenly. Comforting, right? There is hope for a better world! What you may not have expected is those same righteous toddlers didn't care as much about equity when the person who got more matched their own race.

Good news: Toddlers not only notice equity but prefer people who are fair.

Bad news: Unfairness and inequity wasn't so bad for these toddlers if those people getting preferential treatment look like them.

Let's not be hard on the little tykes. From an evolutionary standpoint, this all makes sense. Our species needed in-group bias to survive. It is not an evolutionary accident that by six months of age babies associate those of their same race with happy things (Xiao et al., 2018) and by the end of their second year start to prefer to play with children of the same gender (Hirschfeld, 2008). We all tend to favor those who look like us! This isn't something feel bad about, but it is something to know in terms of what occurs at the earliest stages of child development.

I don't know about you, but I have seen babies break dance on YouTube, seen TikTok videos of little ones building complex towers to reach a bag of cookies from a high shelf, and watched my own children each fall at least once because I didn't realize when I placed them on our bed that they knew how to crawl yet! I say all this to illustrate the fact that I have three degrees (one in child development with a specialization in infant studies) and at times I too have been surprised by what babies know and are able to do. I have mistakenly fallen into the trap of believing that a child's inability to speak equates to their lack of knowledge. Babies know way more than they can say and are really amazing thinkers and learners. I also want to take this opportunity to apologize to each of our four children for allowing them to fall. Mommy is sorry! And in case any readers were worried, they are all healthy and happy young adults today.

> Do you have any surprises to share about babies? Any funny stories? Research is valuable, but so is your knowledge of infants, toddlers, and two-year-olds. Take a minute and write down what you have seen babies, toddlers, and two-year-olds do.
>
> Next, I want you to go back to the list you made of all the words you use with babies, toddlers, and two-year-olds. Think more about how you respond and what you say to them and what you know about them.

I will share what I noticed when I did this activity.

> ME: When I was first tasked to think about infants, toddlers, twos, and equity, I wasn't certain whether the topic was age appropriate. Ideas around gender identity, race, or religion are probably too abstract for infants and toddlers.
>
> ALSO ME: Asking a toddler if they have a girlfriend. Turns out that was my favorite icebreaker when I looked at my list of words I use when I interact with this age group. [Snickering to self] "Do you have a girlfriend?" I crack myself up!

Then I realized there is space for both ideas: I could think two things at the same time. I didn't need to choose. I don't need to have in-depth sophisticated conversations with babies about gender, race, ability, or religion because that isn't age appropriate. Research shows that babies are at a very rudimentary level of understanding these ideas. I came to the conclusion that I was already talking to this group about some basic concepts around equity:

- "Are you being fair with the Legos?" to a toddler
- "How many crackers do you have?" to a two-year-old
- "Is that your husband?" to a six-month-old [amusing self again]

I was brought up with the idea young children were to be seen and not heard, and I sometimes viewed babies as if they were a blank slate. The research really helped update my thinking. As a result, I decided I wanted to be more intentional with what I said and did around babies, considering what I had learned about them.

*Important note: You will notice I talk about development in terms of ages, but also keep in mind that developmental stages might not always correspond to a child's age. Some children might be six years old and have some areas of development similar to that of an infant or toddler. Typical child development is not uniform, and all children have variances in certain areas. Be cautious in your understanding of development. Use your observations of children to decide what level of development they might be demonstrating, then decide what level of equity might fit for them. For example, you might be surprised by what Vanessa Hus Bal and colleagues (2020) found when they studied more than a thousand children. Almost half of the children described as "minimally verbal" had high intelligence for language-free skills. In other words, don't confuse the ability to talk with the ability to think. I am describing skills by age purely for organizational flow. Please look at each child in your life as an individual with skills that may fall within varying ages.

You have read my take on things and have looked at evidence from research, as well as evidence from your own observations and interactions. What are you thinking? Keep in mind I am not here to tell you what to think. I am here to help you discover what level of equity you can offer to a baby, toddler, or two-year-old.

Preschoolers

> Close your eyes and think about yourself as a preschooler, or think about children ages three to five whom you know or have observed.
>
> Next, take a piece of paper and draw or create a collage that represents this age group.
>
> On the back, write down all the words or interactions you typically have with this age group. If you don't interact with young children often, think about what you would or could say when given the chance. Reflect on any memories you have of yourself at this age, or use your imagination to picture yourself as a preschooler. Now, don't act like you don't revert to using an overly cutesy voice and start dispensing tickles or those affectionate hair tousles with the just-out-of-diapers set. So, consider the words and interactions you might engage in with a preschooler.

What do preschoolers know about the world around them? Around the age of three, children begin to understand gender. Research by Kristin Shutts and colleagues (2013) shows that as soon as children make this discovery, they use this new information to decide whom to be friends with and who might share their interests. These three-year-olds are not trying to cause inequity; they are just trying to figure out how to make friends.

> "We had a four-year-old enrolled [at a preschool] who spoke mostly Spanish. He told us, 'I don't want to speak more English because I am afraid I will lose my voice.'"
>
> —Tina Kukla, teacher

Retired teacher and white woman Marilyn Peterson shared, "I was really good friends with my teaching assistant, a very Black-skinned woman, and one of the preschoolers asked, 'Are you sisters?'" Her anecdote illustrates that children will see attributes, but three-year-olds tend to focus on one attribute at a time and do not have a sophisticated understanding of what those attributes mean. According to Swiss psychologist Jean Piaget (1952), *centration* in cognitive development is when young children might attend to one aspect of a person while ignoring the others. It is not that that the preschooler in Mrs. Peterson's class didn't recognize that the two women were of different skin colors; it just means the three-years-old's ability to focus on multiple attributes at one time is still developing. The same way every animal with four legs is always a "doggy."

Research by Fabes, Martin, and Hanish (2003) shows that by preschool fewer than half of children's play interactions involve peers of other genders. Their research, as well as that by La Freniere, Strayer, and Gauthier (1984) and Xiao and colleagues (2019), demonstrates how preschoolers prefer playmates of the same gender. Moreover, it is not just that children at this age have preferred playmates; they also might be internalizing negative stereotypes. For example, a study by Alexia Albert and Judith Porter (1983) showed that, as early as four years old, children had a difficult time associating positive gender stereotypes with those of the opposite sex and negative characteristics with their own sex.

On the one hand, I am glad the little crumb snatchers feel good about themselves. On the other hand, their thinking about those who aren't of their gender might not be as positive. A research study by Harry Reis and Stephanie Wright (1982) showed that, at three-and-a-half, children are already internalizing gender-role stereotypes. Another study titled "Boys Just Don't! Gender Stereotyping and Sanctioning of Counter-Stereotypical Behavior in Preschoolers" by Milica Skočajić and colleagues (2020) shows that preschoolers are not only aware of gender norms but are also ready to tell children playing outside the boundaries of gender-stereotypical toys, "Leave that!" or "That's for girls."

Around the time the preschool playground starts buzzing with phrases such as "No boys/girls allowed," research by Kristin Shutts and colleagues (2013) shows that four-year-olds have taken a new cognitive leap forward and can use more than one attribute to understand those around them. For example, they might use race and gender to figure out who might be friends that share the same interests. Every child is different, but typically when children are able to sort objects by more than one attribute, they are also sorting and classifying everything around them and using that information to make decisions about the world as well as people.

Research by Mako Okanda and Shoji Itakura (2008) found that preschoolers have a bias toward familiar objects, but it turns out they have a bias toward familiar people as well. Studies by Frances Aboud and Shelagh Skerry (1984), Rebecca Bigler and Lynn Liben (1993), and Mary Kircher and Lita Furby (1971) all show preschool-age children prefer same-race to other-race children as long as their own racial group is high in status. The preschool set is not known for their capacity for sharing, but a study by Maggie Renno and Kristin Shutts (2015) showed that preschool children share even more with those who are their same race and gender.

I know what you are thinking. Someone must have taught them this, Angela! And they may have. But I also want you to consider: If you have, know, or work with young children, have they ever surprised you by saying words or engaging in actions you never explicitly taught them? I mean, I never taught my two-year-olds to bite people, but they did. And I didn't teach my children to blurt out, ahem, *colorful* language they heard at church or school functions, but they did. Just like the acquisition of swear words or hitting their playmates, learning societal constructs around race, gender, and ability can occur spontaneously and automatically without any formal instruction. Speaking of words, educators should keep in mind that language is also a key component of identify formation. For example, several studies point to the implications for bilingual preschoolers when their identities are seriously challenged and they create new identities for the classroom (Fernández, 2006; Martin and Stuart-Smith, 1998). The conscious and unconscious messages from children and adults about the status of languages and language prestige can result in tensions that result in a child losing a language and the identity that goes along with that language (Liebkind, 1995; Orellana, 1994).

Identity is not just language but also appearance. For example, Phebe Cramer and Tiffany Steinwert's research study titled "Thin Is Good, Fat Is Bad: How Early Does It Begin?" (1998) found children as young as three had already internalized stereotypes about weight. The researchers told children stories and then presented them with pictures in which they had to pick which picture represents the mean child of the story and which represents the nice child. When the only difference between pictures was body size, the children consistently chose the picture of the person with the greater body weight as the mean character. Similar results presented themselves in a study of preschoolers by Shayla Holub (2008) and again in research by Jennifer Harriger and colleagues (2010).

Preschoolers even have a bias about who they think is honest. In a study titled "In Beauty We Trust: Children Prefer Information from More Attractive Informants," Igor Bascandziev and Paul Harris (2014) found that preschoolers are more likely to trust information from people whom society would consider attractive. Research even shows they can have a preference toward those who display more dominance (Charaffeddine et al., 2016). Researchers Mubiar Agustin and colleagues (2021) describe this as "pre-prejudice" and "symptoms of stereotyping.... in early childhood." Those symptoms include stereotypes about race, gender, appearance, intelligence, and ability.

Keep in mind, I am not suggesting preschoolers have any moral understanding of these topics or the implications of their behavior. They are just sorting and classifying information based on what they notice about how people respond to physical attributes, just as they would sort and classify shapes and colors.

When looking at research, anyone could easily cherry pick a few studies that match their agenda. So in my effort to ensure equity, I researched many studies and looked at overall trends. For example, one study by Raabe and Beelmann (2011) that summarizes 128 studies around children and adolescents found that prejudice among children peaks at ages five to seven, before most adults even discuss these ideas. Also, a study by Jessica Sullivan and colleagues (2021) found that parents underestimate their children's understanding of topics like race, and talk about race four-and-a-half years later than is suggested by child-development experts. The younger the children in this age group, the more they are influenced by stereotypes. Prejudice changes from explicit expressions in the younger years to more implicit or subtle forms in elementary school.

What Preschoolers Know About Equity

Anyone who has ever dispensed pizza slices at a preschooler's birthday party already knows this age group cares deeply about equality. Researchers from across the globe have demonstrated there is a psychological shift from focusing on equality to focusing on equity that occurs in preschool (LoBue et al., 2011; Rizzo and Killen, 2016; Schmidt et al., 2016; Smith and Warneken, 2016; Svetlova, 2013; Wörle and Paulus, 2018; Blake et al., 2015; Essler, Lepach, Petermann, Paulus, 2020; Baumard, Mascaro, and Chevallier, 2012; Olson and Spelke, 2008). *Equality* means "each individual or group of people is given the same amount of resources or opportunities" (Milken Institute School of Public Health, The George Washington University, 2020). Preschool children not only understand equality but also understand equity. They are even able to communicate how each person has a unique set of characteristics and circumstances that determines how resources will be allocated to them. For example, researchers Kristina Olson and Elizabeth Spelke (2008) found that when preschoolers are presented with limited resources, they will give more to family and friends than to strangers. But before you worry about the generosity of these little tykes, when these same children have more resources, they give an equal amount to family, friends, and even those they don't know.

Next, let's travel to Sweden to see more equity in action with a study involving preschool children watching a puppet struggling to achieve its goals (Kenward and Dahl, 2011). The puppet is helped by a second puppet and hindered by a third. Later, when asked to distribute treats between the helper and hinderer, most of the children gave more to the helpful puppet. Moreover, these young children were able to give reasons why they gave more to the helpful puppet based on its actions.

It is reassuring that a study by Hannes Rakoczy and colleagues (2016) found preschoolers will speak up—some might even say loudly—in protest on behalf of others when things are unfair. However, what is concerning are the studies that show preschoolers perpetuating inequality and giving more resources to those who are wealthy. Why are some preschoolers more sensitive to equality than others? Turns out the child's own unique characteristics might be an influence. For instance, a study by Markus Paulus and Bibianna Rosal-Grifoll (2017) found that preschool children with autism spectrum disorder (ASD) along with lower cognitive abilities and more severe symptoms of ASD were more generous to the rich than to the poor. Another study by Jonas Miller and colleagues (2020) went even deeper to look at many individual differences and how those influenced generosity in preschoolers. They explored the socio-environmental, psychological, and biological factors that influence children's behavior around equity. They found children from families with a lower socioeconomic status were more generous than children from wealthier families, and children with compassionate mothers also were more generous.

Hold on to your chair, because this next characteristic is mind blowing! Miller and his team decided to explore children's nervous systems to see if there was a biological influence on their level of equity. Those who had healthy activation in the parasympathetic nervous system (PNS), which is the part of the nervous system that helps us relax in stressful situations, were more generous regardless of socio-economic status. What does this mean? One part of our nervous system controls the fight-or-flight response, which takes us out of dangerous situations. That part raises the heart rate and blood pressure, dilates the pupils, and keeps the body on high alert (Long, 2022). The PNS slows our heart rate and breathing and tells the brain that the body can relax because we are not in danger (Long, 2022). So, if children have a nervous system that is out of balance, they might struggle with equity. In other words, when children are on high alert and their danger dial is turned up all the way, they might not have the bandwidth to be as generous as a child who does not have that challenge. For example, I have experienced this when I work with children who have experienced trauma. Instead of asking them to share toys, a strategy that has worked is to make them feel safe before trying the skill of sharing. One way to do that is to put a large plastic hoop on the floor and let the child play in the hoop. It is not restricting the child; the hoop is there to help a child feel safe. I tell the child, "Everything in your hoop is yours, and if you play outside of the hoop you will be asked to share." This provides two things: the ability to still teach the skill of sharing if they play outside the hoop and the ability to play in the hoop without sharing.

Taken altogether, preschoolers around the globe all go through a natural developmental sequence from understanding *equality* (everyone gets the same) to understanding *equity* (each person gets what they need). It is in preschool that children begin to use their observations, logic, and emotions to determine what equity is (Essler, Lepach, Petermann, and Paulus, 2020; Paulus and Essler, 2020). However, a preschooler's individual socio-environmental, psychological, and even biological characteristics can potentially affect his ability to *exhibit* equity. Children's relationships in their lives and their mental and physical health each play a part in their development of skills associated with equity.

> Do you have any surprises to share about preschoolers from your own observations? any funny stories? Research is valuable, but so is your knowledge of preschoolers. Now, I want you to take a minute and write down what you have seen and heard from preschoolers around equity.
>
> Look back at what you drew and wrote about what you know about preschoolers and what you say to preschoolers.

I will share what I noticed when I did this activity.

> I was again surprised by what preschoolers knew about equity. But, in regard to their behavior around equity and fairness, I also think I had my expectations set too high. For example, I noticed I will often respond to lack of sharing with, "You know better," forgetting that children younger than seven or eight are too young to act on their understanding of fairness without adult support. I realize now that most children aren't able to act on everything they know about equity. I'm a walking contradiction myself: I know there is a clear gap between what I understand intellectually about topics such as exercise and my abilities and willingness to act. (I promise I will start exercising tomorrow.) I don't know why I thought children should children be different. I am more aware of what researchers Peter Blake, Katherine McAuliffe and Felix Warneken call the knowledge-behavior gap (Blake, McAuliffe, and Warneken, 2014).

I was not always considering the individual needs of each child when it came to equity.

> My thought process: "We all need to share and follow the rules or else you're going to jail when you grow up. I am sorry. I don't care if you have autism or trauma—we all need to share and be friends." I had this mindset, and then I would become frustrated and start calling the mental-health consultant whenever children resorted to physical and verbal aggression when asked to exhibit these skills.

> In my defense, this research was not available in 1990 when I began as a teacher. Some of the research I have shared used technology that wasn't available in the twentieth century! I was just operating off what I knew at the time. But now that I know more, it makes sense to me that I had to give extra support to children who had special needs or trauma. Preschool children could have an emotional, cognitive, and/or physical reason that results in them struggling to exhibit equity.

> I would never get upset with children who struggled with math or literacy skills, so why is it when children struggle with equity skills, I become so frustrated? Because that is the reaction I received and others typically

displayed when children struggled with equity. I suddenly realized I needed to update my ideas just as I update my phone. I support children with academic skills; I also need to support them with skills involving equity and inclusion.

You may be thinking, "Okay, let me just stop you right here, Angela. If I need to teach all of this, can I have this child's social security number? Because if I can't claim them on my taxes, then I am not teaching them anything around equity. That is the parent's job and should be taught at home."

Well, yes, I agree these skills should be taught at home, and I do think they could be taught at school. And if you disagree, I accept and understand your concerns. I mean, what credential even allows you to teach equity? There is no equity if we think there is only one way to accomplish a goal. I am sure some readers wouldn't be opposed to a formal curriculum on equity, but others would be, and still others would fall somewhere in the middle. But the real takeaway for me is that equity is not so formal. Remember the studies I shared earlier demonstrating that each time a child is in your presence, he is learning something? It's not as if anyone wakes up and says, "Today is the day we are going to make sure gender roles are clear to the preschoolers." The reality is far less dramatic. The studies show learning is a dynamic process that occurs through observation and everyday interaction. Preschoolers are learning something about language, something about math, something about the world, and something about equity whether you intentionally teach it or not. So even if I don't intentionally teach a lesson on equity or have an "equity curriculum," I am sending important messages about equity in my everyday actions. As a result, even if I never teach a formal lesson on the topic, I must make sure my everyday actions are intentional examples of equity. Lead by example.

> **Preschoolers are learning about equity from you whether you intentionally teach it or not.**

Educator Pamela Obazee shared, "When a seed is planted nobody sees it. It goes through the process of growth silently." As a young teacher, I never considered that along with the ability to sort letters or shapes came the ability to sort people. We don't need to say anything for children to see everything around them. For example, they will see that children with wheelchairs are not in their school, just like I did as a child. From that observation, a seed will be planted about people in wheelchairs. What did I learn about people who used wheelchairs as a child? That they belong in a different place. My high school, for example, had a different building for children with special needs. We didn't have stairs in my high school, so I was never sure why things were this way. This was never explained; it was just something I observed and came to my own conclusions about.

Bias and inequity aren't always intentional. Preschoolers can see something on TV or hear a passing comment from an acquaintance or even a stranger in public and come away with inaccurate observations that lead to inequity in their behaviors. Children in the United States, for example, can see there has been only one Black president and never a woman president and can come away with an understanding about what that means in terms of gender and race. When I saw only men as president, that left me with an impression that there was an unspoken criterion for the presidency. Because adults around me didn't address it, I came away thinking that women somehow were not up to the task. As a young child, this conclusion left me with a sad feeling. When something is not discussed, children can potentially come away with inaccurate understandings and must endure any upset feelings alone, without the support of adults. Silence around only certain topics could inadvertently send a message to young children that those topics should not be discussed. This could lead to feelings of shame for being a part of a community no one is supposed to talk about. Children then rely on each other or popular media for information, which can lead to inaccurate understandings of what these events might mean without any input from the adults that care for them. I also didn't consider how young children who just want to make friends would absorb the world around them in an automatic way that could lead to inequity. Whatever your thoughts on the subject, preschoolers are learning—whether we formally teach a topic or not.

Children in Kindergarten through Third Grade

> Close your eyes and think about children in early elementary school. Now draw on a piece of paper or create a collage that represents this age group. Think about yourself at the ages of six to eight years. On the back of the paper, write all the words or interactions you typically have with this age group. If you don't interact with young children often, think about what you would or could say when given the chance. If you are like me, you have made many observations of this age group and how they behave in public! If you are at a loss for what to write, tap into the SMH (shaking my head) comments you might have shared on social media or your conversations at the kitchen table or local beauty salon about what is right or wrong about with this age group.

Swiss psychologist Jean Piaget's book *The Origins of Intelligence* (1952) provides insight into what children this age know. During this stage of development, children are more logical and less egocentric than preschoolers but are still concrete learners and are still very literal in their understandings of the world. For example, educator Denise Henry, who identifies as white, shared a not-so-funny story about race:

> The first time I realized there was animosity between people with different colors of skin, I was probably seven or eight years old and swimming at our public pool. I was having a great time playing with another child I had met that day. (The other child happened to be African American.) We were splashing around and laughing. From the pool deck, another African American child started yelling at me out of nowhere, "Stick to your own race!" I had absolutely no idea what he was talking about. We weren't racing; we were splashing and playing. There was no swim race happening. I can't remember if someone at the pool explained it or my parents explained it at home that night.

Early-elementary-age children are beginning to gain deeper understandings of race, gender, ability, and even religion. They are aware of the world around them, and their ability to see things from another person's perspective is growing but is just not perfected yet. For example, one study by Larisa Heiphetz and her colleagues (2013) found children ages six to eight already show religious preferences. Studies by researchers such as Selin Gülgöz and colleagues (2018) show school-aged children prefer to interact with peers who are the same gender, and several studies, such as one by Kimberly Powlishta (1995), show early-elementary-age children are more positive toward their own gender.

But many children at this age still want to make friends and want to play with children of all abilities. For example, researcher Kyriakos Demetriou (2020) found, when given a choice, children aged six to eight chose children with a physical disability as playmates even for activities involving mobility. The reason? The children explained that they didn't want to exclude the child in a wheelchair even if the child was not able to fully participate.

Before you pull out the confetti and we start congratulating ourselves on a job well done, consider the following. Studies by Jennifer Steele and colleagues (2018), Andrew Baron and Mahzarin Banaji (2006), and Anna-Kaisa Newheiser and colleagues (2014) show children tend to prefer socially advantaged groups. For example, school-aged children are quicker to pair positive pictures with white faces and negative pictures with Black faces. Just like adults, children are complex. Yet, before you think we have lost the fight toward racial equity, if we take a closer look the Steele et al., 2018 study, we see it also notes that older children show less bias than younger children. Perhaps this is because the younger the children, the less adult support they receive around the topic of bias.

Potential bias should be addressed with children as young as six because it can also affect their academic outcomes. For example, in a study by Ambady and colleagues (2001), children as young as kindergarten were found to predict that an Asian student would be more likely to excel in math than a white student. Research by Lummis and Stevenson (1990) showed that, by first grade, some children already think boys are better than girls at math. Remember, the younger the child, the more inflexible they are in their thinking. As a result, the youngest children are more likely to believe stereotypes that might affect their academic performance and to need the most support when it comes to breaking down those stereotypes. In her exploration of attitudes around stereotypes, Carol Martin (1990) reminds us that by age seven children are beginning to look at the individual person and include information about the characteristics they observe in their judgments.

In early elementary school, children observe any positive events happening to members of groups in the majority and negative events happening to members of groups in the minority. Through these observations, they learn to view minority groups in a negative way and majority groups in a positive way. At this age, children are very aware of their status as related to gender, class, race, ability, language, and so on (Cho and Wang, 2020).

Ambady and colleagues (2001) theorized that children want to distance themselves from any negative stereotypes around their minority identity and to fit in with the majority so they can make friends. Keep in mind, these stereotypes affect children socially as well as academically. As children grow, prejudice becomes more differentiated and multifaceted, so their own social status, whom they have contact with, and their environment play roles in their understanding of equity. The good news is research shows that both one-on-one interventions (Ülger, Dette-Hagenmeyer, Reichle, and Gaertner, 2018; Christ et al., 2014) and interactions with diverse groups (Pettigrew and Tropp, 2006) can reduce prejudice. Sarina Schäfer (2020) found that these interactions can have a powerful impact on equity.

What Early-Elementary-Age Children Know About Equity

Rational Adult: (Purchases and distributes identical cupcakes)

Eight-Year-Old: (Eyeing your cupcake) You have more icing on your cupcake than me.

Rational Adult: What? No, we all have the same amount of icing on our cupcakes.

Eight-Year-Old: I want your cupcake.

Rational Adult: You can't have my cupcake.

Eight-Year-Old: I want a new cupcake.

Rational Adult: I am not buying any more cupcakes.

Eight-Year-Old: (Moaning) Whaaaaaaat? This is soooooo [wait for it, wait for it... say it with me now] UNFAIRRRRRRRRRRR!

If you work with, care for, or are in any proximity to children ages six through eight, you are probably familiar with this scenario. If your child or the children you care for are like mine, they have probably unleashed a truckload of "It's not fair!" on you at some point. To find out more about why this phrase has become the unofficial theme song for this age group, researchers Peter Blake and colleagues (2015) used Skittles—yes, you read right, Skittles—to learn more about equity and young children. The researchers placed Skittles on trays in front of children. They found that children of all ages love the sugar rush of eating the candy. But the most interesting finding is that, by age eight, if a child was offered a larger amount candy than another child, the first child rejected the offer stating, "That's not fair." This was experiment was tried with children in Canada, India, Mexico, Peru, Senegal, Uganda, and the United States with similar results. This supports earlier research by Blake and McAuliffe (2011) showing that children would rather throw resources away than distribute them unequally. Another study by John Corbit and colleagues (2017) with children from rural India and from rural Canada demonstrated the children's willingness to sacrifice their own advantage to achieve equity for all.

> **Do you have any surprises to share about this age group from your own observations? any funny stories? anything that might tug on our heartstrings? Research is valuable, but so is *your* knowledge of early-elementary-aged children. Take a minute and write down what you have seen and heard from children around equity.**
>
> **Next, think more about how you respond, what you say, and what you know about children aged six to eight around equity.**

I will share what I noticed when I did this activity. I was surprised by how much children at this age know about equity! I learned that the construction of gender, language, ethnic, and racial identities are important developmental milestones and there is a correlation between positive mental-health outcomes and the degree of acceptance children receive around their identities (Rivas-Drake et al., 2014).

I feel more comfortable with identity being the focus of my discussions with young children. For example, I was relieved when I realized I am not talking with children about sex but about gender identity. One of the most touching stories of gender identity for a young child is the book *Raising Ryland: Our Story of Parenting a Transgender Child with No Strings Attached* (Whittington, 2015). In the article "When Your Young Daughter

Says 'I'm a Boy'" (Wallace, 2015), Ryland's mother Hilllary Whittington states, "Everything changed the day Ryland announced, 'When the family dies, I will cut off my hair so I can be a boy.'" I realized after watching the documentary *Raising Ryland* by Sarah Feeley (2015) and hearing Whittington ask herself, "Do I want a living son or a dead daughter?" that I could potentially be helping families in need and saving the lives of children. I do not need to teach children about sex or poverty, but I can support positive identity development. As an educator, I can communicate to families that I support the positive identity development of young children in my setting, which is an important aspect of social-emotional development and social studies. Think, for example, how a child might feel when everyone has a new Halloween costume or a new toy that he doesn't have. Not talking about social and socio-economic elements that young children notice just means they process those feelings alone without adult support.

> **"We can't solve problems by using the same kind of thinking we used when we created them."**
>
> **—Albert Einstein**

Ahem. Can I interrupt here? Voice of Reason again. Why can't we just leave this to families? Well, thank you for that great question. A report titled "Identity Matters: Parents' and Educators' Perceptions of Children's Social Identity Development" (Kotler, Haider, and Levine, 2019) provides insight into why "leaving it to families" might mean leaving the topic unexplored.

The study of families from all fifty U.S. states and the District of Columbia found only 10 percent of parents reported that they often talk with their children about their race or ethnicity. Eight percent of the parents reported that they often discuss their socioeconomic class with their children. The report went on to explain, "Parents are not, by and large, focusing family conversations on children's social identity formation."

We can have discussions with children based on where the children are developmentally. For example, teachers can bring up geometry at any age, but geometry for a baby might include saying, "That ball is round." For a preschooler, teachers can form shapes with playdough and name them and their characteristics. With an older child, teachers can use rulers to experiment with angles. We can apply the same principles with equity. Discussions should be based on the child's level of development. Equity at its most basic is the understanding that people's identities should be heard, understood, celebrated, and supported.

It is interesting to me that the youngest of children who need the most guidance around equity get the least amount of support. Jessica Sullivan and colleagues (2021) point out that when adults censure dialogue around identities, for example by saying "It's not polite to say things like that"; adopt a "colorblind" approach; or emphasize the commonalities between humans, for example by saying "We're all the same inside," these approaches are detrimental to race relations for both adults and children. Instead, Sullivan and colleagues say that several research studies show that talking about topics such as race constructively with children helps them "develop empathy, learn about new perspectives, understand their own identities, avoid engaging in practices that reproduce structural inequality, and exhibit less racial bias."

It is clear that children can experience psychological stress when they are not among a group that is in the majority. It is the adult's role to support children or find people to support children in their social and emotional development. For example, research supports the understanding of the damaging physical, psychological, physiological, and academic effects of having an identity that is not part of the majority (Wong, Eccles, and Sameroff, 2003; Wang and Huguley, 2012; Chavous et al., 2008; Jernigan and Daniel, 2011; Higa et al., 2014). Educators and families must be on the lookout for stereotypes and bias that can affect self-esteem, mood, and academic self-concepts and can lead to less school engagement and lower academic performance.

◆ ◆ ◆

Now that you have read my take on things and have looked at evidence from research, as well as from your own observations and interactions, what are you thinking? If you are thinking, "So if children model behavior they see, why don't they model my cleaning up after them every day?" I get it that this will take some time to process. Keep in mind, I am not here to tell you what to think. I am here to help you discover what level of equity you might consider for young children. You may be thinking, "Angela, what does all this mean for early childhood educators?" Glad you asked! Let's delve into that in chapter 3.

CHAPTER 3

What This Means for Early Childhood Educators

Did you know students who are labeled as overweight have more school absences (Segal, Rayburn, and Beck, 2017)? Did you know that LGBTQ youth in socially unsupportive environments have a greater risk of attempting suicide (Hatzenbuehler, 2011)? Elevating equity is all about healthy development and self-esteem. Research shows children can experience psychological stress when they are not among a group that is in the majority. Children who encounter discrimination can have more challenging behaviors, lower levels of school engagement and motivation, and more anxiety and depression symptoms (Dotterer, McHale, and Crouter, 2009; Seaton et al., 2011). As an educator, I want to support and/or find resources to support children who might be experiencing stress in positive identity development. I also want to help children learn how to support each other and become allies. Now that I know elevating equity has to do with healthy identity development and social studies, rather than endorsement of a particular lifestyle, I feel ready to take the next step toward thinking about what all this information might mean for early childhood educators.

What Do Educators Know about Equity?

Research shows educators are often uncomfortable with classroom discussions around identity. For example, in a survey almost half of educators say social class is not an issue they are comfortable talking about (Kotler, Haider, and Levine, 2019). This makes sense because data also shows few teachers are encouraged by school leadership to discuss identity with their students. Yet at the same time, that same survey revealed about one-third of educators who work with young children have heard negative remarks regarding students' identity in their classrooms. Researcher Jennifer Kotler and colleagues (2019) contend, "healthy social development—including a strong appreciation of individual and group identity factors—can be influenced (both positively and negatively) by home and peer interactions, as well as in community and school experiences."

Caregivers of Infants, Toddlers, and Two-Year-Olds

Remember, when it comes to equity, I want to empower you to choose what level works for you.

Look inside yourself. Are the infants and toddlers you care for seeing positive messages about equity? What is your body language when someone of a different culture sits next to you? Do you stiffen up? turn away? hold a child's hand more tightly? Do you become visibly frustrated when someone speaks in a language that is different than yours? Do you use negative labels or tell "off-color" jokes when you see someone who is overweight? How about when you see someone who has a different level of ability or income? Can children play with any toy regardless of their gender? Or do you pick toys by the color, as I did when my children were young? Do you look in the mirror and complain about how "fat" you look? Are you requiring children to make eye contact to show they are paying attention or making them sit crisscross applesauce to show they are ready to learn? Some cultures don't require eye contact and making eye contact with an adult could be a sign of disrespect. Instead, let children look at whatever they need to in order to learn. Allow children to sit or stand while learning, as long as they are safe and everyone can see. These ideas honor the diverse way children learn.

Look outward in your community. Are the babies you care for only around people who look and act like them? What about a virtual playdate? What about having a two-year-old "write" to a pen pal outside of your class and your neighborhood? It is so easy to make connections with technology. Instead of creating an activity about a culture you are not a part of, what if you invite families from a variety of lifestyles, religions, family structures, cultures, and so on, to tell a story to your class or create a parent advice book on social media?

Does your school include children with diverse abilities? If your church or community organization has sign-language interpreters, pairing them with people who could benefit from that skill is a twofer—equity *and* language skills. Did you know researchers have confirmed babies can learn sign language starting at approximately nine months of age (Goodwyn and Acredolo, 1993)? I recommend teaching sign language to all children. Equity goes both ways. Teach sign language to the children who have a challenge with oral language. Also teach it to the children who have oral-language skills, along with teaching them to support and accept children who don't. Is your local school intentionally teaching sign language to all children, whether they are deaf or not, to enhance communication with anyone who struggles with oral language? A study by Susan Goodwyn and colleagues (2000) suggests that signing can actually facilitate, not hinder, the development of vocal language. An approach that helps children who are diverse learners enhances learning for everyone (Thompson et al., 2007). Why don't we make language interpreters more commonplace? Are the signs in the community as multilingual as the signs in the airport? If babies can point to a McDonald's sign, they are already noticing what languages are on signs. Are we all striving to create multilingual interactions and spaces for our babies?

Look at the books, toys, and media in your classroom. Do they reflect a wide range of people in terms of race, ethnicity, ability, gender, language, religion, immigration status, and families engaging in a wide range of activities?

Heather Taylor, one of the teachers that I have worked with as a consultant and trainer, told me that she was reading a board book to one of the two-year-olds in her class. Each page spread had a simple photograph of only one subject on one page and the words, "Where's the…?" on the other page—for example, "Where's the lion?" with a picture of a lion on the opposite page. On the page with the words "Where's the baby?" the child she was reading to was unable to identify that there was a baby in the photo on the opposite page. The photo was of a Black infant.

Look for stereotypical media, and limit it or acknowledge it. Yes, I do still love and watch old Disney movies that I grew up with; I also take warnings about some Disney movies seriously. I might say something like, "Princesses look a variety of ways. Let me show you more examples." I know older books might bring back cherished memories of your own childhood, but consider that with those books there may be opportunities for lessons on differences in how we behave now compared to back when you were a child. Older books or media also might not be accurate. For example, many of my family members have naturally red hair, and my mother had naturally sandy blond hair but was Black. However, in popular media, redheads or blonds with light green eyes are typically white. Evaluate older books and media that might show inappropriate representations of groups based on race, gender, and so on. Offer books and media that show a wider range of people and characteristics.

Selecting Books on Equity

In the groundbreaking work "Mirrors, Windows, and Sliding Glass Doors," Rudine Sims Bishop (1990) provides guidance for choosing books. She reminds us that books should sometimes be windows "… offering views of worlds that may be real or imagined, familiar, or strange." Sliding glass doors that "… readers have only to walk through in imagination to become part of whatever world has been created or recreated by the author." And mirrors that "… reflect (life) back to us, and in that reflection we can see our own lives and experiences as part of a larger human experience. Reading, then, becomes a means of self-affirmation, and readers often seek their mirrors in books." Dr. Bishop contends all children need diverse literature. If children *don't* see themselves, it sends a powerful message about their value. If children see *only* themselves, they can come away with an exaggerated sense of self. If children see negative images, that can leave them with a distorted image of themselves.

Louise Derman-Sparks has a useful guide for selecting anti-bias children's books. You can find it here: https://socialjusticebooks.org/guide-for-selecting-anti-bias-childrens-books/

Here are some questions to consider when choosing literature:

- Does the book show children with recognizable differences from each other who engage with one another in positive ways?

- Does the book depict characters as equal partners with equal status? In the article "Diversifying Your Classroom Book Collections? Avoid these 7 Pitfalls," Kara Newhouse (2020) warns readers to beware of the "sidekick cliché" in which the person who is not typically dominant in society is a sidekick character to the main character or is a victim the main character has to help. Also beware of books with a lead character who is part of the same group as everyone else (with no diversity). On the same note, historical books are great, but beware of books that show individuals who are not part of the dominant group only during periods of suffering.

- Are you just purchasing books based off some imaginary "diversity" list? No group is monolithic; there is diversity within groups. If you have one book about a child with Down syndrome, you have one book about one child with Down syndrome. If you have one book about a family with two dads you have one book about a family with two dads.

- Consider: Is this a quality book about a meaningful topic you and the children would have a genuine interest in? Choose books to match the interests of the individual children you care for.

- Does the author share the cultural identity of the lead characters? Author Corinne Duyvis coined the hashtag #OwnVoices as a way to recommend books written by people who are members of the groups they write about (Lavoie, 2021).

- Consider the children's ages and abilities. For example, using animals to talk about issues of diversity and culture is asking young children, who are concrete thinkers, to take a big leap in cognition they are not ready for. They might not understand how a book about ducks is supposed to teach them how to treat people. We, as adults, can see the analogy, but for young children that book about ducks is teaching them how to treat ducks.

The Cooperative Children's Book Center (CCBC), part of the School of Education at the University of Wisconsin–Madison (2022), offers data on the number of books by or about Black, Indigenous, or People of Color published in a given year*. The data show that a child of color is more likely to see a book featuring an animal than they are to see a character that looks like them. In 2021, 27 percent of children's books were about animals and other nonhuman characters, and only 23 percent were about people of color; more than half the books featured white characters (Sol, 2021). A child of color might not be excited to read or look at books that don't reflect them or their experience. As of 2019, data show only 1 percent of books featured Indigenous characters, 5 percent Latinx characters, and 7 percent Asian/Pacific Islanders, which means we are all losing out when it comes to looking into the window of these cultures (CCBC, 2019).

> "Books may be one of the few places where children who are socially isolated and insulated from the larger world may meet people unlike themselves."
>
> —Dr. Rudine Sims Bishop

Books aren't enough. Let babies, toddlers, and twos actually play with children of cultures different than their own. Babies need to see you interacting with people of cultures different than your own too, so they can see how to interact with people of cultures differing from their own.

Listening for Equity

Has a toddler ever blurted out a word you never taught her, and you're pretty sure her parents never did either? Were you embarrassed? (I know I was!) Listen for equity in your conversations that infants and toddlers are exposed to. I can guarantee based on the research that toddlers are absorbing everything you say and do. Babies are learning whether or not the language or actions are directed toward them.

Listen for any questions toddlers might have. Be sure to acknowledge and answer the questions in a matter-of-fact way. You already know the examples children will understand; for example if a child declares, "She's fat!" you can reply, "She weighs more than you do, but *fat* is a mean word." Or when a child sees a feeding tube that another child must use and asks, "What that tube?" Acknowledge and answer the question: "That is a feeding tube. He uses that to eat, and you use your mouth to eat."

---

*Data on books by and about Black, Indigenous and People of Color compiled by the Cooperative Children's Book Center (CCBC), School of Education, University of Wisconsin-Madison, based on its work analyzing the content of books published for children and teens received by the CCBC annually.

Learning about Equity

Look to see what the infants and toddlers in your care are noticing. What catches their eye? Is it a feature such as a beard, a hair color or style, skin color, a wheelchair or crutches, or gender? What are they pointing at? Sometimes, in an effort to be kind, we might inadvertently ignore someone or not acknowledge a child pointing toward someone out of curiosity, which can send the wrong message. For example, if a baby notices that an adult has a hearing aid, instead of asking the baby not to notice that person, explain, acknowledge, and teach (EAT). In other words, eat up that equity and make learning delicious!

- **Explain** in simple language that the baby will understand, "You are noticing a device called a *hearing aid* that helps that person hear."

- **Acknowledge** by nodding and smiling at the adult wearing the hearing aid. The child will follow your lead.

- **Teach** by following up with a book or activity. For example, look at an educational video about hearing aids with the child. Read books about all types of babies, toddlers, and twos. Create a space where learning about people and differing ideas is valued: "Yes, everyone is different, and Jovan needs more time to eat his snack." Purposely point out differences in a positive way. If an infant looks toward someone of a different race ask, "Did you notice his beautiful brown skin?" or say, "Yes, you are right. Her skin looks different than ours. Isn't it beautiful? Everybody's skin is a different color. Isn't that amazing?" Share positive observations with observations with babies, such as, "Her hair has lovely curls." Or, "Yes, his hair is different than your hair and is beautiful."

Keep in mind it would not be appropriate to ask someone why they are using assistive technology or initiate a conversation about assistive technology. Instead, go to someone who wants to teach on the topic. As for me? I love to teach about race and diversity! But it would be presumptuous to think all Black women want to teach everyone about race or diversity just because they are Black and female. It is up to us to do our own research and learn from trusted and reliable sources that are trained to teach on the subject matter.

Leading Activities in Equity

For infants, toddlers, and twos, activities in equity are easy to implement. The key is to intentionally use clear, accurate language. Keep in mind that children this age are learning language quickly and understand much more than they can say. For example, use words such as *fair* and *equal* when dividing snack: "I'm giving two crackers to each friend. That is fair. Brionna has two crackers. James has two crackers. Ming has two crackers. You each have an equal number of crackers."

Similarly, use accurate language around race, ability, gender, and languages: "Your friend has brown-colored skin that people call *Black*. And your skin is peachy, which people call *white*." Or "Yes, those are called *crutches*. They help him walk." Or "Marisol is asking for the ball. She says the word *pelota*, which means 'ball' in Spanish."

Keep activities developmentally appropriate. This means adults should make sure an activity is geared to match the children's current stage of development. Infants, toddlers, and two-year-olds learn with hands-on activities. One well-meaning teacher thought teaching equity meant giving the infants, toddlers, and twos in her classroom coloring sheets with Dr. Martin Luther King, Jr. on them. I understand this wonderful teacher's intentions—she is a hero in my book! I greatly admire and respect her. Yet, I am wondering how coloring with brown crayons would teach children this age anything about Dr. King. The toddlers looked at the drawing and kept asking "Daddy?" as she handed them brown crayons. Yes, coloring is a hands-on activity, but it supports fine motor skills more than it teaches about equity. Instead, talking about equal portions of snack, teaching children to use gentle hands, having duplicates of popular toys, or singing a song about friendship might work well as appropriate first steps toward understanding Dr. King's principles. I have also heard of teachers who have used objects such as M&Ms or an egg to show children how people of different colors are still the same inside. Children this age don't really understand the idea of the inside of a person. They are very concrete thinkers, so they might think we all have chocolate or yolks inside of us!

So what can you do? Share books with infants, toddlers, twos that feature characters who are of different ethnicities. Ask the children to look in a mirror and compare characteristics between themselves and the characters. For example, "The little girl in the story has brown skin. What color is your skin? That's right! Brown!"

Encourage a baby or toddler to notice if someone needs help or isn't getting what they need. In a classroom while getting ready to go outside say, for example, "You have on your coat already. Now check to see if anyone needs help with their coat, and I will do the same."

Do you live in an area with little diversity? Get a pen pal—or shall I say "scribble pal"—or set up a zoom playdate. Just like many of us keep young children connected to Papa or MeeMaw with a FaceTime call, we can connect them with other children in different locations. We can also connect with moms' groups on social media to make those connections.

April Leigh, a woman who identifies as white, shared some simple ways she supports her son's understandings around equity.

> My son is only two and a half, but he notices skin color. He will see another child and say, "Oh, it's a brown baby!" I don't ignore it. I acknowledge, "You're right! People can be different colors!"
>
> My son is also noticing signs around our neighborhood—stop signs, street signs, and BLM signs.
>
> When he asks me, "What does that mean?" I tell him, for example, that it says "Black Lives Matter," and I tell him, "That means that Black people are very important." I have brought a white male into this world. It's my responsibility to raise him so that he uses his privilege to be an ally to others. I want him to be a man who will stand up for others, not tear them down.

You may be thinking, "Angela, what if I don't want to talk about a particular group or lifestyle because I don't agree from a moral standpoint or don't endorse that type of lifestyle?" You don't have to agree. You can simply be kind and get along with people. Activities are not an endorsement. Just because you don't endorse a particular type of group or lifestyle doesn't mean you can't display empathy toward individuals who differ from you. Disagreement doesn't warrant disrespect or pretending that a person doesn't exist. Something as simple as "I don't _____, but I am still kind to those that do" is a good way to elevate equity while communicating the beliefs you want to pass down to children in your life.

> **"Nothing in life is to be feared, it is only to be understood. Now is the time to understand more, so that we may fear less."**
>
> **—Marie Curie, physicist and chemist**

MAKE A DIFFERENCE WITH A DONUT

We tend to judge the actions of others harshly in areas we judge ourselves harshly. Judgment can be a coping tool that can potentially make us feel better about our own decisions. Hearing someone talk about ideas you profoundly disagree with can leave you feeling vulnerable or stressed. To indulge in judgment might feel good—it is almost as delicious as chocolate—but, like chocolate, it can have a negative impact on your health. The goal of any healthy discussion should be to gain understanding instead of agreement. Judgment can be corrosive to relationships and can divert us from empathetic responses that are at the core of elevating equity.

Take judging whether someone else's choices are "right" or "wrong" off your plate; instead, add a donut. This doesn't mean an action is never wrong. It just means you acknowledge that you don't have authority over others and have not been tasked with the job of judge or juror. (Unless you actually have, and then by all means carry on.) The donut tool is meant to help focus your energy on the delicious donut rather than on the hole, which just leaves you empty. When you (and when I say *you* I mean *me*) are busy judging, it leaves little room for loving or understanding. You will be surprised by focusing on the donut is even more delicious than judgment and provides a joy that fills you up inside.

Push Past Conflict by Focusing on the Donut, Not the Hole

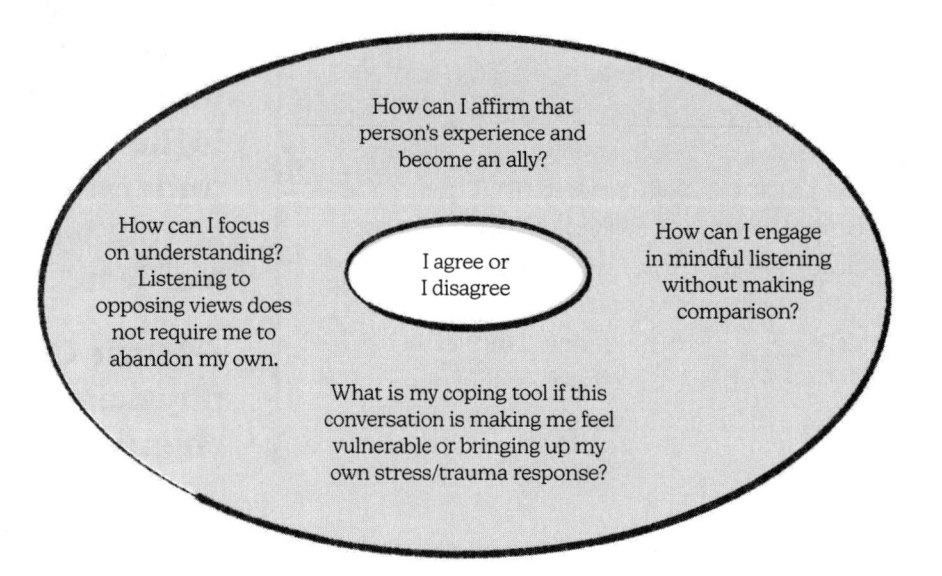

- How can I affirm that person's experience and become an ally?
- How can I focus on understanding? Listening to opposing views does not require me to abandon my own.
- I agree or I disagree
- How can I engage in mindful listening without making comparison?
- What is my coping tool if this conversation is making me feel vulnerable or bringing up my own stress/trauma response?

68 | Elevating Equity: Advice for Navigating Challenges in Early Childhood Programs

Choose Books to Support Equity Activities

In collaboration with the Erikson Institute for the Advanced Study in Child Development, I created Literature Links to Equity (Lit Links). These are simple activities that link quality children's literature to equity activities. The following are several Lit Links for books that are commonly found in infant, toddler, and twos classrooms.

Williams, Vera. 1997. *More More More Said the Baby*. New York: Greenwillow Books.

This book introduces us to three families of different races whose children run until they are scooped up by the adults. Even though they are getting tickles, kisses, and affection showered on them by grownups, the children in Vera B. Williams's Caldecott Honor Book cry out for more, more, more!

Link this tale to equity by pointing out descriptions of the families of different races featured in the story. This picture book with repetition is perfect for infants, toddlers, and twos, and as a board book it is easy for little ones to hold, chew, and manipulate.

- **Introduce the story:** Let the children explore the board book using all their senses.
- **During the story:** Talk about the color and physical attributes of people in the book as the baby manipulates it. Point to characters and say things that explicitly name race, such as, "That is Little Guy. He is a peach color called white." "That is Little Pumpkin. He is a brown color, but we call him Black."

Vocabulary: *peach, white, brown, black, middle, catch, throw, belly button, swing, either, fast*

Babies do not always explore books with any order, so it is okay to start wherever the baby starts. You may be able to read a sentence here or there for a toddler, but a two-year-old might have the attention span to sit in your lap and listen to much of the story. No matter what stage the child is in, point out physical characteristics of the characters: "Look! Little Bird's hair is smooth and straight, and Little Pumpkin's hair is curly. I like them both!" Point out that Little Pumpkin's skin is darker than his grandmother's: "Little Pumpkin is brown, and his grandmother is lighter. Black people come in many beautiful colors."

Let children explore an unbreakable, child-safe mirror, and then encourage them to compare what they see in the mirror to the babies featured in the book: "See, your skin is white like Little Guy's skin." Next, look at yourself in the mirror and point out the differences between the adults in the book and you: "I have curly hair. Little Pumpkin's hair is curly too."

Fill an empty water bottle with items such as beads. Seal the top so children can't open the bottle. Invite the child to shake the bottle every time they hear, "More, more, more!"

- **Pushing past challenging behaviors:** If you are frustrated that a baby is chewing on the book, keep in mind that board books are designed for sensory exploration and perfect for little fingers to turn pages or grab, mouth, or chew. I know it may seem as if the baby is being inappropriate by chewing on or throwing a book, but babies are multisensory learners. It is important for them to explore books with their entire bodies. If you are frustrated that a baby won't sit while you're reading a book, remember that babies learn when they move. They don't have to sit to learn or listen to a story.

  If a baby or toddler takes the book away from you in the middle of reading, that is also normal. It is fine for a baby to hold a book or toy while you read another book to them. It is okay for a young child to want to mimic you and "read" on their own. This is a good time to listen to what they know.

  If a child asks so many questions you can't get through the book, remember you don't have to read the entire book in one sitting. It is also okay if a child walks away from a book and then comes back, walking or moving in a back-and-forth manner. Young children have short attention spans. Their attention will grow the more they experience book reading.

———— **Manushkin, Fran. 2018.** *Happy in Our Skin.* **Somerville, MA: Candlewick Press.**

This picture book is a celebration of families of all races. Full of rich description and rhyme, the book includes and celebrates everyone from the human family. Link this tale to equity by pointing out the poetic descriptions of the families of different races featured in the story.

- **Introduce the story:** Point out the different skin colors, ages, genders, and abilities on the cover. Wonder aloud what the book might be about.

  Provide an unbreakable, child-safe mirror and start by looking in the mirror and talking about the child's skin and your skin. If you have a mirror that magnifies, point out the child's fingertips and fingerprint and let her explore seeing her skin, hair, and nails from a new lens.

  Have a basket of baby dolls of different ethnicities for children to explore. (If you don't have dolls like this, consider purchasing some.)

- **During the story:** Point to characters, and point out physical characteristics of the child: "Do you have any freckles, dimples, or birthmarks? Birthmarks are marks on our skin that make us special and unique."

  Explicitly name ethnicity. "Cocoa brown" might describe an African American or a Hispanic American person's skin.

  Encourage the child to look in the unbreakable mirror. Then make comparisons between the child's features and those of the families featured in the book.

  If you have baby dolls of different ethnicities, let the child hold one or two while you read the story. Pause and point out characteristics of the baby dolls.

  Talk about how our skin protects us and is often called a "birthday suit." Talk about how the colors of our skin vary based on how much melanin we have in our bodies. Explain how at your fingertips your finger print has swirls and lines that are unique to only you. Very young children will not understand all of this information, but simply talking with them supports their language development.

  Vocabulary: *birthday suit, bouquet, ginger, melanin, birthmark, freckles, fingertips, goosepimples, nestle, melanin, colorism*

- **After the story:** Trace the children on large paper, and let them use multicultural paint, markers, or crayons to decorate their outline. Remember that, at this age, children enjoy simply exploring art materials. They do not need to create a specific piece of art. As they explore, name the colors they are using and the body parts they are coloring.

  Provide multicultural playdough with colors representing a variety of ethnicities for the children to explore. Name the colors they are using.

- **Pushing past challenging behaviors:** If you are frustrated because a baby tries to chew on the book while you read, be sure to give her something appropriate to chew on while she listens. Some babies love to listen to books as they eat a snack.

  If you are frustrated that a baby or child throws books or damages them, remember it takes time for children to learn how to be gentle with books. Be patient as they learn this skill over time. The more opportunities they have to explore books, the more opportunities they'll have to learn to care for books.

  If a baby or toddler takes the book away from you in the middle of reading, that is also normal. It is fine for a baby to hold another book or toy while you read a book to her.

> Go back to that drawing and the words you wrote down that you currently say to babies. Is there anything you would add or change to elevate equity?

Caregivers of Preschoolers

Remember, when it comes to equity, I want to empower you to choose what level works for you. You are always in charge your own level of engagement with equity. Your equity journey is not static. Be sure to come back to review levels as you grow and shift in your journey toward equity. And remember to accept others in their journeys. This isn't a debate, so you don't need to decide what is right or wrong for someone else. Just find the level that is right for you and embrace a spirit of equity that supports others in whatever level they choose.

Look inside yourself. Are the preschoolers you care for receiving positive messages around equity? What is your body language when someone of a culture different than yours sits next to you? Do you stiffen up? turn away? hold a child's hand more tightly? Do you become visibly frustrated when someone speaks in a language that is different than yours? Do you use negative labels or tell "off color" jokes when you see someone who is overweight? How about when you see someone who has a different level of ability or income? Can children play with any toy regardless of their gender?

Look long and hard! Honestly, I had to take a hard look at phrases I have said many times, such as, "I am the adult, so you should listen." This could be harmful because it creates a situation where a child might think she should listen to people who are older even if they are abusive. Instead, I now say, "Respect everyone regardless of their age, and please speak out if any one of any age is not respectful toward you." Does this mean I have to compromise values that I grew up with? No. I still respect my elders and anyone of any age—the youngest of infants also deserves my respect. I had to re-evaluate statements like, "These millennials are so crazy!" Be cautious of saying something that results in an oversimplified image or idea of a particular group of people.

Look inside your classroom. Are all activities accessible to all the children? Putting popsicle sticks on book pages can make book pages easier to turn for children who have fine motor challenges, and they work well for children who don't have these challenges, too! For a child who is wearing a cast and cannot participate in a game, consider including her as the scorekeeper. Do you have tactile visuals for children that need to see and touch directions in your preschool?

Three-year-olds (and even some four-year-olds) are just beginning to be able to observe many attributes at one time. Children may comment in surprising ways about a characteristic they notice. Teacher Jamie Dolezalek Vozenilek shared the following example.

> A child overheard a friend of his asking why another friend was brown but that friend's mother was white. The friend's mother explained, "Because his daddy is Black."
>
> The child later commented, "I've never seen a Black person." I told him, "Of course you have! What color is Carlos [a Black friend]?" He replied, "Skinny." So I asked him what color I am. "Skinny," he said. This was my favorite conversation!

Use opportunities such as this one as teachable moments to clear up any confusion a child may have.

Look for early signs of stereotyping for the purpose of fitting in and making friends. Strategies as simple as asking preschoolers how they make friends could be a great way to look for strengths or misconceptions in this area. Build children's skills in inclusion and equity by inviting preschoolers to become inclusion and equity detectives. Have them look out for anyone who is not included or given equity.

Look at children's artwork and play. Research shows that children can begin to internalize negative stereotypes about themselves in preschool (Clark and Clark, 1939). In their article "Teaching about Identity, Racism, and Fairness," Derman-Sparks and Edwards (2021) remind us, "Pay attention to indicators of confusion or self-rejection. When children make self-portraits or family drawings, sometimes they choose colors that do not correspond to their actual skin, eye, or hair coloring. It is important to ask the child about these choices."

Look for children in preschool who might exhibit a knowledge-behavior gap in terms of equity. For example, children might know about fairness but might not be able to explicitly talk about fairness until the ages of five or six. They might not be able to exhibit fairness (outside of their own best interest) without adult support. Research by Vanessa LoBue and colleagues (2011) shows preschool children understand the principles around fairness by about three years of age, but research by Blake, McAuliffe, and Warneken (2014) shows that knowledge of fairness does not always align with behavior. You know this knowledge-behavior gap all too well. You understand that it is important eat healthy and exercise, but how much do you eat healthy and exercise?

Consider the books, toys, and media in your and classroom. Monitor the books, toys, and media in your classroom the same way you monitor your diet and waistline to see if they reflect a healthy range. Consider these materials in terms of how they portray people in appearance, ethnicity, ability, gender, language, religion, and immigration status. Consider whether they show different families engaging in a wide range of activities. Consider intersectionality and include accurate images of children and families with various identities. Make a list of books and other media you would like to have in your classroom while also considering what the children like and their individual interests.

Look for visibility, and always be on the lookout for children or adults who are not being represented. Being highly visible when others are not can lead to an inflated sense of sense of self for those who are represented, based on appearance, gender, family income, abilities, or family structure, and can undermine equity for those who are never seen.

Look for tokenism. In her 2016 article "Guide for Selecting Anti-Bias Children's Books," author and social-justice advocate Louise Derman-Sparks reminds us to look for "the one only message." She says, "Regularly seeing only 'one' person of any group teaches young children about who is more or less important. It only allows children to see one view of a group of people, rather than the diversity that exists among all groups." Do I still

74 | Elevating Equity: Advice for Navigating Challenges in Early Childhood Programs

love the *Facts of Life* TV show in which the character of Tootie was the only person of color? Interestingly, yes. And, I also have a higher standard for shows on television today. Embrace what mothers-in-law across the globe have always known: You can love something dearly and still maintain a critical eye.

Ask what materials are appropriate for learning. For example, I thought building using marshmallows with toothpicks was a harmless learning activity until I realized that the marshmallows commonly found in grocery stores are not considered kosher by people of the Jewish faith or considered halal by people of the Muslim faith. In addition, I would put rice and beans in a sensory table for children to explore without considering that some families found this insensitive to those who were hungry.

Look outward in your community. Are the preschoolers you care for only around people who look like and act like them? Continue to consider virtual playdates or pen pals to give them opportunities to interact with a variety of people. Does the school include children from diverse cultures and with diverse abilities? What about adopting a "grandparent" for your classroom and visiting the grandparent once a week to learn about varying age groups?

Listening for Equity

Listen for any misconceptions preschoolers might have around equity. Instead of focusing on where they "got that from," keep in mind that anyone might use inequitable words at any time. Equity is not something people "have" or "are," it is a continuum we all fall along. In the same way you would clarify if a child mistakenly called a square a circle, clarify any misunderstandings around equity. Cultivate an environment that embraces mistakes as opportunities to learn. For example, if a child says, "That person is dirty," respond calmly with something like, "You are so observant. That person is clean. They have more melanin in their skin that gives them more color." Or if a child says, "I went to chubby Mike's house," respond, "I am glad you and Mike are friends. Remember, we focus on who people are instead of how they look. I think you mean you went to Mike's house." Or if a child declares, "No girls allowed!" reply, "Every place is for everybody." Keep in mind that, for preschoolers, the simplest explanation is usually the best. Don't overthink it! You are already an expert. Only you could know the words and examples that will resonate with the children you care for.

Listen to how you reinforced and use languages during instruction. When you have bilingual preschoolers, you need to be what I call "biliberate," which is a play on the word *deliberate*. How an educator uses language could send important messages about which language is more prestigious to young children. Researcher Madeline Fernández (2006) advises that, when working with bilingual children, teachers should reinforce and strengthen the two languages. She adds that bilingual children perform best:

- "when they are able to maintain the skills that they have acquired in their first language while acquiring the second,

- when their first language is valued and fully used in the household, and

- when their culture is promoted."

Listen closely for any questions preschoolers might have. Remember, some children might use words to ask questions; others might show confusion with their actions. Questions are how preschoolers engage in the learning process, so be sure to embrace these entries into equity. When you hear statements like, "I have more blocks so I am the boss," pose your own questions: "So just because you have more of something you get to make all the rules? Why do you think that?" Questions such as "Is that fair?" and "How would everyone feel if you had all the toys?" are great entry points into discussions of equity. Use the Explain, Acknowledge, and Teach (EAT) approach to support their journey.

- **Explain** in simple language that the child will understand.

- **Acknowledge** by inviting children with varying skills to pair up for buddy play or by asking a multilingual child to teach you some new words. The children will follow your lead.

- **Teach** by following up with a book or activity.

Learning about Equity

Hopefully, preschool-age children have had some previous discussions from ages zero to three that support their understanding of equity. If not, that is okay. You can help them learn. For example, when a child asks why someone has brown skin you can say, "Her skin is brown because she has more melanin. Melanin can make someone's eyes, skin, and hair look darker."

Expand conversations by explaining when you have a new visitor in your classroom for example, "Some people might be frightened that others will not be nice to them because they look different—let's show them how nice we are."

As a consultant, when I was observing a classroom, some preschool children noticed my curly hair and started to point and laugh. I didn't think much of it at the time—they are just preschoolers, right? But, now I think it could have been a great learning opportunity. One way to do this is get yarn or ribbon to represent varying hair textures and have children draw faces and add hair. You can use scissors to "curl" ribbon. Use sponges to represent tightly curled hair or string for very straight, fine hair. Then let children cut the "hair" or wash it using a variety of hair products, and talk about hair texture. Talk about how boys and girls can be hairstylists. Talk about how some people put oil in their hair and some people brush the oil out. Show hair picks and different types of combs and brushes. Challenge preschool children to be includers and challenge them to be on the lookout for anyone who is not being included, to notice them and include them. Make it a job to be the includer of the day.

Continue to read books about all types of preschoolers. Choose books that celebrate all religions, ethnicities, abilities, languages, genders, and family structures. Instead of Mother's Day or Father's Day, celebrate children's Favorite Grown-Ups Day, since they might be raised by a grandparent or be in foster care. This is also a perfect solution if a parent has died.

Create a space where learning about people and differing ideas is valued. For example, if a child notices that a classmate uses a fidget toy, you could explain, "Your classmate needs a fidget toy while they listen and learn, and you don't, because all people learn differently." Just like it may take a while for children to learn letters and numbers, it may take several repetitions for children to understand this concept. However, research shows children this age have capacity to learn this idea and it is developmentally appropriate for this age, so get ready to be a broken record (LoBue et al., 2011; Rizzo and Killen, 2016; Schmidt et al., 2016; Smith and Warneken, 2016; Svetlova, 2013; Wörle and Paulus, 2018; Blake et al., 2015; Essler, Lepach, Petermann, Paulus, 2020; Baumard, Mascaro, and Chevallier, 2012; Olson and Spelke, 2008)!

Learning about equity should be developmentally appropriate. Preschoolers are still hands-on learners. This means that, instead of a worksheet on equity, a peace area/table or giving a few children the job of "peacekeepers of the day" to help each other when disputes occur among classmates is a hands-on way to teach equity. Assigning peer buddies is another way to have children with differing skills support one another.

A teacher I greatly admire decided she would have children color with red, black, and green crayons for Black History Month. I am so grateful this teacher felt comfortable enough to share her idea at a workshop with me. I respect and appreciate her intentions, yet Black history is so much richer than that idea. Perhaps asking Black educators what they would like children to know about Black history might be a good start. I wonder how Black history can be embedded into this teacher's everyday curriculum. For example, she might point out items we use every day, such as the traffic light, which was invented by Garrett Morgan, a Black man.

Remember the discussion of how the parasympathetic nervous system (PNS) helps the body relax? (If you missed that part or need a refresher, it's on page 49.) Meditation, yoga, and mindfulness activities help to balance the nervous system so children can acquire skills that support equity.

Leading Activities and Activism in Equity

UNTIE THE KNOT

Using a skein of yarn or length of fabric, tie a loose knot. Have the children work together to untie the knot.

When they've done it, talk about how they had to use teamwork to succeed. Talk about how challenges with equity can also be hard to unravel and it takes all of us working together to fix them.

Keep using words such as *fair*, and talk about the difference between *equal* (everyone gets the same) and *equity* (each person gets what they need) when dividing up roles and materials.

ADDRESS ISSUES HEAD ON

Don't be afraid to discuss gender and ethnicity head on. In fact, authors Bronson and Merryman (2009) found directly talking about racial friendships improved race relations among young children.

Encourage preschoolers to notice if someone needs help or isn't getting what they need and to help them or speak up. Teach children to become allies.

Teach children about peaceful protest. You want more pizza for lunch? Let's send a letter of protest!

CHOOSE BOOKS TO SUPPORT EQUITY ACTIVITIES

In collaboration with the Erikson Institute for the Advanced Study in Child Development, I created Literature Links to Equity (Lit Links). These are simple activities that link quality children's literature to equity activities.

——————— **Clements, Andrew. 1997. *Big Al*. New York: Aladdin.**

I am always cautious about using animals to teach about equity. However, I do like this book. *Big Al* is lonely and is excluded from the other fish because of his size and appearance. But when a fisherman's net drops silently around all the fish, Big Al has the chance to show his kind character. In the end, the other fish change how they view Big Al and understand what a good friend he is.

Link this story to equity by pointing out that Big Al is nice, but that his physical attributes lead to his not having friends and being lonely despite his character.

Talk about how Al tried to change and hide his physical attributes to be accepted by the other fish. Talk about how the other fish steered clear of him and how that can make anyone feel. Point out how in the end Al used the same attributes that made him scary to help the other fish. Note that it wasn't Al who needed to change, but the other fish.

- **Introduce the story:** Talk about the fish, and have the children predict what they think will happen in the story based on the cover.

- **During the story:** Point out Al's size and physical features and ask it why those attributes are perceived as scary. Point out that Big Al is big, dark, has big eyes, teeth, and so on. Ask if these attributes exist in people. For example, ask, "Can you give me some examples?" Then observe,

    "You bring up good examples; so do you think those examples are scary?" Ask why or why not to gain an understanding of the children's reasoning. Be sure to ask how these attributes connect to equity. It is clear that Al is dark and big. Talk about how people who have dark skin or big might worry others will misread their actions or not welcome them. To get a better understanding of their reasoning, ask, "Do you think this same scenario could happen to a person? Why or why not?"

Talk about how someone would miss out on a friend if this happened.

Consider giving the children paper and having them draw as they listen to the story without seeing the pictures. During the story, pause to comment on their drawings and give them encouragement.

Vocabulary: *scary, lonely, salty, friends, tremendous, wonderful*

- **After the story:**
    - Art: When the story is over, have the children share their drawings and talk about how they imagined the fish in the story and why they imagined them that way.
    - Social-emotional: Ask the children, "If you were Big Al, what would you have done? Would you change the ending in any way?
    - Language and math: Help the children make a graph comparing all the different types of fish in the story.
    - Literacy: Have the children dictate their own story about the animals. Or invite them to dictate a story about what they look for when they choose friends. For example, do they look for friends who are fun? who think of good games to play? who will share and take turns? What else do they look for?

DISRUPTING STEREOTYPES

As children interact, listen for any biased statements. For example, when you discuss Big Al, if you hear, "Black is bad and scary," try to find out about how the children came to that reasoning. The goal is not to punish or scold but to learn more about their reasoning skills. Ask, "Why do you think that?" Listen to their responses. Then ask, "Was Big Al really scary, or was he helpful and kind?"

——— Williams, Vera. 1997. *More More More Said the Baby*. New York: Greenwillow Books.

While perfect for infants, toddlers, and twos, this book also has a catchy refrain that is great for preschoolers or early readers to remember. The book introduces us to three families of different races whose children run until they are scooped up by the adults. Even though they are getting tickles, kisses, and affection showered on them by grownups, the children in Vera B. Williams' Caldecott Honor Book cry out for more, more, more!

Link this tale to equity by pointing out descriptions of the families of different races featured in the story.

- **Introduce the story:** Ask a child to predict what they think the story might be about by looking at the book cover. Ask them what they notice about the cover.

- **During the story:** Point to characters and say things that explicitly name race: "That is Little Guy. He is a peach color, but we call him white." "That is Little Pumpkin. He is a brown color, but we call him Black."

Vocabulary: *peach, white, brown, black, middle, catch, throw, belly button, swing, either, fast*

Ask the children how they think the children in the story feel.

Point out physical characteristics of the characters: "Look! Little Bird's hair is smooth and straight, and Little Pumpkin's hair is curly. I like them both!"

Point out that Little Pumpkin's skin is darker than his grandmother's: "Little Pumpkin is brown, and his grandmother is lighter. Black people come in many beautiful colors."

Let children explore an unbreakable child-safe mirror, and encourage them to compare what they see in the mirror to the babies featured in the book. Next, look at yourself in the mirror and have the children point out the differences they see between the adults in the book and you.

Fill water bottles with items and seal the tops so the bottles can't open. Invite the children shake the bottles every time they hear "more, more, more."

- **After the story:**

    - Math: Make a graph with children showing all the colors present in their families, the class, their neighborhood, church, and so on.
    - Literacy and writing: Help children create their own story about families in your school or the neighborhood.
    - Art: Invite children to cut out photos of diverse children and families and glue them to a piece of paper to make a collage.

- **Pushing past challenging behaviors:** If a child asks so many questions you can't get through the book, remember you don't have to read the entire book in one sitting. If children are talking a lot, have them turn to a partner, then you can set a timer and let then talk for a minute or two to a friend about what they are thinking. Then come back to large group. If a child walks away from a book and then comes back, walking or moving in a back-and-forth manner, understand that this is normal for young children with short attention spans. Their attention will grow the more they experience book reading.

Manushkin, Fran. 2018. *Happy in Our Skin*. **Somerville, MA: Candlewick Press.**

This book is a celebration of families of all races. Full of rich description and rhyme, this picture book includes and celebrates everyone from the human family. Link this tale to equity by pointing out the poetic descriptions of the families of different races featured in the story.

- **Introduce the story:** Begin by asking children to predict what they think the story might be about by looking at the book cover.

    Ask them what they notice about the cover. Have an unbreakable child-safe mirror for children to explore. Start by looking in the mirror and talking about their skin and your skin.

    If you have a mirror that magnifies, and point out their fingertips and fingerprints, and let them explore seeing their skin, hair, and nails from a new lens.

Have a basket of baby dolls of different ethnicities and skin colors for children to explore. (If you don't have dolls of different ethnicities, consider purchasing some.)

- **During the story:** Point to characters, and point out physical characteristics. Ask the children,

"Do you have any freckles, dimples, or birthmarks? *Birthmarks* are marks on our skin that make us special and unique."

Explicitly name race or ethnicity. "Cocoa brown" might describe an African American or Hispanic American person's skin.

Encourage children to look in the unbreakable mirror and make comparisons to the families featured in the book.

Talk about how our skin protects us and is often called a "birthday suit." Talk about how the colors of our skin vary based on how much melanin we have in our bodies. Explain that our fingertips have fingerprints with swirls and lines that are unique to the individual person.

Vocabulary: *Birthday suit, bouquet, ginger, melanin, birthmark, freckles, fingertips, goosepimples, nestle, melanin, colorism*

Ask the children how they think the people featured in the story feel.

Ask what the children know about racism. Explain, "*Racism* is when people are not nice to each other because of their skin color or other features related to race." Or "Racism is when laws are made that don't allow people of certain colors to do things others can do."

If children ask why, take out a ball of string and wrap it around your hand over and over again. Then explain that the string is like racism—it has been intertwined in our society since it began. Just like this string, it will take time and hard work to unravel it."

Introduce the topic of colorism. Explain, "*Colorism* is when people of the same race are not nice to those with different skin colors." Ask, "Have you ever experienced this?" "How did it feel?" Children of color might be open to sharing how even people of the same race or ethnic group can be prejudiced against each other.

Give children paper and read the story without the children seeing the illustrations. Have them draw as they listen to the story. During the story, pause to comment or give encouragement. When the story is over, ask them to share their drawings and talk about what race or physical features they imagined the characters having, and why.

Talk to the children about how each family in the book shows affection. Ask, "What is the same and different about each family?" "How are they like your family?"

- **After the story:**

    ▸ Math: Make a graph, chart, or tally sheet with the children to show all the colors present in the class, their families, the neighborhood, church, school, and so on. Make a graph showing all the colors present in the book and compare that graph to the one of the class.

    ▸ Literacy and writing: Help children create their own story about families in the school or neighborhood. Write about how what races they are and how they are different and similar.

    ▸ Science, language, and literacy: Explore melanin with the children. What is it? Why do we have it? Explain how melanin protects skin from sunlight. Talk about how it shows up in the gums, nails, eyes, hair, lips, and skin of some people. Talk about how some people have freckles. Explain those are just cells that have color that show up on light skin. Anyone can have freckles. Find more books that explain the role of melanin.

    ▸ Art: Have the children trace themselves on large paper, or have them make a self-portrait or family portrait. Give them multicultural paint, markers, and crayons.

    ▸ Explain that how much melanin you have depends on how much your parents have. Mix and match and experiment with the different colors with the children. Multicultural playdough with colors representing all races is another way to explore.

    ▸ Get some old magazines and have children cut out people of different ethnicities and glue them on paper to make a collage. Notice what types of people are in different types of magazines, and point out whether or not those magazines are diverse.

- **Pushing past challenging behaviors:** If children have damaged some of the books in the classroom, consider creating a "book hospital." Teach the children how to fix any hurt books. Remember, it takes time for children to learn how to be gentle with books. Be patient as they learn this skill over time. The more opportunities they have to explore books, the more opportunities they'll have to learn to care for books.

Mother Bridge of Love. 2007. *Motherbridge of Love.* **Cambridge, MA: Barefoot Books.**

This book includes a poem that celebrates adopted children and parents. Link this tale to equity by pointing out the poetic description that explains adoption.

- **Introduce the story:** Begin by asking the children to predict what they think the story might be about by looking at the book cover.

  Ask them what they notice about the cover. Ask, "What is a bridge?

- **During the story:** Talk about the different ways the mothers contribute to the character in the poem. Ask children about the people in their homes and how they each contribute something special. Ask children if they know where they were born or their birth story.

  Vocabulary: *adoption, birth place, mother, home*

- **After the story:**

    - Math: Ask children to list and count all the people who contribute to their lives. The list might include family, friends, neighbors, and so on.
    - Literacy and art: Invite the children make their own poem or song about their family. Help by writing down the words the children dictate.
    - Science: Explore what characteristics you get from family members, such as hair or eye color, the ability to play music or dance, and so on.

- **Pushing past challenging behaviors:** Acknowledge this activity can be triggering for children who are adopted or in foster care. Allow children the option to participate or just listen. Have supports ready if needed for social and emotional needs.

―――― **Brown, Monica. 2011. *Marisol McDonald Doesn't Match/Marisol McDonald no combina*. New York: Children's Book Press.**

This book is about Marisol McDonald, a biracial Peruvian-Scottish-American girl whom people try to categorize. They say she doesn't match, and that is okay with Marisol. The author is a mestiza Peruvian American of European, Jewish, and Amerindian heritage. She wrote this tale to bring her own experience of being mismatched to life.

Link this tale to equity by pointing out the descriptions of skin tones, hair color, and physical attributes of the characters. Point out languages featured in the story, and describe code switching. *Code switching* is when people switch between languages or modify dialect, register, accent, or behavior to adapt to cultural norms or circumstances.

- **Introduce the story:** Begin by asking the children to predict what they think the story might be about by looking at the book cover.

  Ask them what they notice about the cover. Have an unbreakable child-safe mirror for the children, and start by looking in the mirror and talking about their skin and hair color and texture as well as yours.

  Practice words from different languages. Talk about being multilingual. Talk about the similarities and differences between English and Spanish words, sounds, and spellings.

- **During the story:** Point out physical characteristics of different characters.

  Talk about how Marisol mixes foods of different cultures together.

  Vocabulary: *code switch, mismatched, cursive, abuelita, Peru, biracial, multilingual*

  Ask the children how they think the people in the story feel.

  Ask the children what they know about code switching or have seen other people do.

Ask whether children have experienced feeling like they are a "mismatch." How did it feel?

Give the children a voice recorder, and record them saying words in different languages and compare the sounds.

Talk about being biracial and bilingual.

- **After the story:**

  ▸ Math: Make a graph, chart, or tally sheet with children with all their different identities.

  ▸ Science: Explore what being biracial means.

- **Pushing past challenging behaviors:** This discussion could be triggering, so make sure children have support if they are feeling strong emotions around this topic.

Seuss, Dr. 1961. "Too Many Daves." *The Sneetches and Other Stories*. New York: Random House Books for Young Readers.

This book is a collection of stories about that focus on diversity and tolerance. The story "Too Many Daves" describes how a mother's choice to name all her sons the same name when they also look the same causes problems. She wishes she had chosen more diversity. Like most Dr. Seuss books, this story uses rhyme.

Link this tale to equity by pointing out that all the Daves in the story have the same name and look the same and how not having diversity can cause problems.

- **Introduce the story:** Begin by asking the children to predict what they think the story might be about by looking at the book cover. Ask them what they notice about the cover. Tell them that the book contains several stories, but you will read just one.

- **During the story:** Point out characters' physical characteristics. Ask, "Are there any differences between the Daves?"

Talk about how Mrs. Cave feels about having all the Daves.

Ask the children how they would feel if everyone looked the same. What kinds of problems do they think it would cause?

Vocabulary: *Difficult, imagine, racism, diverse, diversity*

Talk about how being different can be fun and interesting. For example, "You get to learn new things, eat different foods, learn different sounding names and words, learn new games, new music, different points of view, or different ways of doing the same thing."

Ask the children, "Has anyone ever not wanted to include you because of how you look?" "How did it make you feel?" "How do you think others feel when they are excluded?" "How can we speak up if we see or suspect someone is being excluded because they are not the same?"

Talk about how and why someone should not change themselves to be the same as everyone else. Talk about how our differences are what make us special and things more fun.

Talk about the variety of names (first and last) in your family or whether you have the same name as someone else in your family or at your school.

Ask the children if they have any worries associated with their name, such as it being hard to pronounce. Ask if they know anyone with an uncommon name or one that is hard to pronounce.

Talk about the different spellings of their name.

Ask the children if anyone ever made them feel bad or sad about their name. What did they do? Talk about the origins of the children's first or last name.

Give children paper and read the story without the children seeing the illustrations. Have them draw as they listen to the story. During the story, pause to comment or give encouragement. When the story is over, ask them to share their drawings and talk about what race or physical features they imagined the characters having and why.

Ask the children what kinds of diversity they see around their neighborhood or school. Why is diversity important?

A DISCUSSION ON DR. SEUSS

On March 2, 2021, Dr. Suess Enterprises released a statement acknowledging that some of the works by Dr. Seuss (real name, Theodore Seuss Geisel) portrayed people of some ethnicities in harmful and hurtful ways. You can read the entire statement here: https://www.seussville.com/statement-from-dr-seuss-enterprises/

They decided to cease publication of several books that contain harmful, offensive content.

As a result, I have taken those books out of my library. March 2 is also Read Across America Day, which was established by the National Education Association. This is a good example of how equity action steps are always evolving. I still read "Too Many Daves" due to its message, but it is always a good idea to periodically reassess your classroom or home library.

I find that many people can have strong opinions about Dr. Seuss and children's literature in general. In case you haven't noticed, I value all people. I do not necessarily agree with all people, but I believe in people choosing their own equity action steps. So, remember the donut from page 68? Strive for understanding rather than agreement.

- **After the story:**

  - Math: Make a chart or graph of different names of friends and family.
  - Literacy: Help the children create their own story about being different or diversity, or invite them to dictate a story about how it feels when people mispronounce their names or comment on some way that they are different.
  - Social Studies: For older children (grades one and two), read books about the names of people who were enslaved or about the history of slavery. Talk about how imposed names can make someone feel bad.
  - Art: Invite the children to draw or paint a picture symbolizing what their name means. The website Behind the Name (https://www.behindthename.com/) offers explanations of the meanings of names from many cultures. Keep in mind that a child's name may mean something different in their family.

- **Pushing past challenging behaviors:** This discussion could bring up strong feelings for children and families. Be prepared to provide children with support if needed. Collaborate with your school mental-health consultant or social worker; if you don't have one, reach out to one in your community for a consultation.

In a blog post on the National Association for the Education of Young Children (NAEYC) website, Karen Hollett writes about a center's journey toward teaching an anti-bias curriculum (Hollett, 2019). She shares that teacher Jenn Hoovan's preschool classroom offers some great examples of how this might look in action. Hoovan wants children to view each piece of who they are positively. For example, she knows that some children in her class "come from families of lower socio-economic status, and so she intentionally uses language and play to frame parts of these families' lifestyles in positive ways. When playing with a doll, for instance, she pretends the doll lives in an apartment and talks about how fun it is for the doll to have so many friends who live right down the hall from her."

I remember a well-meaning teacher changed her dramatic play area into a store, but when I spoke to the children, it turned out they had no background knowledge of a store because they often got donations from a food pantry. It is a good idea to introduce new ideas by starting with what children already know and then link new ideas to the old one to build on their background knowledge. In the blog post, the teacher helps children understand the concept of prejudice by connecting it to familiar experiences with fairness, which most preschoolers have strong feelings about. Hoovan relates that she gives children an emotional connection to the topic of understanding people who have been marginalized by talking to them "about things that have happened to them that are unfair, and it can create a sense of understanding."

> Now go back to that drawing and the words you wrote down that you currently say to preschoolers. Is there anything that shed a new light on things? Is there anything you would add or change to elevate equity?

Educators Who Work with Early Elementary Children

Are you getting the hang of this? What level of equity might you consider for children in early elementary school? Reflect on what might work for you as you elevate equity. Just as jumping up and touching the doorframe makes children at this age feel powerful, I want to empower you to find the level that is right for you. Look, listen, and learn.

Looking Inward and Outward for Equity

Look inside yourself. Are you open to making sure all aspects of identity are acknowledged and celebrated?

Look inside your classroom. Consider, for example, the perspective shared with me by a mom:

> Just because two Asian kids are in the same class doesn't mean they are friends or best friends, and just because my son is Asian doesn't mean that you should seat him with the only other child of color in the room all the time and assume they are BFFs. The teachers always put my son with this very pretty Black girl. She did not want to be sitting next to my son. She wanted to sit with her girlfriends. Can you blame her? Boys are yucky when you're in kindergarten and first grade.

This is an example of how a well-meaning teacher considered only race instead of intersectionality. We must consider multiple identities. Instead of assuming what a child needs, activate the Q in *equity* by surveying families to see what supports they think their child needs in terms of identity development and/or culture.

- Look for children's natural tendency to group themselves based on gender (or any other characteristic), and have a "Mix It Up" day during which, for 10 or 15 minutes, they play or interact with children they don't ordinarily interact with.

- Look for any bullying or exclusion. Have a "Buddy Table" during lunch or a "Buddy Bench" during recess, so children who need a buddy will know where to find one. Have children volunteer to be buddies to ensure they do find one.

- Look for any indication a child is feeling stress or anxiety around any aspect of their identity. Look for signs a child is internalizing any negative stereotypes about their identity. This photo is one I drew for a class assignment in about 1979 or 1980. It might look good, but if you take a closer look, you'll notice that the drawing of my father does not reflect the reality of a wheelchair. My father never wore hats and had a large afro, but if you look to the left you'll see that I scratched out my first attempt to draw him because I wanted to cover his hair. An afro was not a characteristic from the dominant group of children I went to school with the time.

- Look for any signs of stereotyping. Have first-, second-, or third-graders pick a group such as "grandparents." Ask them to write down (or say and you write down) everything that comes to mind for 60 seconds. Then talk about what they said and wrote. Introduce the word *stereotype*. Put simply, a stereotype is a description that assumes an entire group all act the same way. For example, "All boys are good at sports," or "All girls wear pink." Do all grandparents fit the children's descriptions? Do some? Asking children this age how they make friends is a good way to look for stereotypes or exclusion.

- Look outward in your community. Is the community diverse? Research shows exposure to diverse groups helps with equity and inclusion. There's no need to go far to find diversity. You can offer virtual experiences, field trips, and connections to schools from other cities or parts of your town or state. Finding pen pals from different schools is a great way to include diversity. Pair younger students with an older peer mentor who speaks a different language or is of a race or culture different than their own.

- Look at the dates that books, learning materials, and media were created, and continue to assess the level of relevance and sensitivity to equity. Just as you update your phone or computer, continue to update your books, learning materials, writing prompts, and lesson plans. Your lessons should show a variety of people in terms of appearance, race, ethnicity, ability, gender, language, religions, and immigration status, and families doing a wide range of things from a variety of places. Make a list of books, learning materials, and media you would like to have in your classroom while also considering what children like and their individual and natural interests.

Listening for Equity

- Listen for any bias or internalized bias your students might have around equity. Listen in class, but don't forget to listen also on the bus, in the cafeteria, or at recess. For example, researchers Van Ausdale and Feagin (2001) noticed as early as preschool that children had developed the capacity to be "highly selective about the adults with whom they share their racially oriented language, concepts and behavior." Van Ausdale and Feagin said that this behavior demonstrates children's sophisticated knowledge of their own thought processes as well as the interpretations and understandings of others, especially adults.

- Listen to make sure children and staff are not shortening names to make them "easier to pronounce." Instead, teach students and staff to say, "I am going to work hard to learn your name," or "Keep correcting me. It helps me learn your name."

- When you hear bias—even subtle forms—take it seriously. For example, if a child has a nickname given by others, ask the child privately if she is comfortable with that nickname. For example, it took me years to live down the nickname "Olive Oyl," given to me by a teacher because I was so skinny. The teacher wasn't a bad teacher. Anyone who has the courage to teach is a hero in my book! But the teacher didn't consider my comfort level with the name.

  It is not just nicknames. In his 2021 book *Uncomfortable Conversations with a Black Boy*, Emmanuel Acho describes being called an Oreo and being told, "You don't even talk like you're Black." Children from families who have immigrated or are part of a community that is not dominant may struggle to figure out how to maintain their cultural identity and language while embracing a new culture. Have students make a list of how they feel when they don't meet stereotypical expectations of how they should be based on their different identities. For example, a girl can be good at sports, and anyone can wear pink. Ask them how they balance all their identities and their intersectionality. Keep in mind that they don't have to share these ideas with the entire class. Writing about those ideas, drawing them, or making a song or play about them and brainstorming how to combat them is important for equity. Children learn more about inclusion when they analyze their own exclusion.

Continue to use the Explain, Acknowledge, and Teach (EAT) tool to support your journey. Listen for learning organizations that are also elevating equity, and be sure to bring those examples into the classroom.

Learning about Equity

Raise your hand if you are thinking, "I don't have time for this! Angela, I have enough to do!" Here is the good news: Activities around equity don't have to be some elaborate experiment or activity. Learning about equity should be embedded in the activities and lessons you *already* do. Make a list of what happens in your everyday routine. Then think about how you can include equity. For example, having students reflect on a reading passage or story and pick out inequity can support understanding. Having students vote on activities in the classroom can support the understanding of equity. Embedding equity into what they do each day is the most powerful way for children to learn about it. Just asking a question such as, "Is that an example of equality or equity?" is a good start! Begin with two minutes a day. Small ideas can lead to big changes. One new prompt, one new activity is enough. You've got this!

> **"If you think you are too small to make a difference, try sleeping with a mosquito."**
>
> —Dalai Lama XIV

- Use cooperative learning groups to encourage collaboration consistently as part of your daily routine.

- Young children are concrete learners, so have them try by themselves to solve a problem, such as building a tower with blocks or a math equation. Then have them work in teams or work in centers to solve the same problem. Talk about which was easier and which was harder. Have them think about the diverse strengths they bring to the group. Talk about how we have to work on solving issues with equity as individuals but also work on systematic inequalities in the world as a collective.

- Challenge children to be includers. For example, choose different students for the job of "includer of the day." For example, assign the includer for certain activities to make sure everyone who wants to be heard is heard. The includer could point out, "Amy had her hand up." Make sure the includer is a defined role with a list of appropriate tasks. If you don't define what to do, students might just do something else.

- Create activities to help children learn the difference between equality and equity. Remember *equality* is when everyone gets the same thing, and *equity* is when each person gets what they need. A great activity is to ask the children what they think about giving everyone a peanut butter sandwich or ice cream. Ask if this would be fair to someone who has an allergy or is lactose intolerant. Or distribute an adhesive bandage to each child regardless of their "injury." Discuss how a little bandage would be very helpful for a scrape on the leg but not for someone having an asthma attack. You can find different versions of this activity online (see, for example, Niaura, 2018). This activity can also introduce the idea that help can hurt (literally) if the help doesn't take into account each person's individual situation.

- Model equity by allowing students to show their understanding of schoolwork in a variety of ways. For example, to honor and showcase diverse learning styles, play assignment Tic-Tac-Toe, and let students choose three activities from the list.

Draw a picture of the main character.	Act out the conclusion of a story.	Write a song about one of the main events.
Write a poem about two main events in the story.	Make a poster that shows the order of events in the story.	Dress up as your favorite character, and perform a speech telling who you are.
Create a Venn diagram comparing and contrasting the introduction and the closing.	Write a sentence about the main character.	Write a sentence about the setting.

- Encourage students to let each other know if they are struggling with something in their lives by using the words "Handle with care." This will let everyone know the individual needs extra patience and support while maintaining privacy. Equity is about understanding that maybe that person needs more compassion today.

- Have students bring in pictures of popular ads, and let the children give each one an equity score. Or let them give equity scores to articles or textbooks. For example, does an ad for clothing include various body sizes? people with disabilities?

- Set a goal to turn down the stereo… types! Reframe or acknowledge stereotypes anywhere in your classroom: books, content, student statements, and so on. Be cautious not to shame students, and make it clear that you always challenge the discriminatory attitudes and behavior by "calling students in" privately rather than relying on the people who were excluded to do so. Understand that people are more than their behaviors

- Play the Reframe Game. Reframe any teasing around race, gender, ability, language, or immigration status, such as "You are smart for a girl," with "All people are smart. That statement reinforces stereotypes." If someone says, "I thought all Mexicans spoke Spanish," reframe the statement with "People of color talk many different ways." If someone asks, "Aren't you supposed to be smart? You are Asian," reframe with, "Let's look at each person as an individual." You would be surprised what intentionally setting the expectation can do. In my classroom, I would reframe even when students said, "Shut up." I'd say, "If you hear my voice, take a deep breath."

- Offer opportunities for children to respond to prompts such as, "What does a part of your identity say about you?" or "How are you unique?" or "What does your accent say about you?"

- Address stereotypes head on: "I know women are often underrepresented in science because they were often excluded from schools until recently. But let me share about some women who are at the top of the science field now." Instead of simply stating that a group might be underrepresented, address *why* a group might not be represented and *the systems* that excluded them.

- Establish equitable standards for working collectively with others in your classroom.

- Make an allies board. In the first few days of school, have students brainstorm how they can be allies to each other based on their different identities. Keep the examples up *all year long* for students to refer to.

- As a teacher, I would acknowledge and celebrate cultural awareness months. But please do not reserve activities about a particular group for only one month out of a year. Equity should be ongoing all year long. The purpose of a month such as Asian American and Pacific Islanders Heritage Month is to showcase the work and activities around the topic you have done all year long. Let me repeat that for the people in the back. The month is mean to highlight the activities you have done all year long. It is not meant to do those activities only during that month.

- Have students complete a confidence level before an assignment: "On a scale of 1 to 10, how confident are you, and why did you pick that number?"

Leading Activities and Activism in Equity

Create opportunities for cultural self-expression by letting students share stories and perspectives with you or the class. In my class, students could share once each month for extra credit. Also allow students to opt out of experiences they don't feel comfortable with or give them the option to not share with the entire class.

- Tap into diversity and activism in and outside the community with guest speakers in person or via video conferencing.

- Showcase and partner with projects, programs, or organizations that focus on race, equity, or social justice.

- Offer discussion prompts, such as: How connected do you feel to your heritage? How do you maintain cultural ties? What encounters have you had with exclusion?

- Have an inclusion club with inclusive activities. Provide support groups for children who are experiencing the stress of exclusion and inequity.

CHOOSE BOOKS TO SUPPORT EQUITY ACTIVITIES

Khalil, Aya. 2020. *The Arabic Quilt: An Immigrant Story*. Thomaston, ME: Tilbury House.

This book is about Kanzi, a third grader who has moved from Egypt to America, and she wants to fit in. She has a quilt that is a treasured reminder of home. She soon realizes that her quilt will help her make new friends. Link this book to equity by helping children to learn about immigration and trying to fit in. The book includes a glossary of Arabic words and Arabic letters with their phonetic English equivalents.

- **Introduce the story:** Begin by asking the children to predict what they think the story might be about by looking at the book cover. Ask them what they notice about the cover. Ask them if they have ever been anxious fitting in or making friends. Ask children what an immigrant is. Give each child a piece of fabric to hold during the story or a piece of paper they can draw on as they listen.

- **During the story:** Ask the children if they have ever felt different due to their identity.

    Ask them if they know what a hijab is and why it is worn. Ask what other cultures cover their hair.

    Use a map to talk about the location of Egypt.

    Ask what it means to be bilingual. Ask them if they know what code switching means. *Code switching* is when individuals alternate between two or more languages, dialects, accents, or behaviors to adapt to cultural norms or circumstances.

    Vocabulary: *hijab, immigrant, code-switch, bilingual, quilt*

    Ask the children how they think the people featured in the story feel.

    Ask if they have experienced anything similar. How did it feel?

- **After the story:**

    - Math: Make a graph or chart of all the names in the class.
    - Literacy and writing: Help the children create their own quilt. Talk about translating to different languages.
    - Art: Have children create visual representations of how to help someone fit in.
    - Geography: Look at the map and talk about immigration.

- **Pushing past challenging behaviors:**

    Talk about creating a welcome committee for new students at the school. Pair new students with an older or same-age mentor student.

    If some children feel emotionally triggered by the story and conversation, talk about ways to cope with those emotions and use breathing exercises. Reassure them that they can talk about their strong feelings.

—————— **Choi, Yangsook. 2003. *The Name Jar*. New York: Dragonfly Books.**

This book is about a little girl who is trying to fit in at a new school and is anxious about whether her name will fit in too. Will children be able to pronounce it? Link this book to equity by helping children to consider the meaning and importance of names and languages.

- **Introduce the story:** Begin by asking the children to predict what they think the story might be about by looking at the book cover. Ask them what they notice about the cover.

    Invite the children to write the names they have—first, middle, last, and nicknames—on slips of paper. Let them put the papers in a jar. Ask them if they have ever been anxious about their names.

- **During the story:** Point to the characters, and point out languages in the book.

    Have children draw while they listen to the story. Later, they can voluntarily share with the rest of the class about their drawings and post them in the classroom if they like.

    Encourage the children to talk about their neighborhoods and make comparisons to the families featured in the book.

    Vocabulary: *introduce, graceful, signature, neighborhood, nicknames*

    Ask the children how they think the people featured in the story feel. Have they ever experienced this? How did it feel?

- **After the story:**

    ▸ Math: Make a graph or chart of all the names in the class.

    ▸ Literacy and writing: Help children create their own story about families in their school or neighborhood. Invite children to write the phonemic pronunciations underneath their own written names on name tents so all students can learn how to pronounce everyone's name.

    ▸ Art: Have children create visual representations of the significance of their names.

- **Pushing past challenging behaviors:**

    Notice in this activity from third grade that I originally wrote my mother's name as *Mary*, and my teacher had to prompt me to write my mother's name accurately. Her name was *Mathrell*, but Mathrell is not a common name. I was worried children would not be able to pronounce it. Notice whether children or adults are shortening names to make them "easier." Easier for whom? Adults should not ask children to alter or adjust their names. Assure children and families that if you make a mistake you will keep trying until you get their name right.

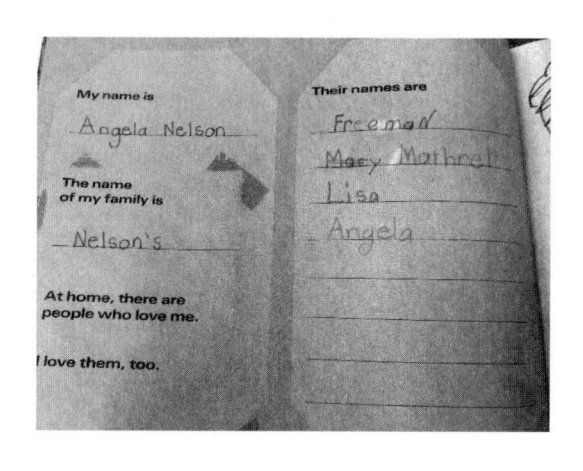

DesJarlait, Maria "White Cedar Woman." 2021. *I'm Not a Costume!* Self-published.

This story features Ayasha, a five-year-old girl who moves to Chicago from Fort Berthold reservation and encounters cultural appropriation. Link this book to equity by showing examples of cultural appropriation and talking about how to respect all cultures.

- **Introduce the story:** Begin by asking the children to predict what they think the story might be about by looking at the book cover. Ask them what they notice about the cover. Have some costumes or photos of costumes and ask what types of costumes are appropriate to wear for fun or a party.

    Have photos of various cultures and the clothes they wear. Ask the children about what clothes they might wear for different events or important ceremonies.

- **During the story:** Ask the children whether they have ever changed schools or moved. Ask what that was like. Did they worry about anything?

    Ask if the children have clothing that represents their culture.

    Explicitly name *cultural appropriation* and explain that it is the inappropriate use or adoption of an element or elements of one culture or identity by members of another culture or identity.

    Vocabulary: *cultural appropriation, Ojibwe and Arikara languages, costume, regalia*

    Ask the children how they think the people featured in the story feel.

    Ask what the children know about cultural appropriation. Have they ever experienced it? How did it feel?

- **After the story:**

    ▸ Writing, literacy, and art: Invite the children to draw and write about a special part of their culture.
    ▸ Literacy and math: Make a Venn diagram comparing cultural celebration and cultural appropriation.

- **Pushing past challenging behaviors:**

    During this book, a child comments, "Well, this happens all the time in my culture. People dress up as leprechauns—what is the big deal? I know someone who is Native American, and they said they don't care. Why can't we have any fun?" Praise the student for bringing up that point, and explain there is context around this example: "If you decide you no longer want anyone to dress as leprechauns, you can choose that, just as this woman is saying her culture is not a costume. We always will listen to those who are from a culture and will respect their wishes. Native Americans are not a monolithic group. If one person who is Native American does not like for you to dress up, then you should adjust." As you might have guessed, this book and discussion might be emotionally triggering for some children. Talk about ways to cope with those emotions and do breathing exercises. Explain that they can talk about their strong feelings.

————— **Celano, Marianne, Marietta Collins, and Ann Hazzard. 2018.** *Something Happened in Our Town: A Child's Story about Racial Injustice.* **Washington, DC: Magination Press.**

Published by the American Psychological Association's Magination Press, this story features questions children might have about traumatic events. The authors offer guidance with thoughtful questions and answers that can be used to open up a discussion with children about violence, injustice, and racism. Link this book to equity by answering children's questions around community violence.

- **Introduce the story:** Begin by asking the children to predict what they think the story might be about by looking at the book cover. Ask them what they notice about the cover.

    Ask children if they ever see news stories that scare them or that they have questions about.

- **During the story:** Explicitly name *community violence* and show children the community helpers who help in such a situation.

    Ask children how they think the people featured in the story feel.

Look at the Note to Parents and Caregivers section for detailed ideas for discussions after reading the story.

Vocabulary: *community violence, bias, mistake*

- **Pushing past challenging behaviors:** This book might be emotionally triggering for some children. Talk about ways to cope with those emotions and use breathing exercises. Explain they can talk about their strong feelings.

——— **Nyong'o, Lupita. 2019. *Sulwe*. New York: Simon and Schuster Books for Young Readers.**

This story features Sulwe, who is darker than everyone else in her family and school. She wants to be beautiful and bright like the other members of her family. Then a magical journey in the night sky opens her eyes and changes her mind. Link this book to equity by discussing colorism and how it feels.

- **Introduce the story:** Begin by asking the children to predict what they think the story might be about by looking at the book cover.

  Have mirrors available, and invite children to talk about their skin color.

- **During the story:** Ask the children whether they have ever heard of colorism. Explain that *colorism* is when people are not nice to individuals with a dark skin tone, typically among people of the same ethnic or racial group.

  Ask the children if they have ever felt excluded due to an aspect of their appearance. How did they feel? What did they do?

  Vocabulary: *colorism, inseparable, brightness, darkest, melanin*

- **After the story:**

  ▸ Literacy, writing, and art: Have children write and draw about when someone teased them due to their appearance.

  ▸ Art: Invite the children to use paint and crayons in a variety of skin colors to make self-portraits.

THE 4 Cs FRAMEWORK

In collaboration with the Erikson Institute for the Advanced Study in Child Development, I created the 4 Cs Framework as a model for clear, easy actions that can turn any moment into an equity learning opportunity. Start with everyday conversations and experiences, and use this simple method to help guide your conversations:

- Get **comfortable** with being uncomfortable. For example, try to avoid dismissive responses such as, "Shhhh!" or ignoring the children or laughing. This could send the message that discussing race is somehow associated with something bad, awkward, or funny. Before correcting any misconception, try to find out more about the child's reasoning. "How did you come to that idea?" That might give information about how they came to that misunderstanding so you can avoid it in the future. For example, "Oh, you saw that on TV. Remember how I said TV shows don't represent everyone who is that race?"

- **Connect** with what the children already know about race. Babies and toddlers tell us what they know with their behavior, facial expressions, and body language. Young children might blurt out what they notice. For example, does a toddler stiffen up when someone of a different race is nearby? Acknowledge what you notice and give words to what you think the child might be feeling. "I see you are nervous because you notice someone different than you. Our differences make us special."

- **Celebrate** and acknowledge differences. Say, for example, "All skin colors are special!" or add new words to the children's vocabulary. For example: "You are both brown, but she is darker because she has more melanin in her skin. Melanin in your body gives you more color."

- **Challenge** stereotypes. Match your words with actions, and reflect on the messages you might be giving the children. Do you comment only on children or adults with certain features? For example, do you tend to compliment children or adults with light eyes or certain features or hair textures? Be intentional if the children's features are not a part of the dominant group. "All hair is good hair! Let's write down all the good things about your hair together."

- Science: Talk about melanin and how it adds color to skin, eyes, lips, gums, freckles, and so on.
- Literacy or music: Invite the children to create a poem or song about their unique appearance.

- **Pushing past challenging behaviors:** This book and discussion might be emotionally triggering for some children. Talk about ways to cope with those emotions and do breathing exercises. Explain they can talk about their strong feelings.

Considerations for Lessons around Equity

Voice of reason: "Angela, this all sounds very nice and good, but I have enough too do! I am trying to support children with special needs, children who are multilanguage learners, and children with intense challenging behaviors with no help!" Okay, I get it! This was a challenge I also encountered! How do I balance the needs of all the children? I created a *Push Past It!* tool called "What About the Other Kids? Balancing the Needs of All Children: Multitiered Systems of Support" to help educators working in groups think about children at the different tiers of support they need in a school day. You can find this tool at https://www.gryphonhouse.com/our-authors/author-detail/angela-searcy-edd

List children's names in each box on this form according to the levels of support they need: tier 1, tier 2, tier 3. In the other column are suggestions for potential supports. Note that the list of supports in the downloadable form is not comprehensive. They are just ideas to get you brainstorming. The following is a sample.

Arrival/Departure	
Time of Day/Activity	**Types of Support**
Tier 1	Tier 1: • Make children greeters to support other children in tiers 2 and 3 • Pair this child with a child in tier 2 as a greeting buddy • Give this child a visual to show other children who struggle in tiers 1 and 2
Tier 2	Tier 2: • Place in child's cubby visuals of what to do at arrival • Create a social story of what to do at this time • Have family put pictures of teachers, school, and favorite activity on a key ring. Attach to backpack if child takes bus • Place a calming basket in cubby for child to use as he enters room • Pair child with a child in tier 1 as greeting buddy • Send visuals of arrival steps home to family (no one reads newsletters) • Sing behavior steps as children arrive
Tier 3	Tier 3: • Plan to be close to this child for the first 5 minutes after she walks in the room. If children enter at once, have their cubbies near each other so you are in close proximity. If you have more than one adult, divide this responsibility • Leader comes in room for 5–10 minutes at this time to push in support and fade as children gain skills • Have visuals of that specific child during transition, and send those visuals home

Jane Elliott is an educator who has received an award for excellence in education from the National Mental Health Association. I emailed her to ask what advice she would give early childhood educators today. Guess what happened. Something I never considered. The next day—yes, the very next day—Ms. Elliott replied! Thus began a series of email exchanges that still warm my heart and garnered me the title of *cousin*. Yes, Jane Elliott considers me, Angela Searcy, her cousin. Following are some excerpts from those exchanges:

Dear Angela,

I am pleased that you call yourself an 'educator'... You are obviously doing what educators are supposed to do, which is to...[be] encouraging [children] to read books about people who are different from themselves... Skin color, as you know, is not the problem; negative reactions to different skin colors cause the problem, and those reactions must be changed.
In order to relate to students [educators don't] have to pretend that the students all look alike. Differences are important. It's time to see them, to recognize them, and to appreciate them.

You can ask me any question you want to, just as long as you are willing to listen to my answers. You don't have to agree with them. You just have to listen to them.

Keep up the good work. Someone has to do it, and it might as well be us. And you're not a bother. You're a cousin, and I enjoy hearing from you.

Busily,

Jane Elliott

Jane Elliott made a good first attempt toward equity education in 1968. Fast-forward more than fifty years later. We have learned so much about how to cultivate equity with young children. It is important for activities to address the systemic aspects of the issue or root causes behind it. For example, can students write a letter to a TV show they watch about being more inclusive? Or have students write or draw letters to the school board about adding a holiday to the school calendar. For example, New York City Schools added Diwali, a holiday known as the Festival of Lights, which is celebrated primarily in South Asia and the Caribbean, as an official school holiday in 2022.

Activities around equity should be individualized, and there are some pitfalls to consider. In their article "Viewpoint. Creating Anti-Racist Early Childhood Spaces," Rosemarie Allen, Dorothy Shapland, Jen Neitzel, and Iheoma Iruka (2021) describe how equity activities are often approached in education:

> More often than not, early childhood educators and programs think or teach about race, bias, and equity from one of two approaches:

Chapter 3: What This Means for Early Childhood Educators | **107** the "colorblind approach" or the "celebration of differences approach" (Doucet and Adair 2013). These stem from beliefs that if educators teach love, kindness, and fairness only, then they do not need to point out or discuss racial bias or inequities with our young learners.

These approaches can potentially distort reality for young children experiencing inequity, who need explicit and intentional support, and for children who could be potential allies and support their friends. Because young children are such concrete learners, we must remember they often can't make the cognitive leap to understand metaphors, such as eggs are different colors on the outside but are all the same on the inside. Instead, I advocate for providing activities that directly teach children how to implement equity or inclusion on a regular, ongoing basis. Young children need to engage with content over time for the most meaningful learning to occur.

As you develop activities, consider the following goals from *Anti-Bias Education for Young Children and Ourselves*, second edition, by Louise Derman-Sparks and Julie O. Edwards with Catherine Goins (2020).

Goal 1: Identity

Teachers will nurture each child's construction of knowledgeable, confident, individual personal and social identities.

Children will demonstrate self-awareness, confidence, family pride, and positive social identities.

Goal 2: Diversity

Teachers will promote each child's comfortable, empathetic interaction with people from diverse backgrounds.

Children will express comfort and joy with human diversity, use accurate language for human differences, and form deep, caring connections across all dimensions of human diversity.

Goal 3: Justice

Teachers will foster each child's capacity to critically identify bias and will nurture each child's empathy for the hurt bias causes.

Children will increasingly recognize unfairness (injustice), have language to describe unfairness, and understand that unfairness hurts.

Goal 4: Activism

Teachers will cultivate each child's ability and confidence to stand up for oneself and for others in the face of bias.

Children will demonstrate a sense of empowerment and the skills to act, with others or alone, against prejudice and/or discriminatory actions.

I came up with some ideas of my own to consider, as well:

- Do your activities consider the individual needs of your students?
- What are your observations of your students around equity?
- What areas of equity might they need support in?

Wendy Walker-Moffatt, author of *The Other Side of the Asian American Success Story* (1995), suggests regarding your students as a source of information. "Teachers should learn from their students, and they should stress that importance of learning about their students' cultural priorities, cultural influences on learning behavior, and tapping existing knowledge and diverse backgrounds."

- Do you have strong emotions around equity that are influencing the activities you try? Remember to look at a diverse number of ways to meet the unique children in your care.
- Do your activities encourage empathy?

- Do your activities include listening to and learning from the people who are experiencing the inequity? Does the activity put the voices of people who are experiencing injustice at the forefront?

- Do your activities equip children with everyday actions for equity?

- Do your activities strengthen your classroom community? Does it strengthen your relationship with children as their teacher?

- Do your activities address any potential misconceptions and/or stereotypes?

- Do your activities occur once or occasionally? It is important for activities to be embedded within your everyday curriculum (for example, cooperative learning groups, includers of the day, and so on) so that children can have many opportunities to learn and practice equity. Learning about a culture cannot be confined to a month. Cultural-awareness months are meant to celebrate the work you have done all year long around that topic.

- Do your activities suggest ways to support children who are experiencing inequity and offer guidance on how to be allies?

- Do your activities include authentic human connections?

- Do your activities go beyond individual acts of kindness or meanness to address systemic issues?

- Do your activities take into account children's stage of development? It is not until upper elementary that children can really understand abstract ideas and metaphors

- Do your activities include families and the community?

Derman-Sparks and Edwards (2019) note, "Just about every subject area in the typical early childhood program has possibilities for anti-bias education themes and activities. For instance, early childhood education themes of self-discovery, family, and community are deeper and more meaningful when they include explorations of ability, culture, economic class, gender identity, and racialized identity."

Prevention is the best intervention, and we as educators want to be mindful of the best ways to elevate equity in a classroom setting. Derman-Sparks, Edwards, and Goins (2020) remind us, "Even when intentions are good, you can expect missteps as you grow as an anti-bias educator." They warn, for example, against "visiting" a culture by exploring the food, clothing, and celebrations for a day or two. Instead, consider embedding all types of people and ways of being into all activities with young children. Engage in what Derman-Sparks, Edwards, and Goins describe as "ongoing learning about how people are the same and different."

Another pitfall to avoid is "token materials." Derman-Sparks and Edwards warn against the tokenism inherent in providing one item—a doll, a book, a poster—to represent an entire culture or group. Instead, activate the *I* in *equity* by looking at many individuals in a group and embracing human diversity within groups.

Walker-Moffat (1995) advises teachers "to avoid the approach that features such attitudes as 'Now we'll talk about African American scientists or the contributions made by immigrants.'" She says teachers should, "[i]ntegrate this information throughout the program." She further warns against what she calls "cookbook strategies": simply adding a few references or terms to try to make a standard curriculum "multicultural."

Another misstep to avoid is misrepresentation. An example might be using materials about Vietnam to describe the lives of Vietnamese Americans, whose lives could be very different. Derman-Sparks, Edwards, and Goins (2020) warn against focusing on historical ways of life instead of how people are now: "For example, all Native Americans live in tipis and wear only ritual clothing," or thinking Black people from America have the exact same culture as Black people from Haiti, or that Hispanic people from Spain have the same culture as Hispanic people from Cuba.

Don't forget to re-assess "classic" books, films, and classroom materials every year. Be on the lookout for one-dimensional "diverse" characters that typically only serve the purpose of supporting the central dominant character. What is the diverse character's back story? Be cautious of characters who might not have their own agency and need the help from the "compassionate" dominant character. Do we know their motivations, or do they serve as the moral compass for the dominant character? Is there a hierarchal dimension to the relationship between characters? When reading children's literature, whom does the story center on? What purpose do the characters serve? Be cautious of "diverse" characters who have some special gift that separates them from others within the same group or use their special gift only to help the dominant character. Consider pairing a classic work of children's literature with an updated story, such as a version of *The Princess and the Pea* with *The Very Smart Pea and the Princess-to-Be* by Mini Grey or *The Princess and the Pea* by Rachel Isadora.

In the article "Diversifying Your Classroom Book Collections? Avoid these 7 Pitfalls" (Newhouse, 2020), teacher and author Lisa Stringfellow advises that own-voices authors bring something to stories that "someone who is outside of that community, no matter how much they've researched, would never be able to capture fully." For example, I was yesterday years old before I knew the author of *The Snowy Day*, Ezra Jack Keats, was a white man. This book is still one of my favorites, but it is also important to remember Stringfellow's advice: "[A]uthenticity has a powerful effect, especially for students who share that identity." As a result, it important to intentionally showcase the ideas, creations, and voices of people who have the identity you want to teach children about.

❖ ❖ ❖

Now that you have learned about what children know about equity and considered what you could do to elevate equity, are you ready to keep going? You might be feeling excited, energized, or just plain overwhelmed. I get it! But consider: Elevating equity might be hard, but experiencing inequity is even harder. Let's continue our journey with looking at the families that the young children belong to. Bring your pen and paper and get ready to test your knowledge.

> **"The difficulty lies, not in the new ideas, but in escaping the old ones."**
>
> **—John Maynard Keynes, British economist**

CHAPTER 4

Equity and Families of Young Children

It is important to make sure we aren't viewing young children in isolation; they come to us in the context of a family and community. As a result, an effective early childhood educator can't be good only at working with young children but must also be skilled at working with families. Working with young children is in tandem with effective collaborations with each child's family and community. As educators, we can't elevate equity for children without elevating equity for the families and the communities they belong to. Let's start with an activity to reflect on how we can move toward elevating equity.

Look at this list of goals children should achieve in the left-hand column. Next to each, write the age at which that goal should be accomplished.

Developmental Goal	Age at Which the Goal Should Be Accomplished
Sleep alone	
Be weaned from the breast/bottle	
Eat with utensils	
Potty train during the day	
Potty train during the night	
Play alone	
Have chores	
Be left home alone	
Go on first date	
Drive a car	

Did you finish? Good job! Now that you have wracked your brain and considered all the possible answers, it might surprise you that there is just one answer. Yes, you read right—one answer: "It depends."

Why Does It Always Depend?

When I do this exercise in person at my presentations, I enjoy watching participants confidently write their answers. When I ask them to gather in groups from various cultures, I take delight in listening in on the discussion as they debate the complexities of each goal. As I describe "various cultures," some of you might be imagining a 1980s

Benetton clothing ad with "all the colors of the world." But culture is not just race. It is age, gender, language, traditions, and, well, viewpoints.

"What if a child has special needs? Won't that change the timeline?"

"I have multiples, and when you have triplets, that timeline changes!"

"Boys! I think they are easier to potty train."

"No way! Girls are easier for me."

"It varies based of the age of the parents and whether it is their first child or last child, too. Sometimes the last child accomplishes tasks faster because they see their older siblings doing something."

"Yes, birth order makes a difference!"

"What if the child has been exposed to trauma? That can impact the timeline, too."

Each, participant shares their answers based on their own cultural experience. So, how do we choose who is right? Because culture is always changing and evolving, the only constant in the list of milestones will be change. Human beings are complex, and often each perspective includes an important way to view development that builds on our understanding. Just as both 2+2 and 1+3=4, there is usually more than one way to get to the right answer. It is important to look at various ideas. And even if you think 3+3=4 and your answer clearly isn't correct, it is still important for me to treat you with respect and kindness and to be curious and listen to why you think that way—without fear, anger, or judgment.

As I stated earlier, when I mention culture, participants often just think about race. But the beauty of this activity is that it really helps everyone to consider all aspects of cultural identity, from ability to birth order, without my ever instructing them to do so. For example, what do different religious doctrines dictate as the age a child goes on their first date? How do timelines for skill development differ if an educator, as opposed to a parent who is a banker or hair stylist, is thinking about them? What happens to the timeline for eating with utensils when a family eats hand-held foods? For example, an Ethiopian family might serve food with flatbread. A Mexican family might use tortillas. An American family might use a sesame seed bun. Where you live in the world may dictate whether your food is on a banana leaf or scooped from communal platters.

The age at which a child is considered old enough to care for siblings or to be left home alone also differs. In the United Kingdom, it is considered an offense leave a child younger than the age of fourteen home alone. In the United States, the standard is even more complex. According to the Child Welfare Information Gateway (2018), in the state of Oregon a child can't be left home alone until the age of ten; in the state of Maryland a child can be left home alone at age eight. For some readers, leaving an eight-year-old child home alone might sound reasonable; for others this sounds downright irresponsible, and for still others this might sound dangerous. In terms of the law or in terms of developmental milestones, there could be a right or wrong answer to each of these milestone accomplishments. However, from an equity-based lens, it depends on your own cultural experience.

In her book *The Cultural Nature of Human Development*, professor of psychology Barbara Rogoff (2003) contends that our variations in answers "make sense once we take into account different circumstances and traditions." If our purpose is to gain new understandings, there isn't a right-or-wrong dichotomy when we are considering equity. Always being on the same page could make for a short book of knowledge. Value judgments might be needed in terms of law enforcement or social services (and equity is not absent from those judgments, either). However, if we are focused on the *U* in *equity*, Rogoff reminds us that to "impose a value judgment from one's own community on the cultural practices of another—without understanding how those practices make sense in the community—is ethnocentric. Ethnocentrism involves making judgments that another cultural community's ways or decisions are immoral, unwise, or inappropriate based on one's own cultural background without taking into account the meaning and circumstances of events in that community." When there is a focus on who is right, that interaction stops being an exercise in equity and turns to an exercise in ego. Of course, something could be wrong, and I could be right. But, will being right help someone gain new understandings? Will it help me learn about that person and why they hold that way of being? Let me confess that being right is a guilty pleasure, but after celebrating my sense of superiority at being right, I need to regroup, buckle down, and push myself to focus my energies on *acting* right. Acting right is all about engaging in equitable actions to support children and families. My goal is to always support children and families, which doesn't mean I necessarily agree with families.

Barbara Rogoff asks us to consider not only the research behind developmental milestones but also a cultural approach that "notes… different cultural communities may expect children to engage in activities at vastly different times in childhood." Age can play a central role in understanding child development, but so can culture. In their article

"Viewpoint. Creating Anti-Racist Early Childhood Spaces," Allen, Shapland, Neitzel, and Iruka (2021) remind readers that preschool was sometimes viewed as a place to fix families. For example, in some programs Black preschoolers were seen as:

> a population that could be fixed, whose deficits could be corrected, and whose future lives could be improved… Black families, especially Black single mothers, were viewed as… inept and incapable of providing an optimal environment for their children. It was believed that Black families needed to be taught how to parent their children by the white teachers in the program (Derman-Sparks, 2016[b]). The fear of unruly, uneducated, and socially deviant children led to the implementation of preschool curricula focused on improving IQ scores, learning "socially appropriate" behaviors, and responding positively to those in authority.

This type of viewpoint is grounded in a lens that sees struggles associated with inequity as the result of personal choices and seeks to address perceived deficits instead of fixing the structural inequalities that led to those choices. As educators, we cross a boundary when we think we are in control of families' decision making.

I always found it interesting that when school districts are successful, they attribute that success to the schools, but when school districts struggle, they attribute those struggles to individual families or the community. This seems a bit nonsensical, kind of like pockets in baby clothes. Pockets for babies make no sense! Just as babies don't hold anything for which they need pockets, an equity approach means children, their parents, communities, and educators should not hold any blame.

Instead of finding fault, it is important to find families' *funds of knowledge*. Researchers Luis Moll, Cathy Amanti, Deborah Neff, and Norma Gonzalez (1992) describe funds of knowledge as "the historical accumulation of abilities, bodies of knowledge, assets, and cultural ways of interacting." According to Moll and colleagues, this approach "represents a positive (and, we argue, realistic) view of households as containing ample cultural and cognitive resources with great, potential utility for classroom instruction… This view… contrasts sharply with prevailing and accepted perceptions of working-class families as somehow disorganized socially and deficient intellectually; perceptions that are well accepted and rarely challenged in the field of education and elsewhere."

What exactly are funds of knowledge? Allison McDonald (2018), in her blog No Time for Flash Cards, says, "funds of knowledge can include learning how to make gnocchi from scratch or keep score at a curling match. It could be quilting or spinning wool into yarn. It could be how to fix a car, care for a crying baby, or prepare a Seder." To be equitable, it is important to find the funds of knowledge families bring to each learning experience. It takes no skill to find fault. When you see flaws—and when I say *you*, I mean *me*—you are accessing the most primitive part of your brain, the lower brain, which is our default. However, it takes great effort and skill as a professional to find funds of knowledge. When you do, you are using your thinking brain or higher-order thinking skills. In fact, all people (including yourself) are complicated mix of flaws and funds of knowledge. Seeing both is the only way to become an effective professional and to elevate equity. This works not only for families but for anyone you meet.

> "Everyone you meet knows something you don't know but need to know. Learn from them."
>
> —Carl G. Jung, founder of analytical psychiatry

Think of a family you are struggling with. (This can exercise can work for a colleague as well. It can even work for members of your own family or your significant other.) Next—oh, you are going to enjoy the next step—write down all the flaws you see in that family. No holds barred! This worksheet is like Vegas—what happens in this list stays there. I promise I won't tell anybody. I start with flaws because, doggone it (excuse my language), that is how my brain works! This isn't an exercise in feeling bad. Embrace it! Normalize it! All activities should honor how our brains work.

Now, take a moment and consider why you perceive each item on the list as a flaw. If you move too quickly to funds of knowledge without examining your perception of flaws, you will miss an important step in understanding yourself. It is through your own cultural lens that you view others. Usually, we judge people harshly in areas others have judged us harshly or in areas we judge ourselves harshly.

The next step will take a bit of effort as you move from your lower brain to your higher-order thinking skills. Oh, you are still writing down flaws? Okay, I get it. It feels good to be in that lower brain, doesn't it? But before you get carried away, you might want to slow your roll because there is a catch. For every flaw, you have to write down one piece of knowledge that family brings. What did you say? I did *not* trick you! (And watch your language!) Can't think of any knowledge that family might have? Then accept the fact that You. Don't. Know. That. Family. If you only see flaws, you don't see that family. If you are still working on knowing that family, skip the funds of knowledge column, and move to the next column to write a plan on how you will find out some funds of knowledge.

Family Flaws	Why Do I Perceive This as a Flaw?	Family Funds of Knowledge	How Can I Find Out about Knowledge This Family Knows

Be aware that finding funds of knowledge can be a slippery slope. For example, one of the participants in my workshops said a student's fund of knowledge was his "street smarts." Out of curiosity, I asked, "What are street smarts?" She listed skills such as how to play basketball and how the child was able to navigate his neighborhood and take care of his younger sibling. I asked, "Why can't we just call them *smarts*? Doesn't the same math that appears on a box of mac-and-cheese that he makes for his sibling also appear on a math worksheet?" *Street smarts* and *book smarts* seem to fall under the category of smarts. It all takes the same cognitive skills and abilities. This is important. In her article "Street Smarts vs. Book Smarts: The Figured World of Smartness in the Lives of Marginalized, Urban Youth," researcher Beth Hatt (2007) explores both types of "smart." She reminds us how smartness is tied to the formation of identity for children, and schools play an important part in this identity formation. "Smartness is what makes the institution of schooling so powerful in our society in assigning status and privilege because it is connected to identity. We

> "As you focus on clearing your generational trauma, do not forget to claim your generational strengths. Your ancestors gave you more than just wounds."
>
> —Ruben Harris, CEO of Career Karma

use smartness to tell us about ourselves and to tell us about other people." Moreover, to support children as they develop, "It requires a critically, reflective teacher willing to challenge her/his own assumptions and biases and "(re)envision smartness… and help students reframe their lives."

Wendy Walker-Moffatt (1995) shares a warning about myths such as the "tiger mom." For example, the "success" of Asian Americans is used to justify the idea that "ethnic minorities can succeed in… schools without affirmative action, in-service teacher preparation, or special program support" and, if so, then "student failure lies not with the schools, but with the student"—or is something we can't change such as genetics, the home environment, or motivation. For instance, in the United States, Asian American students "are not regarded as 'at-risk' students regardless of the reality of their situations… The reality is that recent immigrants and refugees from Southeast Asia, China, the Philippines, and the Pacific Islands require the same special attention that any member of a cultural minority in America requires."

Another example is the trap of thinking that special needs children have "special families." Carla Moore (2021) shares, "I wasn't 'meant' to be a special needs mom. I wasn't 'given' a special child because I am some sort of ultra-special, amazing, strong person. I have a daughter and son with special needs because genetics didn't play out in our favor. I am your average person who has two children who require more… Special needs parents are not superhuman. We're just parents taking care of our kids, loving them just as you love yours."

Viewing families of children with special needs as martyrs is just as damaging as viewing Asian American families as "model" minorities. These biases—even those perceived as positive ones—stop us from really getting to know the individual characteristics of families. Now go back and make sure your funds of knowledge are bias free.

For example, let's take a deep dive into one task on our development goal list: toilet training. Some cultures, such as caregivers in Vietnam and East Africa for instance, start taking on the potty-training task in early infancy and have cultural traditions that don't include diapers. Researchers Duong and colleagues (2013) found that Vietnamese children are typically trained by the age of two. Another study by researchers deVries and deVries (1977) found that caregivers in the Digo culture of East Africa also begin training at birth. There, day and night dryness is accomplished the first five or six months. Wow!

I have to admit I am a bit envious! If you live in a world without diapers or lived in a time before washing machines, it makes sense that you would want children to get trained as soon as possible. This might explain why in the mid-twentieth-century statistics show around 95 percent of children in the United States were potty trained by eighteen months. In contrast, a more recent study by Timothy Schum and colleagues (2002) found that only 10 percent of children are trained by this age in the United States. Just as I am not "bad" or "lazy" for not using a sundial to tell time, families today are not "lazy" or "bad" for using tools that come along with evolving technology. Culture and circumstances influence choices and approaches.

Our Potty-Training Journey

When I would see old classmates from high school, I realized they had made some astounding accomplishments! And while my fellow classmates were climbing Mount Everest (seriously—one of my classmates is the first Black woman to climb Mount Everest), cowriting TV show pilots, and presenting TEDTalks, I remember feeling accomplished that the last of our four children was potty trained on her third birthday. (Some of you are not thinking much of that accomplishment, and others of you are in shock!)

For those of you clutching your pearls, raising an eyebrow, or thinking, "Why did it take so long? Don't you just sit, pee, and wipe? How hard can that be?" I don't blame you! A few years earlier, if I had overheard discussions about potty-training struggles, I would have responded by quickly assuming a sense of superiority—starting with how early my other three children had achieved this skill—and would have commenced to disperse unsolicited advice without any sense of perspective or cultural sensitivity. You are welcome! But now I cringe thinking about these exchanges and realize how important it is to understand someone else's context first. In my case, as a two-year-old/toddler teacher, I had years of experience potty training other peoples' children. Our son Daniel, who was the oldest, was the first to potty train. And boy, he had to learn fast because his sister Maya was on the way, and my husband Reginald and I were not paying for two children in diapers! It wasn't much different eighteen months later when our next child, Lena, was born. But for our fourth child, Zaria, I guess without the impending threat of two children in diapers, I was less motivated. By this time, in our mid-thirties, my husband Reginald and I were different parents. Life when Daniel was an only child learning to potty train was very different from our life with four children with busy school and activity schedules. What people seem to forget is that families grow and develop with their children. The parent or family you see in front of you today might not be the same parent or family you see tomorrow.

My example illustrates how knowing a family's cultural context informs what types of supports might be needed next. The help I needed when, in my mid-twenties, I had one child was not the same type of help I needed in my mid-thirties with four children. The help for a working mother who is an early childhood professional might differ from supports needed by someone who is not. Being a Black mother might also change what supports are needed, and being a two-parent middle-class family also could inform someone's approach. As professionals, it is important that we ask questions around context to support next steps. Empower families to never take advice from anyone who doesn't understand their context. This is true for any advice! For example, friends will tell you to leave your significant other based off one piece of information without knowing any context about your entire relationship. Come on! You know I am only going to share stories about my relationship that put me in a positive light (insert halo here) and leave out tons of vital information. The first thing you do when your friend has a lovers' spat is to listen and ask questions that help lead your friend to find their own answers based on their own unique needs and situation. The same holds true for families.

Family Development

The idea of child development is widely recognized in the field of education. It provides a general framework to guide teachers in their professional practice and a starting point for planning quality interactions with children. Similarly, in her book *The Six Stages of Parenthood*, noted researcher Ellen Galinsky (1987) outlines a growth process for parents. Families as a whole are growing and developing in a variety of ways. Galinsky's framework provides a guide for professionals as they consider actions, engagement efforts, and supports that might be most responsive during each stage. For our purposes, we'll focus on the first four stages.

The Image-Making Stage: Pregnancy

It is during pregnancy that parents form and re-form images of their baby. Image-making is not a linear process and does not end after a child is born. This process is ongoing, and as families move through each stage, they often need support when those images do not match the reality in front of them. If a parent or family does not appear responsive to your ideas, it could be because it requires them to modify an image. It is important to realize as professionals that parents and families are in a parallel process of growth and change with their child.

With that in mind, listen more than you talk to families. Individualize how you move forward based on observations of readiness by parents. Just as you can't potty train a child who is not exhibiting "readiness" skills, you must look for readiness toward new ideas in parents. Ask questions such as, "Are you ready to move to action planning?" "Would you like to hear some of my ideas?" "What do you need right now—someone to listen, more time to think, or are you ready to move forward?" Ask permission before giving advice a family is not ready to implement: "Could I share a strategy, or is this not the right time yet?" Ask them what they imagine for their child. Let families move through the continual process of reframing and modifying their image of their child at their own pace. While educators are experts about child development, remember that parents are experts on their own family history, current situation, and future. Conversation starters can include, "What have you observed?" "What do you imagine for your child?" "How have you dealt with changes in the past?"

The Nurturing Stage: Infancy/Toddler

This stage involves developing bonds of attachment with their child. At this stage, parents are caregivers. Be cautious about directing parents to let their child "do it themselves." There is value in families encouraging interdependence as they work on bonding and attachment. Early childhood professionals may think parents are "spoiling" the child when in fact they are bonding with the child. If there is a disruption or absence from their child, this stage may take longer. It is interesting to consider how a sick child, an absence, foster care, working long hours, or work travel might affect this stage. It is also important to consider how being a teen parent might affect this stage, as their development is coinciding with their child's development.

With that in mind, encourage families to bond with their child. Use language such as, "Take your time to say goodbye," and "You are taking off your child's coat (feeding your child, washing your child's hands, and so on) even though they know how to do it, so you can bond. I get it." Reassure parents and families that feelings of nurturing are normal. Their parenting style will change as their child changes. There is no such thing as "spoiling" a child with too much love or attention. Ask families how they bond with their child; teachers may not always see this bonding or a parent could be struggling to bond. Don't assume; dialogue instead. Keep in mind that bonding looks different across cultures. The bonding process may be happening along with a lot of stress, such as sleep deprivation and uncertainty. Point out the positive signs of bonding you observe.

Authority Stage: Two to Five Years Old

As parents are constantly reshaping their image of their child, the "no" stage begins. Parents are working hard to establish routines and set limits. The parents have made it through survival mode. Now, they might be self-conscious due to the discrepancy between their image of their child and the challenging behaviors that are often associated with this age range. We learned from my earlier book *Push Past It! A Positive Approach to Challenging Classroom Behaviors* that challenging behaviors and parent concerns about those behaviors peak around this age. Families need reassurance that challenges are normal and developmentally appropriate. They may begin to question the effectiveness they have just recently acquired.

With that in mind, remind families that behavior is just another form of communication until their child has mastered language and cognitive skills. Help parents by connecting them with other families to limit isolation. Model positive discipline when children have challenges at school.

Interpretive Stage: Five Years Old to Adolescence

At this stage, parents are interpreting their child's experiences in a social world outside of the family. They're helping their child navigate social relationships and deciding what experiences will help develop their child. They are trying to figure out how involved they need to be as their child grows and gains more experiences outside the home. Families are trying to cope with the fast-paced changes occurring during their child's development. Resist the urge to label families as "lawnmower" or "helicopter" parents. It will take time for families to realize that strategies that were effective during the earlier stages might not be as effective during this stage, as their children slowly gain more and more independence. No one word could ever adequately describe the complexities of any relationship. Similar to how children can suffer when given a negative label, labels for families can restrict our ability to see their full potential and can limit our ability to express empathy.

With that in mind, give families opportunities to reflect on how to balance between helping their child become independent while still maintaining their role as an authority figure. Provide supports to families to help them choose appropriate educational and recreational activities, depending on the age and development of their child. Support families in dealing with the stress of constantly redefining their changing role as their child grows. Reassure families that the feelings of doubt or stress are normal as their child begins to become more independent and make more choices.

Help That Hurts

I was presenting a workshop for educators and discussing context when a participant said, "Now I realize my help was hurting her." She went on, "I was helping her from my perspective and not considering what she wanted or needed. I was giving ideas without asking questions and making assumptions. I was sabotaging my own efforts to help this mom."

Help should be applied in any way that supports equity and inclusion. Before offering help that could be hurting a family or your relationship, apply the Q in *equity* along with some ideas from my book *Push Past It! A Positive Approach to Challenging Classroom Behavior*.

- Ask questions to see if something that is problematic for you is also a problem for a family *before* you begin problem solving or giving advice. What you view as a problem might be a cultural tradition. Ask yourself whether you are viewing a cultural tradition or behavior from a deficit lens. This doesn't mean what you notice isn't a challenge for you as a professional. But it also doesn't automatically mean a behavior is a challenge for everyone and needs to stop or change. It also doesn't mean you abandon your ideas or culture. You may need to collaborate or to let two ideas live in the same place. For example, if a family comes to preschool each day at 9 a.m. and breakfast at the program is served at 8 a.m., the child-care provider might save breakfast for the child to eat once they arrive.

- What are their values? What are your values? Is this just a value difference?

- What is their perspective? What is your perspective? Are you so focused on the family seeing your perspective that you lose sight of understanding theirs?

- Before offering suggestions, give a family a menu of supports to choose from that you can offer if advice is not wanted. For example, give a listening ear, give time to process information or ideas, give them a connection to another professional, or give them a connection to another family who has gone through the same issue successfully.

So, how did Zaria finally get potty trained? I know you're wondering. You might be surprised to learn our youngest child potty trained in one day. We had been trying to potty train for over a year. We had read all the potty books, and "Elmo's Potty Time" was on frequent rotation on the TV. But it wasn't until our daughter Zaria's third birthday that she was finally trained. My trick? I told her the restaurant we were going to for her birthday didn't allow children with diapers inside, so she decided to wear her cloth underpants that I had been coaxing her to wear for *months*. Normally, as a child development expert, I don't recommend lying to small children. But at the time we had a full house of children ages three to thirteen, and to be frank, my husband and I were tired. I figured she wasn't going to college without being able to use the potty, so why stress myself out by forcing it? We just supported Zaria until she was ready. On a funny note, we both thought the jig was up when Zaria spotted a baby at the restaurant that evening! My husband and I held our breath when we both noticed Zaria see the baby. Luckily, when she gestured for me to lean in close to her, Zaria smiled and whispered, "Look at that baby, Mommy. They must not know the rules like we do." Whew! Disaster averted! Zaria is now a happy, healthy young adult.

An Equity Understanding of Child Development Milestones

Just like my husband and me in our journey as parents, culture is always evolving, and practices around the porcelain bowl are no different. For those of you shaking your head about "families today," remember hold onto the idea that "it depends" for all developmental milestones. Equity means everyone gets to choose their own path, free of judgment. Whatever a family's decision, I will be there to affirm their thinking when things turn out well and support them when they don't. My decision donut helps me to focus on understanding rather than agreement. There are many lenses from which to view children, families, and child development, but from an equity lens, all ways of being are to be understood.

Barbara Rogoff (2003) reminds us, "To understand development, it is helpful to separate value judgments from observations… it is important to examine the meaning and function of events for the local cultural framework and goals… It does not require us to give up our own ways… if we can go beyond the idea that one way is necessarily best, we can consider possibilities of other ways." Contrary to what you might be thinking, this doesn't mean a practice or way of being is never wrong; instead, it is a way to activate the *U* in *equity*. It is only though understanding that we can problem solve, support families, and collaborate. As early childhood professionals, we have a responsibility to:

- ensure that collaboration with families and colleagues is equitable,
- seek to understand and include cultures that are different than our own,
- use those understandings to support problem solving when challenges occur, and
- ensure there is no inherent superiority placed on our own cultural values and negative judgments placed on cultures that are unlike our own.

In their book *Knowing and Serving Diverse Families*, Verna Hildebrand and colleagues (2007) remind us that even people from the same cultural traditions are unique and there is variation within groups: "Traditional values are subject to change, and there are various expressions of cultural values and beliefs. Each person appropriates various values in an individualistic way." This understanding of variation within groups is at the heart of the *I* in *equity*.

Circle the value that is more important to you. Please try to choose one or the other on each row. Then write about why you made your choice.

Value	Value	Why You Chose One Over the Other
Living each day as it comes	Goal driven	
Interdependence	Independence	
Cooperation	Competition	
Inner harmony	Outside appearance	
Collectivism	Individualism	
Giving	Saving	
Spontaneous	Punctual	
Respect of elders	Forever young	
Egalitarianism	Elitism	

Adapted from Hildebrand, Phenice, Gray, and Hines, 2007.

Which values did you circle? Was it hard to choose?

In chapter 4 of my book *Push Past It!*, I describe common sources of conflict between educators and families, such as punctuality.

> Why couldn't these family members handle something as simple as getting their children to school on time?
>
> Then I had my own children.
>
> In 1995, when our oldest was born, I thought I would have the whole parenting thing in the bag. I had years of experience as a teacher, degrees in education and child development, and a specialization in infant studies. But by 1998, Reginald and I had three children under the age of five, and as a result I don't remember anything from 1995 to 2002. Reginald and I call them the lost years... So now I help educators and family members understand that young children's behavior is a reflection of age and development, not a reflection of child-rearing abilities or a sign of how children will behave as adults.

As you can see, it was not until I had my own children that I understood that values can change over time. I can now see that values are fluid—and the values of some families don't always match their actions. I understand how as an educator I was called upon to work within the values of the children and families I serve instead of purely within my own.

> **"Being heard is so close to being loved that for the average person they are almost indistinguishable."**
>
> —David Augsburger, *Caring Enough to Hear and Be Heard*

Setting Aside Your Own Perspective

Author Anne Fadiman's award-winning book *The Spirit Catches You and You Fall Down: A Hmong Child, Her American Doctors, and the Collision of Two Cultures* (1997) recounts the medical and cultural struggles of an immigrant Hmong family with a child who has epilepsy as they adjust to living in California. The book provides some important lessons to consider.

- Work within the families' values. The social worker in the account "worked within the family's belief system. She did not carry her belief system—which included a feminist distaste for being forced to deal with the husband instead of the wife—into the negotiations [with the family]. She never threatened, criticized, or patronized." Remember, empathy is not an endorsement. The idea is that, to be an effective professional, one needs to respect the values that a family holds dear in order to help them. Help families in the manner they want to be helped, and treat them like they want to be treated, which may differ from how you would like to be treated. Remember to activate the platinum rule to elevate equity.

- Involve the people you are making decisions about in the decisions. Fadiman writes, "[G]et rid of the term *compliance*." To be effective it is important to do away with the idea that one person is morally superior (even if that is the situation). People don't want commands; they want a conversation.

- Find cultural brokers. In the Fadiman book, it is suggested the medical team "go find a member of the Hmong community" to help support collaborations. "Use interpreters who are both bilingual and bicultural… enlist the support of family and community leaders." This means the interpreter is not just able to speak the language but also understands the customs, values, and beliefs of that culture.

- Anticipate potential cultural misunderstandings. Prevention is the best intervention. Survey families and staff to pinpoint potential cultural differences. For example, if families don't understand the power of play in child development, consider changing how it is explained to them. Families who are not in early childhood education typically have a definition of *play* that means something very different than it does to educators who advocate for play. Make sure you aren't arguing with families over ideas you agree on! It turns out educators and families typically want the same goals but are thinking about those goals in different ways. As professionals with ethical considerations, the onus is on educators to change their words to match families rather than insisting families change themselves to understand educators.

Look at the picture of a family below. Get a piece of paper and a pen. Now, set a timer for one minute. During that one minute, list only the strengths of this family. Ready? Go!

How did you do? Were you able to just look at the strengths of this family? Chillle! Was this activity as hard it was for you as it was for me? At first, all I could see was what was wrong with this family. But there is a lot right with this family. Let's list their strengths.

There is a family.

This family has a home.

There is food.

There are dishes in the sink because someone took time to cook a meal.

Unorganized toys on the floor mean children are playing.

There is a family pet.

There are family photos.

They have clothes.

The family members are in close proximity to one another.

There are books, so maybe this family are avid readers.

There is child artwork on the refrigerator.

There is a calendar on the refrigerator, so maybe they think planning is important.

There is a school paper on the refrigerator, and they appear to value school-home communication.

Have you ever been to this home or one like it? I have. Was it hard for you to see the strengths within so much chaos? Don't feel bad if it was. I too struggled when I visited this home as a home visitor. It is 2006, and Rascal Flatts is topping the charts with their song about a wish. *Pirates of the Caribbean* was tops at the box office when I was working as a child development specialist providing assessment and treatment services for children with special needs.

It was a chilly winter day when I completed an in-home assessment of a two-year-old girl I will call Izzy. Once I complete an assessment, if the assessment shows a child in need of developmental therapy services, I have the choice of adding that child to my therapy caseload. When I added Izzy to my caseload, I didn't realize the assessment had taken place at the Izzy's grandparents' home. I am going to be honest—I added Izzy to my caseload because of the location of her neighborhood and the nice home I thought she lived in. When I arrived at her actual home, I was taken aback by the condition, which was similar to the illustration above. That was the environment where I would have to do therapy once a week with little Izzy. I remember how exhausting it was to lug my therapy toys up to the third floor of the family's apartment building. A group of flies would always greet me as I rang the outside bell at the front door, even in the winter. I would bring an old blanket for Izzy and me to sit on during therapy, so I didn't have to sit directly on the floor. After each session, I would always take a few minutes to shake out the blanket before I loaded it in my car and to spray it and anything else I had brought into the house with disinfectant before I headed home.

> **"All I know is that life is better when I assume people are doing their best."**
>
> **—Brené Brown, researcher, speaker, and author**

My mother was the neatest person I've ever known. When I was growing up, our home was a showplace, and anyone entering our home always told us so. I couldn't even walk into our living room as a child; I think I sat in the room only a few times during those years. We couldn't even wear shoes in our house. Looking back, I initially didn't realize I was judging Izzy's family harshly on things that I would have judged myself on harshly.

After about six weeks of this, I was determined to quit working with this family. Enough was enough. I finally got the courage to tell Izzy's father at my next visit. I will never forget how Izzy's father greeted me with a big smile that day. He said Izzy had "cleaned up" in anticipation of my visit. I looked around in disbelief. The house looked as messy as always. Her father told me that Izzy had been patiently sitting on our spot on the floor waiting for me to arrive. Her father went on to say she didn't listen to any of the other therapists, just me. He also said he noticed Izzy was talking more each day. Izzy would ask for me even when I wasn't there. Her father then told me he didn't have any learning. He wasn't good at school. He was worried Izzy would be like him. But he was happy to see Izzy was learning, and he wanted to thank me. I wiped the tears from my eyes and kept working with Izzy and her family for the next year. I stopped only after Izzy had successfully met all of her developmental milestones.

As I reflect on our relationship so many years later, I now realize Izzy and her family were the ones who taught me a lesson: To always look for the good in people through a strength-based lens and assume good intent. If you can't find the good in a family, then you don't know that family. Looking for the good is not a just an admirable personal trait but a professional responsibility. I was so busy looking at what was wrong, I was missing what was going right. Izzy was learning. I was not just helping a child but also a family. I actually devoted a therapy session to helping the family organize Izzy's toys, and we talked about how to declutter and keep their home for Izzy. I hope our relationship had as big an impact on that family as it did on me as a professional.

What were Izzy's and her family's strengths?

    Izzy had a mother and father.

    Izzy's parents both had jobs.

    Izzy was gaining new skills from my work with her.

    Izzy wanted to learn.

    Izzy's family was learning how to support her development.

    Izzy was loved.

    Izzy's family was kind, appreciative, and caring.

That is all I needed to keep working with Izzy and her family. I am grateful to this day for Izzy and her family and all they taught me. While it is important to address safety issues (which I did with Izzy's family), I learned a valuable lesson in presuming competence; presuming competence involves presuming the positive.

In 1984, researcher Anne Donnellan published an article in the journal *Behavioral Disorders* called "The Criterion of the Least Dangerous Assumption." In it she explains, "in the absence of conclusive data, educational decisions ought to be based on assumptions which, if incorrect, will have the lease dangerous effect on the likelihood that students will be able to function independently as adults." Researcher Douglas Biklen (Biklen and Burke, 2006) elaborates on Donnellan's idea: "Presuming competence is nothing less than a Hippocratic oath for educators. It is a framework that says, approach each child as wanting to be fully included, wanting acceptance and appreciation, wanting to learn, wanting to be heard, wanting to contribute. By presuming competence, educators place the burden on themselves to come up with ever more creative, innovative ways for individuals to learn. The question is no longer who can be included or who can learn, but how can we achieve inclusive education. We begin by presuming competence."

We often judge families harshly on the areas we judge ourselves harshly. In her TEDx Talk "To Transform Child Welfare, Take Race Out of the Equation," social worker Jessica Pryce (2018) describes the impact of race and neighborhood on home visitors. She shares a promising solution to help professionals make bias-free assessments when they see unsafe living conditions. "Emma Ketteringham, a family court attorney, says that if you live in a poor neighborhood, then you better be a perfect parent. She says that we place unfair, often unreachable standards on parents who are raising their kids with very little money. And their neighborhood and ethnicity impact whether or not their kids are removed." Pryce goes on to share that "in almost every state, there are high numbers of Black kids going into foster care. But data revealed that Nassau County, a community in New York, had managed to decrease the number of Black kids being removed." What did they do? When they presented a family in question to the committee, they "delete[d] names, ethnicity, neighborhood, race—all identifiable information. They focus[ed] on what happened, family strength, relevant history, and the parents' ability to protect the child. With that information, the committee makes a recommendation, never knowing the race of the family." After implementation of this "blind" strategy, the numbers of Black children in foster care decreased by 21 percent. This protocol is a tool that, instead of pulling families apart, brings them together.

Equity is not just an individual professional responsibility; it is also important for systems to ensure equity. In the article "Poverty and Neglect Are Not the Same—It's Time to Realign Our Response," Jody Levison-Johnson (2021), a clinical social worker with nearly thirty years of experience in the field of human services, states, "Poverty is a risk factor for neglect, but poverty does not equate to neglect. The presence of poverty alone does not mean a child is unsafe, unloved, or that a parent lacks the capacity to care for his or her child. Poverty can make it more challenging for parents to meet certain of their children's needs. We must be resoundingly clear that a child should never be removed from his or her family due to poverty alone."

> **Get a timer. Set the timer for sixty seconds. Then write down as many words as you can come to mind when I say** *water*. **Ready? Go!**

When I do this exercise with educators, after they write as many words as they can, I ask them to pair up and count how many words they have in common. Usually, they come back with very few matches and are astounded by how many variations they find around the word *water*.

Take a look at your own answers. Some of you wrote words that focused on drinking water; others of you wrote about the temperature of water. Some of you wrote about the ocean. Others of you wrote about water safety or water activities. Still others wrote about what you wear in water, water fountains, what lives or grows in water, vessels that travel in water, water bottles, water-balloon fights, bodies of water, or even your classroom's water table. For some of you, I have yet to list what your answers were. This exercise reminds us how one word can have many meanings. The same is true when we communicate to families.

An example from the book *The Spirit Catches You and You Fall Down* (Fadiman, 1997) illustrates interesting ways the Lee family, Hmong refugees in the United States, interpreted their daughter's Lia's seizures. When asked what they called the seizures, they responded, "*Qaug dah peg*. That means the spirit [*dah*] catches you and you fall down." They attributed the seizures to "soul loss" caused when Lia's sister slammed a door and scared Lia's soul out of her body. The family felt her disorder was occurring because a spirit was catching her. The family thought that Lia should take western medication for a week, along with Hmong medicines, but not any longer. They also said that they should sacrifice pigs and chickens. When asked about their hopes for Lia, they responded, "We hope Lia will be healthy, but we are not sure we want her to stop shaking because it makes her noble in our culture…" The family wondered why they were even being questioned and figured the medical team must not be good doctors.

If you think any of these answers are odd, weird, or even laughable, you are lot like me. At first glance, so did I. What? Sacrificing pigs and chickens? While it is normal for my initial thoughts to contain bias, I can't stay in that space if I want to support families. Could thoughts such as, "That sounds crazy," guide me into helping a family like Lia's with their child's seizures? To see their strengths, I must practice taking a step back and looking at my own identity. For example, how might it sound to someone who has never heard of Christianity to hear that I receive the body and blood of Christ on Sunday? Without any context, it might sound odd or even shocking. Take a minute and think about an aspect of your identity or culture that, on the surface, might sound odd. This thought process can provide a good reminder that our goal is to not judge families but to understand them.

Evaluating the answers from Lia's family would take away from time professionals could be spending talking and thinking about the origin and meaning behind the answers from her family. It is only when we activate the platinum rule that we can elevate equity and provide supports that Lia's family would find helpful for her medical challenge. The platinum rule helps us to treat Lia's family as they would like to be treated. I have had firsthand experiences with families who mistakenly think a referral for special needs services is actually a notice to the U.S. Immigration and Customs Enforcement. I have worked with families who worry our involvement will lead to an arrest or their family being separated. How do we as educators navigate these communication challenges? How can we help families without hurting them and deal with what sometimes seem like huge gulfs in our interactions and understandings? I am going to bring us back to the word that started this whole section, *water*.

Bruce Lee (1971) tells us to be like water:

> Empty your mind, be formless, shapeless, like water. If you put water into a cup, it becomes the cup. You put water into a bottle, and it becomes the bottle. You put it in a teapot, it becomes the teapot. Now, water can flow or it can crash. Be water, my friend.

When working with families, be like water. A true expert in working with families is an expert not just in child development but also in understanding the perspectives of families. To be an expert in perspective taking, one must be like water. Adjust to families. Nothing within you can stay rigid. Empty your mind of your own biases and prejudices. Be like water. A lovely idea to learn from water: adjust yourself in every situation and in any shape, but most importantly find your own way to flow.

Ideas about what is best for children are fluid. For example, in late 1800s, well-meaning professionals advised Hellen Keller's mother to put her in an institution. What was best practice in the nineteenth century is not considered best practice today. It is important to always ask yourself, What if I am wrong? Understand that our professional knowledge is always changing, and some changes have come from learning acquired from families. A professional might be an expert in their field of study, but the family is always the expert on their child. What is best for a family depends on the family.

In the article "Working with Families: Rethinking Denial," Gallagher, Fialka, Rhodes, and Arceneaux (2002) state, "Sometimes when professionals use the phrase 'in denial,' the implied message is that the parents are not being realistic in their expectations of what their child can or will be able to do. Professionals should be careful not to judge a family when the family does not want to do things the way the professionals think is best." The authors suggest that, as professionals, we should "reframe 'in denial' as the parents' way of being 'in hope.'" Other suggestions from the article include going at the pace of the family instead of your pace as a professional. You have had many years to integrate and process the information you share with families, so be sure to follow the families' timeline. "Sometimes parents attempt to slow down the speed of change, particularly when they are integrating new, and sometimes painful and uninvited, information about their child (Gallagher et al., 2002)."

You might be thinking, "Okay, Angela—Voice of Reason here again—that all sounds good, but I am drowning in my attempts to, as you say, 'be like water.' (Insert sarcastic smirk.) Whatever that means. I'm working with an African American family that is resistant to mental-health services. What if they are a hard-to-reach family that is disengaged?"

Good question. It is important that you first process your own feelings about a family. We can be negative or frustrated, but as professionals we work hard to move past that place. To elevate equity, I want you to think about how mental health is often addressed with African American families. What is the context around mental health and families? What are the origins for that behavior? With the group you describe, mental health needs have been historically been marginalized. African American families often go to the church rather than to psychologists or psychiatrists for support. Is there a way to provide mental health support in a church or community setting that the family values or already attends? How can you collaborate with local community programs already in place in the community? How can we all keep in mind that silence *is* communication?

When working with families, Rosemarie Allen, president and chief executive officer for the Institute for Racial Equity and Excellence, asks us to flip the narrative: "There are no hard-to-reach families. There are just hard-to-reach services." Did you catch that? Mind blown! It wasn't until I read this quote from Dr. Allen that I considered I was hard to reach as an educator. From the family's viewpoint, if the parents sleep during the day and work at night, I was the one that was hard to reach. It is easy to label families as "hard to reach" without understanding the reason behind their behavior. Once you understand the reason, you can adjust your program to make it easier for families to access. Consider all the diverse ways to engage to elevate equity when working with families.

- What are the goals of the family or grown-ups?
- What are the goals of educators?
- What are goals that incorporate elements of both sets of goals?
- List ways for professionals to adjust to the family's needs.

As you read the list above, you might be thinking, wait! Why must I adjust to families? Professionals providing a support to others are inherently in a position of power. Author, counselor, and psychotherapist Cedar Barstow (2015) reminds us, "Understanding both the value and the many impacts of the power differential is the core of ethical awareness." She goes on to describe how families or clients "seeking help are in a position in which they must trust in the knowledge and guidance of their caregiver. This results in a greater-than-ordinary vulnerability. Consequently, people are unusually susceptible to harm and confusion through misuses (either under- or overuse) of power and influence." Within a professional capacity, she writes, "it is our role as the therapist [or any helping professional] to create a safe space, empower your client, protect your client's spirit, and to see a wider perspective." *Centering* involves putting the focus only on the values, norms, perspectives, needs, and feelings of the professionals over the families and children they are tasked with serving. This is a serious problem, especially when a professional is working with a group whose needs are pushed to the margins. Let's examine some common causes of challenging conversations with families and potential solutions to navigate them. My friend, fellow consultant, and frequent co-presenter Dr. Antoinette Taylor often uses the phrase "adult assembly required." Each of these ideas listed below is just a starting point that your program must build on its own.

- **Why don't some families help children with homework?** Homework is not easily completed within their schedule. So, offer diverse ways children can practice homework. For example, they can practice math by cooking dinner with a family member and tell you what they cooked and how it connected to adding or fractions. Or they can tell you how many miles their parents drove from school, or write how many signs they passed on the way home on the bus. Make sure homework is voluntary, as some children don't have time or space for schoolwork out of school. Some children are caring for younger siblings, or their parents work third shift and can't provide adult support. Since homework is typically completed outside of school hours, consider keeping it outside the required grades for a course. Homework is a place to practice, learn, and make mistakes; as a result, homework should not be graded for accuracy if an educator wants to elevate equity.

- **Why don't some families respond to school communication or read it?** Methods of communication may not be diverse to meet the needs of families. So, offer video newsletters on a private YouTube link or in apps, and drop newsletters off at community-based programs students go to, such as those at houses of worship or community centers. Make phone calls. (As a teacher I would pick a few families to phone each week.) Send postcards or mail letters. (Yes, mail still exists, folks.) Have porch meetings. (Visit a family at home with a quick porch meeting.) Talk with them at after-school events.

  Voice of every educator reading this right now: "Porch meeting?! Thanks, Angela, for adding more thing on my plate!" I want to give a shout out to all the educators who said they are going to try all these great ideas and already have decided to wait until next school year. I get it! I would suggest you try one small thing now—the one you think would be the easiest and would give you the most success.

- **Why don't some families return forms?** It is too hard to find or has a poor format. So, color-code communication: blue paper for field trips, green for forms about money, red for time-sensitive information, and so on. You can use the same code for online communication and make words in the body of the email color-coded. Or just label the email "Red Email Time-Sensitive." As a parent, I have 3,464 emails in my inbox, and if you don't want your email to get lost among my Bath and Body Works coupons, you need to be creative. Give me some specific reading guidance in the subject line, such as, "Field trip information for July 9th," so I can read it at 11:49 p.m. on July 8th like any good parent. Survey families to find out how to set up a meaningful schedule of communication. Why do some parents miss communication? They don't know when it is coming. Create a consistent schedule when sending out communication. For example, the principal sends emails on Mondays with the week's announcements unless it is an emergency. The teacher sends updates in the child's Friday folder unless it is an emergency. The social worker sends updates on events the last week of the month. Don't assume you can just send communication just willy-nilly without some type of consistency and think that as a parent I am going to read it.

- **Why are some families are not engaged with their child's classroom community?** Many children live within a family that consists of more caregivers than just the parents. Instead of connecting only with parents, ask for permission to connect with a child's grown-ups. Grown-ups can include all the blood relatives and potentially non-blood relatives in a child's life. Sending a newsletter to the parent might mean it is never read. But sending a newsletter to Mee-maw or Nana? It will not only be read, but it will also have a special place on the refrigerator! Consider inviting families to receive communication on apps, newsletters, emails, and so on (with permission from parents or guardians).

- **Why are some families are so disconnected from the school community?** Because there is no organization to keep them connected. Don't wait for alumni to become adults. Set up an alumni club. Sometimes those alumni are siblings or current students. This approach allows for former families and students to stay connected and continue to volunteer and connect with other families. Maybe I will follow through on a referral from a teacher if I see how a referral led to success for a former student. Engage family and community mentors. With permission, pair up families with other families as mentors. This can be done by class or school wide. Let families help each other. Try to pair up highly visible families with those who have busy schedules. Leverage the strengths of families and the community to contribute to the entire program.

Your school isn't the only one dealing with these issues. Divide and conquer and pool your resources. Talk to other schools. Make intentional connections between schools. Is the middle school connecting with the preschools in the local area? My daughter's family child-care home was part of a pod—a group of home child-care providers that shared services. For example, each child-care provider in the pod shared a substitute who worked among all six of the child-care homes in the pod. If one home was closed for vacation, the family could schedule with a different home in the pod during that vacation.

Why do some parents seem as if they don't care? All families care. I've never met a family who said, "I can't wait to mess this kid up!" Make space for families to share their funds of knowledge with your program. This will allow you to learn more about them and their goals and values.

Viewing Children through a Strengths-Based Lens

Just as changing how we view colleagues can alter our perceptions of them, viewing children through a strengths-based lens can help us to see them positively. Children should never be described in terms of a perceived deficit such as "low functioning" or with blanket terms such as *failing*. A group of children might have test scores that are below passing, but children are individuals who each have a unique reason for their performance level. These terms don't help us to understand how to support children if we don't look at the reasons, systems, and barriers behind why they have scores at a certain level.

In the same vein, labeling a group as "above average" doesn't tell me anything about how or why they are performing at a particular skill level, even if it is superior. Because children are never uniformly high or low in skills, I have stopped using phrases like "high group" and "low group." I would not use those phrases to describe adults at work, nor would I "track" adults at work. We all have varying skills that make an organization successful. Similarly, instead of describing a child as *nonverbal*, describe them in terms of what they *can* do: "Child's preferred mode of communication is visuals," or "Child is preverbal." Stick to calling people by the labels they give to themselves. For example, consider the practice of describing a child as "below grade level." I just couldn't imagine a child or their family using that label to describe themselves! Learners are not the skills, emotions, or behaviors they exhibit. Instead, say something like, "When in a testing environment or when using a timed assessment, this student demonstrates at skill at _____ percent."

Sounds wordy? I get it, but if you would please indulge me for a couple of minutes and think of your last teacher evaluation. If you were suddenly hot with fury over an impromptu classroom observation the day before a break, or if negative wording on your evaluation says you didn't so something you *know* you did, I am asking you to go to that place bring that same energy to student evaluations. Treat students how you know they want to be treated.

Chapter 4: Equity and Families of Young Children | **141**

Children need adults to accurately and equitability describe their skills. Programs and systems definitely need economic funding to support children, but remember to highlight the cause. For example, Elena Hung (2022), mother of a child with a disability and executive director of Little Lobbyists, a nonprofit organization that advocates for children with complex medical needs and disabilities, advises that words matter. She suggests that instead of saying, "She can't get inside the building because of her wheelchair," to say, "She can't get inside because the building is not accessible... The wheelchair is not the problem: the building's lack of access is the problem." The focus is on the cause, not the person's abilities.

Assessment of children's current skills speaks little about potential for future skills. What might appear to be challenges now can be assets when they are better understood. For example, children with attention-deficit hyperactivity disorder (ADHD) are often characterized as having a short attention span, but this is not so. They have interest-driven attention and may hyperfocus. According to the article "Hyperfocus: The ADHD Phenomenon of Intense Fixation" (Flippin, 2022), *hyperfocus* refers to an "intense fixation on an interest or activity for an extended period of time. People who experience hyperfocus often become so engrossed they block out the world around them.... adults with ADHD often exhibit hyperfocus when working intently on things that interest them." They have exceptionally long attention spans for activities that engage their interest. Flippin says, "If they're doing something they enjoy or find psychologically rewarding, they'll tend to persist in this behavior after others would normally move on to other things." ADHD/ADD can be a strength that allows a student in your classroom to pay attention longer to something they have an interest in. To elevate equity as educators, we need to include student interests into the educational content. This is coming directly from a solid C student! I didn't start getting solid A's until I found my interest in college.

Creators of assessments and screening tools should make sure they use relevant, age-appropriate words and examples. Along those same lines, no single test can adequately estimate the knowledge of a child. As a result, if a program requires a test for entry, that program should also look at authentic measures beyond paper and pencil tests. Often entry into gifted or talented programs relies on a test or teacher recommendations, meaning some children will never gain entry into those programs. There is a bias that written testing increases with the age of the student. Many cultures have rich oral traditions, and many children are hands-on learners.

Interest-driven lessons are just one strategy to elevate equity. To be inclusive for all children, educators should learn instructional strategies that support all types of learners. Curriculum, classroom routines, school policies, and procedures should also be inclusive. Upon hearing this idea, my husband, Reginald, charged me with creating a "kids' bill of rights" to describe the essential rights that all children should have in any early childhood program. I decided to call the final product the Learner's Bill of Rights to include learners of all ages. Early childhood programs should be inclusive learning communities for children, families, staff, and educators. To anyone who has ever found themselves saying, "If I had been alive when _____ happened, I would have..." or "If I could change the world, I would ...," here is your chance! You are alive now, and we each have an opportunity to change the world every day.

> "Some believe it is only great power that can hold evil in check, but that is not what I have found. I found it is the small everyday deeds of ordinary folk that keep the darkness at bay... small acts of kindness and love."
>
> —Gandalf the Grey, *The Hobbit: An Unexpected Journey*

Learners' Bill of Rights

Learners have a right to have instructors who protect and place their physical and emotional needs at the forefront of learning. Those needs are at the foundation of all learning. In this learning environment, learners are explicitly taught how to get along as a community of learners. Learners have the freedom to express a variety of emotions and are supported when those emotions are strong or overwhelming. Learners are not removed or excluded based on their ability to manage strong feelings. Students are not removed from learning or recess (which is an important learning opportunity) due to dress-code violations or hairstyles or to things they cannot control, such as tardiness. Children are always invited to learn, and if there are compliance issues, exclusion is never the solution. In fact, the entire learning environment supports managing emotional and physical needs. If a preschool-age child needs to sleep, he has a space to do so in the cozy corner. If a child arrives to school after breakfast, food is saved for him to eat when he arrives. For elementary-aged students, they are guaranteed the right to use the restroom without worry of interrupting a teacher's lesson. For adults and children, learning is a social and emotional endeavor that occurs within cooperative learning groups or centers.

Learners have the right to freedom of involvement within the learning process. From a neurological standpoint, humans are hard-wired to learn through interaction and involvement. Freedom to safely move, to ask any question and talk anytime without restriction, and to engage in hands-on interaction with learning materials are important elements in the learning process. Freedom of involvement is learner centered. Instructors develop learning goals *with* students, and instructors encourage creative expression. This environment recognizes learners' need to move when they learn and offers flexible seating and schedules. Learners are encouraged to lead activities. Instructors center activities around the interests of the learners, following their lead, rather than around the interests and schedule of the instructor. The person learning, rather than the instructor, is the person who is talking most often.

Learners have a right to multisensory learning. A variety of learning styles are honored and respected. Each lesson engages all the senses and honors freedom of movement. The teacher offers a balance of quiet, reflective activities and active experiences. The teacher offers a range of instructional strategies and learning opportunities that use a variety of modalities and ways to manipulate or participate with learning materials and activities. Learning is adapted to support various learning styles, cultures, and temperaments.

Learners have freedom to exhibit learning in a variety of ways. Learners can show understanding through song, interviews, writing, portfolios, art, dance, poems, stories, tests, formal assessments, informal assessments, experiments, investigations, role play, journals, demonstrations, presentations, open-ended questions, learner reflections, peer reflections, small group assessments or projects, and games. A variety of assessments honor many learning styles. Family input is used to assess children's learning and development, and for older learners, rubrics, self-assessment, and peer assessment are used. Grading or assessing comprehension is the focus instead of grading or assessing compliance to rules—for example, losing points for not having a shirt tucked in or being excluded from the learning environment for hair being below a collar. The instructor motivates, values connection over compliance, and understands that connection supports following directions. Assessment is embedded into learning and is authentic. For example, an instructor might showcase a learner's work samples over time to assess learning. Learners perform real-world tasks to demonstrate knowledge and skill development. Formal assessments are given in a variety of ways. Elementary-age children can retake assessments, whenever possible, to gain more points and new understandings.

Learners have a right to educators who ask of themselves what they ask of learners: engagement in the learning process, continuous learning, and implementation of evidence-based equitable strategies. Education and the knowledge around it is constantly evolving. Learners have a right to instructors who are in constant pursuit of knowledge grounded in personal and scientific evidence and are actively evaluating strategies and themselves for potential bias.

Viewing Families through a Strengths-Based Lens

The deficit model can rear its head when professionals work with families. If children don't have food or medicine, that can be a hurdle, but exercise caution when describing the experiences of children. For example, I have heard educators describing with anguish children who didn't have toys at home. Toys are just one type of material that can be used for learning. The best foundation for learning is a strong, engaging, and loving relationship. Toys without an engaged adult mean little to a young child. Check out a list of culturally relevant or home-based tools for learning here: https://www.gryphonhouse.com/books/details/elevating-equity

Also, keep in mind that ideas about play vary by culture. For example, a study by Jo Ann Farver and Yoolim Lee-Shin (2000) showed that 96 percent of European American mothers believed children and parents should play together, but only 54 percent of Korean American mothers believed this. Because of those differences, Korean American mothers were rated by their child's teachers as more difficult.

I can relate to how these ratings might have come about. Raise your hand if you are an educator or home visitor who would have viewed this situation as a "difficulty" and would have started "teaching" Korean American mothers the value of play. Yes! I have found my people! Same here! Guilty! Now that I know how to elevate equity, I would instead listen to those mothers and support them to see the value of the playful experiences they were already doing with their children. No, those mothers probably don't sit and play on the floor with toys like I do as a teacher, and they don't have to. But I am sure they have fun with their children every day, and those are important learning experiences they might not even realize they were doing. I would listen, learn, and find commonality.

As a home visitor, I used what was in a family's home to support the acquisition of new skills. Whatever that family had was enough and most meaningful to that child. Don't get me wrong, families can experience poverty, and it can be challenging when they do, but they are never impoverished. We want to acknowledge a need without assigning a value or identity. Poverty is something people can experience but not be who they are. Someone might not have a house but still live in a home.

When Children "Don't Act Like That at Home"

It can be puzzling or even frustrating when you run across a child whose parents say, "He doesn't act like that at home." However, in terms of child development research, you might be surprised to find it is normal for students to behave differently in different settings based on the quality of their relationships and levels of support in their environment. Until children master self-regulation, they are still learning how to maintain their internal emotions despite what is happening in the external environment. As a result, to gain a meaningful understanding of student behavior, there also must be a meaningful understanding of all the adults in a child's life and the context in which all of these behaviors occur.

It is important for adults to help children learn how to navigate different settings. The discrepancy between situational demands, rules, and schedules is to be expected. It is culturally responsive and realistic for environments to differ from one another. Consistency is important; but if overemphasized without caution, it could potentially be harmful if caregivers expect all environments to be the same. *Ethnocentrism* is a term use to describe a cultural bias that involves thinking your way of living is the only correct way. Caregivers must be cautious not to impose the values of dominant culture on underrepresented groups. Honor all types of families and ways of caregiving. What is suitable for one environment may not work in another setting.

Let's engage in a reflection exercise. You can find a blank version of "They Don't Act Like That at Home" on my author page: https://www.gryphonhouse.com/our-authors/author-detail/angela-searcy-edd

Directions:

1. Write down the differences in environments in the spaces below.

At home:	At therapy:	In classroom:
Child is only child. Interacts only with adults. Child listens to older siblings, and family incorporates child's interests. Few demands are placed on the child because they are relaxing at home. There are no behavior challenges, but family repeats rules often. Family follows child's lead.	Child is sometimes alone or in small group of with two or three other children. There are demands, but there is more support in small group. Therapist uses visuals and sign language. Behavior challenges happen sometimes, but the child is redirected with visuals.	Child is with a group of nineteen children. There are tasks and many transitions. The child does not get to pick the order of tasks and often must do tasks independently. There are many behavior challenges that last for 10–15 minutes. No visuals are used.

2. Write down the similarities among environments in the spaces below.

At home:	At therapy:	In classroom:
The family has rules at home.	There are rules at therapy.	There are rules in the classroom.

On a piece of paper, write down problem-solving and support conversations that identify what is feasible in each setting. For example, a suitable support used in the home environment or one-on-one therapy session such as taking a child to the potty every five minutes might be difficult to implement in a classroom setting. In a group setting, transitions are common, so that might be a natural stopping point to help a child individually. An educator might check in with a child during each transition. Reflect on the differences and similarities and ways to work with families to think about what supports best suit each environment.

Suitable Supports in Environment 1

> Add more visuals at home to support understanding of rules. This will reinforce the tools used when working at therapy.
>
> Take photos of the daily schedule in the classroom, and go over expectations and rules at home when child is relaxed.

Suitable Supports in Environment 2

> Pair child with a child who is compliant. Perhaps the child will listen to another child in the way they listen to older siblings at home.
>
> Follow the lead of the child like the family does at home, and incorporate child's interests into tasks like they do at home. To have fewer challenging behaviors, give more choice with choice boards, and use dice with visuals of tasks.
>
> When child is relaxed, there are no challenges. Mindfulness breathing at therapy might help this child.

Suitable Supports in Environment 3

> Incorporate child interests into lessons.
>
> Add visuals and sign language to classroom.
>
> Use peer buddies during some transitions and tasks. Let child pick order of a task. Use peer buddies with children who don't have challenges so teacher can give one-on-one support more often.

> **THINK THRICE BEFORE YOU GIVE ADVICE**
>
> - Did this person ask me for advice? Stating a problem is not asking for advice.
>
> - Did I activate the *U* in *equity* and ask questions to understand how the person who needs support sees the problem? Did I ask questions that help me understand the context behind the situation before giving any advice. What are their goals? What are their strengths? How is this situation different or similar to one I have encountered?
>
> - Remember, no one needs to follow your advice (sorry to all the mothers of the world!). If advice *must* be followed or a consequence will ensue, that is just an exercise in ego instead of an exercise in support

Handle with Care

When working with families, Handle With Care (HWC) is a low-cost model that helps notify schools if a child has experienced a traumatic event. Developed by the West Virginia Defending Childhood Initiative, HWC requires law enforcement to alert school personnel when a child is exposed to a traumatic event during a first-responder call, in case extra support is warranted (West Virginia Center for Children's Justice, n.d.). School personnel are simply asked to keep a caring eye on the student or provide appropriate trauma-sensitive interventions immediately, if needed. You can learn more at https://salud-america.org/toolkit/start-handle-with-care-for-traumatized-kids/

HWC doesn't have to be used for those in trauma. I teach Family and Culture and adopted HWC for my graduate students during the pandemic. This tool elevates equity because it helps someone maintain their privacy and dignity while gaining support. HWC can be used for children, staff, or anyone who needs care. What is your tool or system at your program when there is a sensitive topic that needs to be addressed?

Use Your Perspectacles

Respect is something we all talk about, but rarely do we have concrete tools to help us with the behaviors that define respect. When there is a conflict, put on those strength-based shades—or what a great colleague of mine, Terry Beasley, an educator with more than forty-five years of experience, likes to call *perspectacles*!

In their book *Using Skilled Dialogue to Transform Challenging Interactions*, Barrera and Kramer (2009) contend, "It is not enough to simply know that there is diversity, or even to know the types of diversity associated with various groups. Knowing that someone may be consistently late for scheduled meetings because of their culturally based values and frame of reference, for example, can be helpful." However, they say, educators may still be frustrated. "One person will continue to feel the need for the other to share their value of punctuality, saying for example, 'After all, how else can we get things done? Am I just supposed to accept and indeed respect their consistent lateness?'" Something more is required, and skilled dialogue is the something more. According to Barrera and Kramer, skilled dialogue requires choosing relationship over control, which "reflects our intentional choice to give priority to people rather than to our desired outcomes; that is, to pay more attention to who the other is in relation to me and who I am in relation to him than to what I want him to do." Skilled dialogue requires "willingness to communicate unconditional respect." Elevating equity goes a step further to allow educators to give themselves, as well as their program, love and respect.

Allow yourself to feel and be human without guilt or shame. Give yourself and the staff a space to be emotional, even negative or biased, but don't stay in that space. To filter your thoughts and respond with neutrality and equity, use tools such as this "Cooling Down Strategy for Teachers: Pushing Past It": https://www.gryphonhouse.com/resources/cooling-down-strategy-for-teachers-pushing-past-it or "What Is Said in the Teachers' Lounge": https://www.gryphonhouse.com/images/authors/What_Is_Said_in_the_Teachers_Lounge_Bias_Worksheet.pdf (You will learn more about those tools in chapter 7.)

- Name the problem and identify the mismatch of goals, values, or ideas.

- Think of your strengths as a professional and what you can learn from this conflict. For example:

    I am a good problem solver. I have done this before and can handle this situation. This is hard, but this is just a another opportunity to get better.

- List the strengths of your program and resources. For example, is there someone who can help you through this?

- List the strengths of the adult you are experiencing conflict with. For example:

    I appreciate that the mother of this child takes time to hug her children each morning.

- Now ask a question to create dialogue about the problem to understand the reason behind it. For example:

    I am wondering how we can have a better relationship. I appreciate when you _____. I wonder how we could _____.

- Activate the *U* in *equity* with the Adult Meaning-Making Machine (see page 232). This tool can support you in finding meaning and using that meaning to consider steps for problem-solving supports.

◆ ◆ ◆

Are you still there? Did you get any new ideas? Did I reaffirm ideas you already had? Elevating equity is not about finding flaws or fault. It is about elevating and building on the positive qualities families already have. Behavior analysis includes something called *explanatory fiction*. It is a statement that appears to explain a challenge, but upon reflection, the cause is really the same as the effect. In terms of equity, it is when a person puts the cause of a problem inside the person with the problem, their family, or community. For example, "If he would just pay attention, he would have heard the directions." "She only talks when she wants to." "She's not motivated." "He never follows directions." Instead of stating the obvious, ask yourself, "How can I gain this child's attention?" "How can I get this child to talk more?" "How can I motivate her?" "How can I change how I give directions?" First, change *you*. Then you will see a change in the child. This doesn't work only with children; it works with any person. You want to see a change in your significant other's behavior? Change your behavior. You want to see a change in your employees? Change how you respond to them. Behavior is a complicated mix of give and take.

I remember in the depths of 2020, during the start of the global pandemic, searching desperately for tools for "disengaged" families. Then I realized I had to reframe and focus on what families were doing and build on that. It wasn't easy, especially when families undressed in front of the camera in virtual classes. (That is not how we wanted children to learn about the human body!) But then I realized, at least they are here, so that's a start.

Instead of focusing on compliance, focus on making connections. People are much more than their perceived problems. Now that we understand more about families, we will next consider the context families come from. How did families get here? What was the history that led some families to the space they are in now? How does our past permeate our present? As always, it starts with a reflective activity that looks at historical trauma from the inside out.

CHAPTER 5

Understanding Historical Trauma

> Write down a painful event (death, illness, war, financial collapse, pandemic, etc.) from your or your family's past.
>
> Write down how this event impacted you, your loved ones, and your family based on your own unique characteristics. (Think back to chapter 1 and the discussion of risk and protective factors.)
>
> Next, write down how that event still affects you or your family today.

Like me, I am sure you can name many painful events. My father's multiple sclerosis diagnosis, my mother's kidney failure, the financial collapse of 2008 in the United States, all these events had long-term effects. Even though many of us endured the 2008 financial collapse, and the COVID-19 pandemic was experienced all over the world, our own unique risk and protective factors played an important part in the depth to which those events were experienced. In the same way that painful events can have long-term impacts, so can trauma.

In her book *The Deepest Well: Healing the Long-Term Effects of Childhood Adversity*, Dr. Nadine Burke Harris (2018) explains, "Twenty years of medical research has shown that childhood adversity literally gets under our skin, changing people in ways that can endure for decades. It can tip a child's developmental trajectory and affect physiology. It can trigger chronic inflammation and hormonal changes that can last a lifetime. It can alter the way DNA is read and how cells replicate, and it dramatically increases the risk for heart disease, stroke, cancer, diabetes—even Alzheimer's."

"Well, We All Turned Out Okay"

If you started thinking, "Hey, I know people that have persevered through astronomical obstacles, and they are okay!" Yes, I agree; I am sure many people are okay. And, research also shows that others went on to get sick. Both ideas can be true at the same time. A growing body of research shows trauma "weathers" the body, making it susceptible to illness (Shonkoff and Garner, 2012). For example, researcher Colter Mitchell and colleagues (2014) looked at the telomere length of forty nine-year-old African American boys from social environments associated with adverse health outcomes. Oops! I lost you at "telomere length"? Okay, I want you to imagine a shoelace. What happens if the plastic caps come off the ends of a shoelace? The shoelace becomes unraveled! Well, the telomere serves the same function, but for your DNA. When the telomere is shortened, our DNA can unravel, which can cause chromosome damage. This, in turn, can affect our health and make a person more susceptible to illness or disease. Telomere shortening is typically associated with aging. So what did those nine-year-old boys experience that is leading their DNA to unravel? Stress from poverty, maternal depression, and harsh parenting (yelling, threatening, hitting, and so on). Those events were not just the result of personal choices but also of historical trauma.

The Administration for Children and Families (2017), a division of the U.S. Department of Health and Human Services, describes *historical trauma* as a "multigenerational trauma… related to major events that oppressed a particular group of people… such as slavery, the Holocaust, forced migration, and the violent colonization of Native Americans. While many in such a group will experience no ill effects… others may experience poor overall physical and behavioral health… Parents' experience of trauma may disrupt parenting skills and contribute to behavior problems in children. Compounding this familial or intergenerational trauma, historical trauma often involves the additional challenge of a damaged cultural identity (Sotero, 2006)."

Maria Yellow Horse Brave Heart (1999), an associate professor and mental-health expert who is known for developing a model for historical trauma, describes historical trauma as "a constellation of characteristics associated with massive cumulative group trauma across generations." This type of trauma is different from other types because it involves the collective group who experienced the event(s) and the consequences and who transfer those consequences down to future generations.

How does historical trauma impact future generations? A study by Rachel Yehuda and colleagues (2008) found that children of Holocaust survivors had an increased risk of post-traumatic stress disorder, a finding corroborated by Danieli, Norris, and Engdahl (2017), who found that this group also had an increased risk of generalized anxiety disorder and depression. Researchers Brent Bezo and Stefania Maggi (2015) looked at the impact of Holodomor, the man-made famine in Soviet Ukraine 1932–1933, on three generations of Ukrainian families. They found coping strategies that emerged in those who survived the genocide "were subsequently transmitted into the second and third generations." Living in what is described in the study as "survival mode" included "fear, mistrust, sadness, shame, anger, stress and anxiety, decreased self-worth, stockpiling of food and overeating, inability to discard unneeded items, an indifference toward others, social hostility, and risky health behaviors." A study by Williams, Printz Pereira, and DeLapp (2018) looked at the effects of racial trauma using the Trauma Symptoms of Discrimination Scale, which showed descendants of slaves have higher levels of post-traumatic stress disorder. Researchers Amy Bombay and colleagues (2014) added to the discussion with their study of the impact of Indian residential schools on Native Americans. They found that not just the children but also the grandchildren of those forced to live at the schools saw long-lasting physical and psychological effects.

> Try this activity to better understand historical trauma. List the following on a piece of paper:
>
> - The name of a favorite person you care for
> - Your favorite activity
> - Your favorite place
>
> Now imagine something deeply distressing occurs to your one of your favorite people during a favorite activity at your favorite place. You have a second friend who also loves that activity and place, but who did not experience anything distressing there. Now imagine when you go to this favorite place there are times when you and your favorite person still experience distressing events occasionally, and you can't predict when those events will occur or with whom.
>
> - How would you feel about that activity going forward?
> - Would you be worried about your favorite person?
> - Would you feel the same about your favorite place?
> - What do you think your second friend will think about your feelings going forward? How could they support you? What should they avoid doing or saying?
> - How might this even impact other events in your life?
>
> (Adapted from Brand, 2022)

This activity is a very simplified view of what it might feel like to have historical trauma. Trauma can even affect those who did not experience the trauma (such as the second friend in the exercise above). For example, according to the Administration for Children and Families (ACF), "Historical trauma reverberates across generations. Descendants who have not directly experienced a traumatic event can exhibit the signs and symptoms of trauma, such as depression, fixation on trauma, low self-esteem, anger, and self-destructive behavior" (ACF, 2017). Turns out, along with my eye color and hair color, I also inherited any genetic changes to a family member's DNA caused by trauma.

Keep in mind, historical trauma is not only about the past; it could still re-occur. For example, someone could still experience sexual harassment even though it was determined in the 1980s to be a form of discrimination in the United States. A fact sheet on the topic by the Substance Abuse and Mental Health Services Administration (SAMHSA, n.d.) makes some important distinctions to consider when thinking about this type of trauma.

"*Historical unresolved grief* is the result of historical trauma that has not been sufficiently acknowledged, expressed, or otherwise addressed.

Disenfranchised grief is the product of historical trauma when loss cannot be voiced publicly or is not publicly acknowledged…

Internalized oppression occurs when 'traumatized people… internalize the views of the oppressor and perpetuate a cycle of self-hatred that manifests itself in negative behaviors.'"

Educators may be providing services to groups who experience this trauma. As a result, it is important to understand historical or transgenerational trauma. An essential aspect of equity involves being mindful of unresolved grief and potential distrust of majority groups. There is a long history of individuals and groups being excluded from education based on ability, gender, race, religion, language, class, and sexual orientation.

One historical trauma is not more harmful than another. I remember talking to a colleague at work about slavery, and she started talking about Poland and how her family struggled as immigrants to the United States. We don't need to compare or compete. My hard is hard. Your hard is hard. It is all hard. All trauma needs to be responded to with care and compassion. Let empathy lead the way when you give a response that elevates equity. Try words like, "I hear you. I am listening and asking questions," before you jump to conclusions. Each person who has experienced trauma will exhibit their hurt in their own unique way, to varying degrees. If you are following a train of thought such as, "That person went through X, and they are okay," here are some questions from my previous book *Push Past It!* to consider:

- Is any individual truly objective enough to assess whether an experience has injured or damaged her?
- Can she really see a wide enough picture to know whether her life would have been better with or without a certain event?

- Are we all using the same standard to measure whether someone is "okay"?
- If they were able to tolerate that experience or situation, does that mean everyone can?
- Is it possible that they were able to tolerate a particular situation because of supports that are not available to everyone?
- What about all the people who are not okay?

Are you able to explore an idea beyond your own personal situation? Can something be important even if it does not affect you or those you know? Generalizing a few experiences to all experiences has drawbacks.

Making Sense of What Appears Senseless: Applying a Historical-Trauma Lens

To learn more about historical trauma, I contacted Dr. Bruce Perry, senior fellow of the Child Trauma Academy in Houston, Texas. He responded:

> Hi Dr. Searcy,
>
> We wrote a bit about this in *What Happened to You?* And this link has some discussion about it. https://youtu.be/Yxl1OVVBGSw Best of luck with your book.
>
> Regards,
>
> Bruce P
>
> B D Perry

First of all, I need to pause over the fact that when I contacted him, Dr. Bruce Perry responded immediately. It is important to elevate equity to celebrate and collaborate with one another, no matter how big or small our contributions. *What Happened to You?* is the title of his bestselling book with Oprah Winfrey. In the book, Perry describes "that seemingly senseless behavior makes sense once you look at what is behind it… something happened that influences how their brain works" (Perry and Winfrey, 2021).

Applying a historical lens can help us find the meaning behind behaviors rooted in transgenerational trauma. Behavior is complex and typically does not originate from one reason. The questions below are important ones to consider when trying to make sense of what appears senseless.

What you might see: "Resistant"

Applying a historical lens: Is this individual or group feeling a sense of distrust due to past events? Is this individual from a group that has experienced distressing events around education or social services before?

What you might see: "Disrespectful"

Applying a historical lens: Is this individual or family from a group that has been historically disrespected in the educational community? Have they been silenced throughout history? Have their priorities been pushed to the margins? Is leadership at the school or organization respectful of cultural traditions?

What you might see: "Unmotivated"

Applying a historical lens: Is this individual from a group whose efforts have historically gone largely unacknowledged except for a small few? Could this group or individual be overwhelmed by a place or system that is new to them due to historical exclusion? Is the person in survival mode due to cumulative historical inequalities?

What you might see: "Anger"

Applying a historical lens: Is the person frustrated by a historical past that excludes or has been harmful toward them? Are they feeling unsafe and triggered by events within the educational or social-work setting? Are they frustrated by lack of diversity? Are they angry, or is that your perception?

What you might see: "Harsh self-criticism" or "harsh criticism of those with the same attributes"

Applying a historical lens: First, look outside to see what might be affecting the inside. Does this person have a historical past in which their attributes, such as skin color, ethnicity, language, religion, gender, sexual orientation, and so on, have been devalued by the larger society? Are there systems in the society that allow privileges to those without those attributes?

What you might see: "Harsh parenting/caregiving"

Applying a historical lens: Does this behavior have roots in a historical past that included violent physical punishment or psychological punishments such as humiliation? For example, in her book *Post-Traumatic Slave Syndrome*, author Dr. Joy DeGruy (2017) describes how "in the slave environment, and continuing through reconstruction and the long night of Jim Crow, it was unsafe for a black child to stray or wander [in America]… Such behavior could result in severe punishment or even death." As a result, Black parents might still be hypervigilant today or carry out severe punishments themselves in an effort to protect their children from the even more severe punishments of others. Researcher Stacey Patton (2017) also contends that the cultural tradition of African Americans spanking their children is not a cultural practice that Africans brought with them from Africa to the United States. Patton suggests that it may be the result of hundreds of years of historical trauma from slavery and Jim Crow.

You may be thinking, "Mmmkay, now everyone has trauma? What if it is just bad behavior?" I agree. I do think it could look like "bad" behavior through your own cultural lens. I know some behaviors look this way from my personal vantage point all the time. To be honest with you, my family could attest to the fact that my personal life does not consist of a continuous self-critique of my values and biases at every turn. That would ruin my people-watching time! You know people-watching time—not to be confused with window-watching time, which takes place almost every day behind my window blinds. People-watching time is when you venture out to a public space either alone or with others to observe strangers and make judgments about their actions in a vacuum with no context or perspective while laughing at your, ahem, shall we say "interesting" observations. It is a time when I can secretly indulge in superficial judgments. It's one of my few guilty pleasures that doesn't add any unwanted calories!

But as a professional, I have to intentionally put on my "perspectacles." Perspectacles is a fun way to describe my ethical duty to try to understand the reason(s) behind a behavior so I can know what supports are needed. I don't wear my perspectacles at all times in my personal life, but as an early childhood professional, perspectacles are something I put on each day when I arrive at my place of practice. I follow NAEYC's *Code of Ethical Conduct and Statement of Commitment* (2011). Among other values, this code calls on educators to:

- Recognize that children are best understood and supported in the context of family, culture*, community, and society

- Respect the dignity, worth, and uniqueness of each individual (child, family member, and colleague)
- Respect diversity in children, families, and colleagues
- Recognize that children and adults achieve their full potential in the context of relationships that are based on trust and respect

*The term *culture* includes ethnicity, racial identity, economic level, family structure, language, and religious and political beliefs, which profoundly influence each child's development and relationship to the world.

Whether you are a mental-health consultant and follow the Diversity Informed Mental Health Tenets or an educator who is part of the International Teacher's Association, all professions have some kind of code of ethics that speaks to equity and inclusion. Defining a behavior purely by how it appears—called *surface dwelling*—tells us nothing about why the behavior occurred or how to support the individual exhibiting it. A *surface dweller* is a slang term for person who is unconcerned with the deeper meaning of things and is focused instead on the implications and manifestations (Urban Dictionary, 2023). While it can be important for me to notice how a behavior could potentially undermine a child's or family's development, based on my point of view, this is not where professionals stop. Professionals have a responsibility to move forward in a way that elevates equity.

Elevate equity in the face of historical trauma by the following choices:

- Build a relationship with children, families, and colleagues.

- Affirm feelings of frustration. For example, "You seem upset and rightfully so. Let's talk about what you are feeling and consider some solutions."

- Do not take those negative feelings or behaviors personally. If someone appears negative, she is doing what their brain and body should be doing. Historical trauma impacts individuals physically and psychologically. If you are thinking, "Well, I need to let my body do what it is supposed to do by giving them a piece of my mind," I get it. Take a deep breath, step away, and come back to the situation with the professional supports you can provide. Help families and colleagues channel any negative feelings into constructive collaborations.

- Know the cultural backgrounds of your students, families, and colleagues.

- Make sure you are not buying into a negative stereotype about children, families, and colleagues. Stop clutching your pearls and exclaiming, "Well, I never!" (When I say *you*, I mean *me*.) I will swear up and down I don't buy into stereotypes in one breath and in another say, "Women are so gossipy." Our brains are designed to make shortcuts. Once I understood how the brain works, I changed my *I nevers* into *I am always* on the lookout for potential bias. I stopped viewing potential bias as a character flaw but rather as a natural biological trait.

- Acknowledge you understand the history and why, based on past events, someone might be distrustful or hesitant.

- Consider having someone from that individual's own community discuss or explain the strategy or idea you are trying to encourage, or explain the origins of cultural traditions both positive and what might appear to be negative.

- Ask families and colleagues what you can do to make them feel heard and supported.

- looking beyond the surface behaviors, such as "resistance." Instead, look at the potential reason(s) behind a behavior and dig deeper by asking questions.

- Work to meet survival needs first and build from there.

- Consider potential triggers, based on the person's, family's, or colleague's culture. For example, the "Family Tree" assignment in school might trigger feelings of past trauma. It doesn't mean you will never assign a family tree. It does mean someone would have the option to do an alternative assignment instead. Or supports would be provided to help with any past trauma.

The Impact of Historical Trauma by Age

Infants, Toddlers, and Twos

Young children are coregulators. Life for a baby is like a bike—a tandem bike. Babies' emotions operate in tandem with adult emotions and are affected profoundly by their families and caregivers. In their article titled "How Intergenerational Trauma Impacts Families," Gina Ryder and Tanesha White (2022) state, "Trauma can be transmitted in many ways—from our genetics to conversations at the dinner table." Wait. Wait. Wait. May I interrupt? Voice of Reason here. These are babies! What could babies know about trauma? They are too little to understand anything!

Well, thank you for bringing that up. You are right: babies do not understand the complexities of historical trauma, and no, you do not have a "historical trauma" talk with a baby. Keep in mind that elevating equity is not just about what babies know but what they are experiencing. In the same way a baby would not know anything about war, hunger, or poverty, that does not stop adults who care for babies from having discussions about the supports needed around what they might be experiencing as a result of those conditions. Babies are still absorbing the words and behaviors associated with trauma. For example, the singer Madonna is older than my parents' ability to exercise their right to vote, and as a baby I had no idea a bank could deny my mother a credit card due to her gender, but I experienced the impact of those facts as an infant. When your boss openly jokes that they only hired you because they knew that, as a man, you probably wouldn't be taking off for maternity leave, I can only imagine how uncomfortable that statement might make asking for family leave because you just adopted a baby with your new husband. The emotional experience of frustration could potentially be transmitted to that new baby and impact the stress level of the adoption.

In a review of research on intergenerational transmission of trauma, researchers Rachel Yehuda and Amy Lehrner (2018) found trauma can be experienced by babies though a variety of means:

- DNA modifications
- in utero
- memory
- cultural messages and conditioning
- cultural patterns
- cumulative emotional wounding
- dominant family narratives

- normalization of hatred, cruelty, and dehumanization toward others
- parents bypassing or not coping with their trauma
- aggressions and microaggressions

What You Might See in Children This Age and Their Families

Yehuda and Lehrner (2018) also found higher levels of the stress hormone cortisol in babies, toddlers, and twos, which can impact their emotions, behavior, and attention span. Families might struggle to express their own emotions in a healthy way. It is through their caregivers that babies learn how to express emotions and deal with stress. Because historical trauma is often not acknowledged or talked about, a family might feel uncomfortable sharing their struggles. According to a guide by the National Child Traumatic Stress Network (NCTSN) titled *Addressing Race and Trauma in the Classroom: A Resource for Educators* (NCTSN, 2017), babies are aware of their environments and their caregivers' emotional states. "For young children, their perception of safety is closely linked to the perceived safety of their caregivers... Being exposed to racially motivated traumatic events toward them or their loved ones can be perceived as threats by young children who might respond with physiological or emotional difficulties. In addition... the effects of racial trauma can impact [families'] emotional availability for their children and ability to protect them from danger and stress."

How You Can Respond

Here is the good news! The ways to deal with stress and historical trauma are approaches most caregivers already know how to implement. On her website Parenting Science (https://parentingscience.com/), Gwen Dewar, author and biological anthropologist, offers some examples of ways to support infants, toddlers, and twos exposed to toxic stress:

- Giving physical affection in ways the baby can accept
- Viewing the world from the baby's perspective
- Being sensitive and responsive to the baby's verbal and nonverbal cues

- Engaging in one-on-one communication that the baby can accept
- Calming a baby by walking with her
- Having a soothing sleep routine that includes your emotional availability (Dewar, 2020)

Preschoolers

By the age of three, children have more language than infants, toddlers, and twos do. They can also use creative play schemas to process trauma. However, trauma has a profound sensory impact on young children at this age. They still might not be able to make sense of or have words for the images they remember and emotions they witnessed or absorbed.

What You Might See in Children This Age and Their Families

Children at this age might begin to talk more about what they see and hear as well as re-create traumatic events in their play. Saying, "Stop that kind of play," doesn't stop the child's thoughts, fears, or questions about traumatic events a child may have witnessed or traumatic memories or histories a child have heard. For example, someone asked me one day when I first learned about Emmett Till, the young Black teen who was murdered in 1955 after being accused of whistling at a white woman. I responded that I don't ever remember not knowing. My parents told me his story at a young age. Emmett Till was only one year older than my parents, and my mother grew up in Mississippi where he was murdered. I wonder how that impacted my mother and her own child development. As I look back, my mother typically shared positive stories of her upbringing with me and my sister. I knew she grew up under the segregation of Jim Crow, but I honestly can't share many details other than her stories of school or band trips.

According to *Addressing Race and Trauma in the Classroom* (NCTSN, 2017), if children hear discussions or see discrimination or violence, at this age they "tend to focus on sights and sounds and interpret words and images literally. They may not fully grasp the concept of an image being repeatedly replayed on television and may think each time that the event is happening over and over again." Preschoolers' understanding of time is emerging, so they might think a story or event just happened when it actually occurred many years ago or is a part of their families' cultural past.

Don't get me wrong—I understand hearing young children talk about traumatic events can be triggering to an adult. And I am not advocating for violent play among preschool-aged children. But go a step further than "Stop that kind of play" by asking questions such as, "Tell me about this game," or "Why do you want to play with this toy this way?" or "Is this real or pretend?" Engaging a child in talking about the play can help them process what they are seeing or feeling and make sense of it with the support of a calm, well-regulated adult.

Keep in mind that children at this age primarily express themselves in play. In her book *Under Deadman's Skin: Discovering the Meaning of Children's Violent Play*, Jane Katch (2001)) asks readers to imagine what would happen if we told adults to stop talking or even thinking about violence from a traumatic event. Preschool children, who don't yet have expansive vocabularies, often express their reactions and fears and process their understanding through play.

How You Can Respond

Violent play could be an expression of trauma. Telling children to stop ends the expression but not the fear or worries children might be experiencing. Instead, try to:

- ask open-ended questions, such as, "That looks like a scary game. How does it make you feel?"

- help children to find a safe play way to express their feelings, such as drawing a picture about the experience.

- ask children how they feel about a situation, then ask about the supports they have. For example, if you hear a child say, "Grandma can't get her water pills because the store gone," after racial violence in the community, ask how she feels about this and how people in the community will support her grandma and help her.

- refer a child or family for therapeutic play therapy or resources to deal with trauma.

As a child, I was terrified that my family would not be welcome in places due to our race, and often, the world was not always accessible for my father's wheelchair. But no one ever talked about either, so I endured my fears alone without any adult support outside of my immediate family, who were dealing with a lot of stress due to my father's progressing illness. I was not oblivious to what was occurring, just unable to express or process it. Children are trying to understand their identities at this age, and discussions can support identity development and lessen the stress, which will help them focus on school and learning.

Understand Your Own Historical Trauma

It is important to acknowledge that certain assignments and discussions can be triggering for children (and adults). Provide alternative activities, and offer supports for big emotional responses and processing. I have had many school assignments that revealed my historical trauma, but one I remember most was an assignment in which we had to find out where our last name originated. Well, my maiden name originates from a Swedish man who owned my family. Can you say *trauma* with a capital *T*? That trauma impacts me every day, not because I feel like a victim—far from it. I come from a very proud and successful family. But there were laws that forced my family into a caste system. Laws defined us as less than human and allocated the benefits of our hard work to another family's wealth and comfort for generations. This sanctioned system of exclusion continued in the United States until the 1964 Civil Rights Act. My parents were the first in our family to gain their civil rights in this country. They didn't speak much of their experience, actually, and I was grateful I was spared from that experience.

I guess I was about thirteen when I got the name assignment, and I remember asking my parents what I should say to my class. My father said, "Tell the class your name is *Nelson*, but that was the name of a Swedish slave owner and is not your original name. You come from Africa. Africa is a place of kings and queens! Just like you are in school now, there were universities in Africa." I know that sounds nice and my father was trying to instill a sense of pride in me about my history—and he succeeded. But now imagine me at thirteen, and developmentally I am trying to do what all thirteen-year-olds are doing: trying to fit in.

Let me provide even more context here. You have to understand, my parents were a part of the civil rights movement. At the time of this discussion, my father still wore a carefully manicured afro and was a card-carrying member of the Rainbow PUSH Coalition. (Rainbow PUSH is an international human- and civil-rights organization founded by Rev. Jesse Jackson, who marched with Dr. Martin Luther King, Jr.) I was reminded of this every Saturday morning in my childhood home when, at 10 a.m., my father listened to Rainbow PUSH on our intercom system that played in every room of our house. I knew this was important, but it was also the '80s! My friends were all about preppies and not so much about Black pride. I was trying to be a material girl in my thirteen-year-old material world. I knew what my father said was right, but all I wanted to do at this age was make friends. I was in the process of developing a strong identity, and Africa was something I talked about at home—not at school. The only thing my classmates associated with Africa was pop singers raising funds for famine relief.

My mother provided a slightly different alternative. She said, "Tell them your name is *Nelson* and it is Swedish, but your family comes from Mississippi." This version left some gaps but bypassed the big elephant in the room: I am not Swedish. My family was owned by another family that looked like most of my classmates. And Mississippi is not in Sweden! If memory serves, I went with the latter option. I don't remember what I said or how anyone responded. All I remember feeling was deep shame.

Now, as an adult with a strong, fully formed identity, I feel very comfortable explaining the origin of my name. But as a child, I was still forming this ability and hadn't quite grasped it yet. Interestingly, my shame was not around my name. By the age of six, I had already seen the groundbreaking mini-series *Roots* on TV. This, along with conversations with my parents, helped me process why Kunta Kinte was suddenly called Toby. It was one thing to know something, but it was another thing to explain it to a group of children who could have potentially owned my family. Let's just say I was no Alex Haley. I was still developing that sense of confidence, especially in a setting where I was one of a few people of color and only one of not even a handful of African American girls.

So, I would ask educators to consider what this assignment could bring up for a student who was adopted or whose parents were divorced. I did, in fact, have a classmate who was adopted. I remember thinking, how cool is that! Many of my classmates, who were also self-absorbed teens who suddenly found themselves self-conscious about their families, secretly wished they were adopted too. Could it be these embarrassing people were not my parents? And in terms of our siblings, we thought adoption would explain a lot. But seriously, I now wonder how my friend who was adopted felt about sharing her story.

In another memorable school activity, we had to watch D.W. Griffith's *The Birth of a Nation* (1915) in my high school film class. If you're not familiar with it, this film depicts the U. S. Civil War and reconstruction from the perspective of racist Ku Klux Klan members and sympathizers. Black people are depicted through racial stereotypes popular at the time. Our teacher said she wanted to show the film due to its technological cinematic significance. In writing this book, I decided to reach out to my former teacher. I told her I remember as students, we had a choice to watch the film or leave the room. I remember feeling conflicted and not knowing how to feel or what to do. As I recall, there were three other Black students in the class. One student left the classroom and sat in the hallway. What was that like for her? Why didn't I join her? Why was the person who might have felt the trauma the person who had to leave the room? I just remember not knowing how to feel or respond.

My teacher, whom I hadn't seen in more than thirty years, responded to my message:

> Hello, Angela, I do recall the film, and its importance filmic-ly. I never showed it a second time, and I certainly understand that you didn't know how to respond. I wish I could tell you why I chose to show it at all. I don't even recall if I showed the entire film or if there were only clips. Do you recall?

This message was such a good reminder that what teachers do one year is not what they do the next.

I replied:

> Hello,
>
> I hope my message didn't make you feel bad in any way. But I really took away how this film was a new idea from you and that the idea you didn't show it again shows the changes teachers go through—we are always growing and changing as life-long learners. That is a reminder for me as an educator to really be respectful of that process. Thanks for replying!

She replied:

> What a beautiful response from a beautiful heart. This is the love that is missing in our world; we are so fortunate to have you in the classroom. Best to you and the young people you serve.

My examples highlighted my feelings as a child. But I wonder what my parents felt. As a parent myself, I prefer not to be in a position where I have to explain historical trauma to my child through a class assignment before I am ready to do so. Therefore, in chapter 1, I provide alternatives to the traditional "family tree" assignment. But as you can see, other assignments and even media can bring about stress from historical trauma. Small children might not fully understand the trauma associated with the activity. For example, many educators might think, "A family tree is harmless for a preschooler. They don't yet have an understanding of historical trauma, Angela." This might be true, but it could be stressful for the family to work on this assignment, and if a family is stressed, a child will feel stress. We must remember children are coregulators. What impacts adults directly impacts a child. My film teacher realized this and came up with a way for us to opt out, but I don't think she realized that opting out is another form of exclusion. I didn't want to leave the classroom and be different from the majority of my peers. I am not sure if my teacher considered how opting out can be as uncomfortable as participating in the assignment or activity. It also could have made me and other students vulnerable to bullying or further isolation. Could it be as uncomfortable for the children who opt in? Now they can't share the activity with all of their classmates.

As you develop activities, consider child development. For young children, being included and making friends is a top developmental priority. Anything that jeopardizes that goal can retraumatize a child. If it is the child who has experienced trauma who must leave and adjust, instead of the dominant group, the child can feel isolated and excluded. I do feel that if one child can't participate, I don't think it is an appropriate activity.

You may be thinking, "But wait! Voice of Reason here. That isn't fair to the others!" Remember, in chapter 2, we learned that even preschoolers know that equity is not equality. They understand that it is important to give children what they need. Children ages six to eight want to include children of all abilities, and by age eight they will turn down candy if another child receives less than they do. As adults, we need to catch up to the children and implement equity. Let's take a lesson from the children who already know that if an activity is hurtful to one child then it impacts all children. When children are forced to "opt out," the other children are missing their friend and wishing they were included.

If you are in doubt when creating assignments, consider these questions:

- Could this assignment bring about any stress for a child or family?
- Can all children participate to the fullest level?
- Can this assignment make children vulnerable to bullying or further isolation?
- Does this assignment or activity foster classroom community?
- Does this assignment force children who may have historical trauma or are not a part of the dominant group to adjust?
- Could it be just as uncomfortable for children who are able to participate? Consider that children want to their peers to be able to participate in all activities. If children are worried about their friends, they are probably not gaining all they can from the activity on an academic level.

Secondary Trauma

Have you ever been traumatized by someone else's trauma? When I was a home visitor, I had several families on my caseload who were experiencing poverty, homelessness, and racism. Even though I wasn't experiencing poverty or homelessness myself, I felt as if I was beginning to take on the traits of the families I was working with. I was feeling tired and short tempered each day and felt saddened by the conditions of the homes and families I worked with. What I was experiencing was the impact of secondary trauma. Ever hear of a spouse experiencing weight gain and bloating when their partner is pregnant? Secondary trauma is similar to that.

The National Child Traumatic Stress Network defines *secondary trauma* as "the emotional duress that results when an individual hears about the firsthand trauma experiences of another… For therapists, child welfare workers, case managers, and other helping professionals involved in the care of traumatized children and their families, the essential act of listening to trauma stories may take an emotional toll that compromises professional functioning and diminishes quality of life (NCTSN, n.d.)."

According to *Secondary Traumatic Stress: A Fact Sheet for Child-Serving Professionals* (NCTSN, 2011), signs of secondary trauma can include but are not limited to:

- Hypervigilance
- Hopelessness
- Inability to embrace complexity
- Inability to listen, avoidance of clients
- Anger and cynicism
- Sleeplessness
- Fear
- Chronic exhaustion
- Physical ailments
- Minimizing
- Guilt

The book *Compassion Fatigue: Coping with Secondary Traumatic Stress Disorder in Those Who Treat the Traumatized*, editor Charles Figley (1995) notes, "Therapists begin to exhibit the same characteristics as their patients. That is, they experience a change in their interaction with the world, themselves, and their family. They may begin to have intrusive thoughts, nightmares, and generalized anxiety. They themselves need assistance in coping with their trauma."

How You Can Respond

Strategies for dealing with secondary trauma include ideas such as mindfulness and wellness workshops. If no amount of green juice or yoga poses are going to help your level of need, consider changes to workload and embedding wellness within your program structure to relieve stress. I am a mental-health consultant for several Head Start programs, and many have a "wellness check-in" monthly, bimonthly, or even weekly. On

Tell the Truth Tuesdays, the meetings feature no PowerPoint, no agenda, just us talking, tellin' the truth about the work.

Please don't give me mental-health workshops when you are the one causing me mental-health issues. So, make sure that workloads are manageable and assessed often. Consider ideas such as "No Email Mondays" during which you can email someone only from 12 p.m. to 6 p.m. if there is an emergency. Oh, I mean it! An. Actual. Emergency. Don't email me about the lunch menu on No Email Mondays after 12 p.m., dagnabit! Excuse my language.

Reclaiming My Time Thursdays are times we educators come together and share ideas on ways to conduct quality work in time-efficient ways. And ten-minute meetings are short get-togethers that only last, well, ten minutes! Everyone stands in a circle and shares ideas. The meetings sometimes vary in length between ten and fifteen minutes and have fun names like "Huddles" or "10-Minute Meet-Ups" that focus on a small but specific topic as you stand in a circle or turn to a partner or small group.

I had virtual Wellness Wednesdays during which all participants were located in different sites, but we went for a walk and chatted for ten minutes as we did so. During one meeting, a few teachers realized they were handwriting forms that could have been digital! Whatever format you choose, consider ways to talk about workload efficiencies and reductions in workload that reduce stress. Consistent reflective supervision and referrals to employee assistance programs and mental health supports are also key.

Get to Know Family Identities

> Now let's go back to the house exercise from chapter 1. This time, instead of your own house, you will create a house for a family you work with, or for all your families, or for a family you are wondering about.
>
> Take out a piece of paper and a pen, pencil, or markers. Draw a home for the student and their important grown-ups. The goal is to explore their identity in an inclusive way that allows you to reflect on your students' unique life circumstances and community.
>
> - Who are the people who live in the home? Remember, family members are not always blood related. This is an inclusive view of family that is a compilation of the people who are important to your student.

- Next, label where their home is located. Where do they come from? You could write down their state, province, or country, or the spirit from which they come. When I do this exercise in person, sometimes participants will not label a place but a spirit the family comes from, such as determination. Think about their community and where it is located.
- On the mailbox, label all your student's identities: sister, brother, child, grandchild, niece, nephew, cousin, Black, white, Latina, dog owner, hamster mom, and so on. Who are they? How do they identify?
- Next, at the foundation for the home, list your student's strengths and the strengths of their important grownups (not *parents*; that characterization recognizes only one type of family, whereas *grownups* honors all types of families)
- Draw and label the foods cooking in the kitchen.
- What celebrations happen in the home?
- What books or magazines are in the home?
- What kinds of art do they display? How is the home decorated?
- What is on TV? What music is playing?
- At the top of the house, write down their values. Make a list of things that are important in the way they live their lives.

How did you feel doing this activity this time? Did you know the answers to all the questions? Do you need to get to know certain students and their families more? How will you go about doing so?

✧ ✧ ✧

Now that you have explored what equity means, what equity looks like at varying ages, and how to respond, how to implement equity with families, and how to identify and respond to historical trauma, you are ready to set up systems that support all you have learned. The next leg of your journey will include choosing policies, procedures, and protocols that elevate equity in your early childhood programming.

CHAPTER 6

Elevating Equity with Your Staff

Now that you are elevating equity with children and families, it is important to make sure equity is elevated with staff members. It is heartbreaking and demotivating to see equity being elevated with children and families but not being elevated with the staff who work for the betterment of children and families.

> "Embracing individual differences starts with a company culture. The support of top management to create an environment of inclusivity enables people to feel a sense if freedom in sharing their opinions and beliefs."
>
> —Dr. Adam Bandelli, management and leadership advisor

> Choose an object that represents how you spend your time at your program. For example, choose a fire extinguisher because you spend your time putting out fires all day, or choose a rubber band because you are a floater who is flexible.
>
> Now answer the following:
>
> - Explain how this object represents your experience. Is this how you want to feel?
> - If not, what is an alternative object that represents how you want to feel in your program?

I picked a piano. A piano plays high and low notes. Its sounds get people moving and makes people feel happy and inspired. A piano is also a key instrument in a jazz band, and a jazz band is a perfect metaphor for the collaborative style needed to elevate equity. In his book *Jamming: The Art and Discipline of Business Creativity*, James Kao (1996) reminds us that in a jazz band, leadership "passes among various instruments" but has a shared harmony that guides the direction of the group. In one of my coaching sessions with child-care director and leader Eleanor Northern, she realized, "If I do everything, nothing gets done." To be most efficient, she needed to make sure her leadership style encompassed the same characteristics of a jazz band. So, she made final decisions when necessary, but leadership roles were shared among all her staff. For example, in the book *Reverse Mentoring: Removing Barriers and Building Belonging in the Workplace* (2022), author Patrice Gordon describes a concept in which junior employees mentor those in senior positions: "Reverse mentorship acknowledges that, though [an employee] might lack the experience and institutional or industry knowledge of those higher up the chain of command, less-senior employees often have a wealth of experiences—personal and professional—that could help leaders make better decisions…"

Reverse mentoring is just one way to create an organization in which knowledge at all levels of the organization is valued. Having parents mentor educators could help educators learn more about the needs of families. Having a paraprofessional mentor a new curriculum coordinator or having assistant teachers mentor lead teachers could help educators learn their work from a different perspective. Creating your own "jazz band" that shares leadership as a collective means that teachers might lead staff meetings or that everyone at every level of an organization will provide feedback on a new compliance form to make sure it is user friendly, efficient, and not redundant.

Do you realize being culturally responsive can make your organization more efficient? Research on more than a thousand companies in twelve countries showed that gender and ethnic diversity led to more profitability (Hunt, Yee, Prince, and Dixon-Fyle, 2018). Companies with diverse staff benefit from diverse ideas as well as creativity.

Elevating Diverse Ideas and Creativity

Write down all the places you get new ideas. If you wrote "in the shower, driving, or in the middle of the night," you are my people! My list includes a variety of places, none of which is at work. Why is that? Let me guess. Layers of soul-crushing bureaucracy? Tons of idea-killing rules? Spirit-squelching verbal and nonverbal reactions to ideas?

In her TEDx Talk "How Power Powers Ideas," author and business strategist Nilofer Merchant (2019) describes how and why most innovative ideas go unheard: "Sometimes, it's engineering ignoring the designers or marketing ignoring sales, because every organization has a group that's deemed less worthy of being heard. Young people are dismissed as 'inexperienced' and older people as 'out of touch.' Almost always, commonly marginalized people, for example, the disabled or people of color, had their ideas marginalized too… it's not that the idea is deemed unworthy, it's that the person who brings that idea is deemed unworthy of being heard." She contends that this type of thinking is even engrained in our language: *diverse, unique, left-field* are words she says we use to describe people who do not fit within the normal, mainstream, or majority. "These," Merchant says, "are code—those worthy of being heard, and then the rest of us are the other."

Researchers Joe Magee and Adam Galinsky (2008) describe power and hierarchy as "defining and pervasive feature of organizations…" and "Status, related to the respect one has in the eyes of others, generates expectations for behavior and opportunities for advancement that favor those with a prior status advantage." More specifically, their research shows "hierarchical differentiation might not only have a direct effect on performance but could also play a legitimizing role, inspiring confidence from institutional observers." Bottom line? When people with power in an organization make a suggestion, it is taken more seriously and acted on. Merchant (2019) explains, "When you have power, it means that idea gets early encouragement, so your boss, your friends, whoever hear you, and they say something like, 'That's so original!' They back you, and they shape it so that idea gets developed enough to become a new reality."

According to Magee and Galinsky, the reverse is true for those without status in an organization. Their ideas are more likely to be ignored or not reinforced by colleagues. Power can come from years of experience, fancy titles, or educational credentials. This is not to say all of those achievements aren't noteworthy; however, if organizations want to elevate equity, it is important to be on the lookout for how power can truly power ideas. Whether it is your first day as an educator or you have few educational credentials, you have something important to offer an organization.

Professionally, I am often the only person of color in a leadership role. An article by Marianne Cooper (2018) highlights research by Rosabeth Moss Kanter of the Harvard Business School: "that a one-and-done approach to diversity makes workplaces isolating for underrepresented employees." Cooper quotes the late U. S. Supreme Court Justice Ruth Bader Ginsberg, who was one of nine women in a class of more than five hundred men at Harvard Law School, as describing the feeling of being constantly on display. A report coauthored by Cooper called *Women in the Workplace* (LeanIn.org and McKinsey and Company, 2018) found that being the "only" can make a person feel left out, on guard, and under pressure to perform and conform while being excluded from social groups with colleagues from the workplace.

Do you have any "onlys" in your ECE program? Black men might be an "only" in an early childhood program. Or someone on your curriculum team who has special needs or is multilingual might be an "only." How do you support them? As an "only," I definitely have wondered why it seemed as if no one was understanding me and whether that lack was based on perception rather than the precision of my words or phrases.

Which is why I love this perspective: Ideas are starting points for discussion, research, and testing; throttling them immediately just limits your options… and makes everyone more wary of stretching their imagination. Every truly innovative product or technology was a 'wild idea' at some point. Taming the discussion from the start serves no purpose…" (Nottingham Spirk, 2021). If your staff meetings have become a place where new ideas go to die, or if your organizational leadership only accepts "exciting new ideas" that keep everything exactly the same, consider the following approach:

- Phase 1: Separate your "idea phase" from your "evaluation phase" when brainstorming.

- Phase 2: Evaluate the ideas.

- Phase 3: Put ideas on a path to immediate or later implementation.

Phase 1: Separate Your "Idea Phase" from Your "Evaluation Phase" when Brainstorming

Everyone's role in first phase is simply to listen to each new idea and to affirm creativity and the generation of ideas. Avoid comparing ideas to one another. Establish norms that eliminate idea-killing phrases such as, "When we tried that back in '99…," or "I heard when such-and-such tried that idea, [insert horrible disaster here] occurred." Ideas will not be fully polished at this phase. What will it cost? Great question—*for a later phase.*

During this phase, leaders should be the last to speak so they don't risk swaying the group toward one idea or another. A leader's role is to create space for ideas to flow and to facilitate others speaking. Just like an orchestra conductor, those in senior positions should lead without making a sound. Leaders manage the process and people will manage themselves within your structure.

If your brainstorm has become more of a sprinkle, try brainwriting. Brainwriting allows employees to generate their own ideas without the influence of others by writing down ideas on a sticky note or on a virtual whiteboard anonymously. This practice elevates equity because it provides space for all ideas without the potential bias of knowing who generated the ideas. Brainstorming can feel very uncomfortable for introverts, and often if someone knows who an idea came from, the idea might flop even if it is a good one.

Phase 2: Evaluate the Ideas

This phase involves glowing and growing: describing how an idea is "glowing," or the good aspects of the idea, and describing the places to for that idea to "grow" or improve. To elevate equity, start with how the idea is glowing. Shine a light on what is good about it or how the idea could be beneficial. Then move to what might be needed to grow the idea to implementation. Is the idea redundant? If so, how? Is there something that must be completed before the idea can take root? The evaluation phase is not about shooting ideas down but about thinking of how to help ideas grow into fruition.

A leader's role is to create dialogue instead of debate. If you are a leader who was a teacher, for example, it can be really easy to fall into the trap of considering only your own past experience. Yes, your past experience is important, but it is important to consider what is happening in the present without judgment. For example, in 2020, no leader had any expertise in teaching during a pandemic. Leaders should hold many perspectives to support growth.

Phase 3: Put Ideas on a Path to Immediate or Later Implementation

At this stage, an idea might have grown into an entirely new form, or only one element of an idea might be implemented. *Now* is the time to consider cost. What are the action steps? What is everyone's role? What are doable timelines? How will those timelines fit within competing priorities? What are the potential obstacles? Again, to elevate equity, provide a variety of ways to offer feedback anonymously.

> **"If you haven't hired a team of people who are of color, female, and/or LGBT to actively turn over every stone, to scope out every nook and cranny, to pop out of every bush, to find every qualified underrepresented founder in this country, you're going to miss out on a lot of money when the rest of the investment world gets it."**
>
> **—Arlan Hamilton, author and founder of a venture capital fund**

To further consider systems that create an inclusive culture, let's not neglect thinking about who is at your staff meeting.

Elevating Equity in Hiring

In a *PBS NewsHour* (2017) report by Cat Wise titled "Making the Grade: Anti-Bias Lessons Help Preschoolers Hold Up a Mirror to Diversity," researcher and author Louise Derman-Sparks reminds us, "If all the teachers are white and all the assistants are people of color, that sends messages to kids about who matters, who is visible, and who has power."

We must acknowledge that many groups have been historically excluded from or traumatized by school systems. Schools have not always been welcoming spaces; for example, consider Native American residential schools, segregation based on ability, or laws that excluded women or people of color from schools. As a result, some schools have passed down generational access while others have passed down trauma. Historical and systematic exclusion is an issue rarely brought up when discussing professionals across the educational spectrum. To say, "You can't come here," then turn around and say, "You must come here to be considered professional," is problematic.

A college degree is one measure of a quality candidate, but it should not be the only measure. Now if you are up in arms because you are concerned that this could water down qualifications for early childhood professionals, put your boom box away. This is not the 1980s and you don't need to gather your breakdance crew for a dance battle to show which group is better. Consider that having a degree is not in competition with not having a degree, and experience is not in competition with inexperience. How professionals are defined is an opportunity to activate the Y in *equity* with a "yes and" approach. Yes, a degree is valuable, *and* experience is valuable. Elevate equity by acknowledging, celebrating, and honoring all types of knowledge.

To ensure inclusion, there should be many points of entry into our profession. From a systemic standpoint, how can teaching experience and continuing education be included in addition to college credit? If the enamel on your teeth is starting to itch and you feel there shouldn't be an easy way into the field of education, consider that I have three degrees and more than thirty years of experience in education. What I found out was getting an education is hard work, yes! *And* gaining hands-on experience is hard work. Education is exciting and exhilarating, yes! *And* hands-on experience is exciting and exhilarating. I have observed classrooms as a consultant since 2003, and I have seen teachers with and without degrees struggle. I have seen teachers with and without degrees excel. It is like comparing riding a bus to riding a train—each is different, and both can be an exhilarating and challenging journey toward knowledge. All staff come with knowledge. Just as no child is an empty vessel, no adult is an empty vessel. Instead of thinking about adults as starting from scratch, consider them as starting from experience. A new teacher could come with cutting-edge knowledge of child development that was not available when a seasoned teacher went through training, and an uncredentialed educator might have experience on how to implement each theory outlined in a textbook without reading a single page. New educators and clinicians are important. Seasoned educators and clinicians are important. Credentials are important, and experience is important. Elevating equity means celebrating all those experiences.

Keep in mind, obtaining a degree can be a barrier to entry for many. For example, student teaching is often unpaid full-time work. Raise your hand if you worked some of the longest hours of your career as a student teacher. I was at the school before it opened and was the last person to leave at the end of the day. I prepared lesson plans on weekends and met with families before and after school. I worked long days with no pay. This was hard on me, but for many this is not just hard—it is impossible.

In the blog post "Equality Matters: How to Hire Diverse ECE Staff for Your Preschool" (MomentPath, 2019) Kirk Sykes, a principal, is quoted as asking, "What does it mean to a student when all the black and brown people in the building are the help? They are the janitors, the cafeteria workers, but not the teachers." The post continues: "Start by questioning your own unconscious stereotypes and asking your employees to do the same. It may feel counterproductive to verbalize and acknowledge our biases, but research shows this is actually the sign of a healthy model of inclusivity."

Do your employee demographics mirror the breakdown of the total population at all levels of operations? In her TEDx Talk "The Surprising Solution to Workplace Diversity," Arwa Mahdawi (2016) says, "… the face of our cities is changing, but what is not changing is the face of power… the people in the big board rooms, upper management. That is still exactly the same." This in spite of the fact that "racially diverse teams outperform non-diverse teams by thirty-five percent," according to Mahdawi. To tackle this issue, take advantage of technology! Consider a blind interview. Use a platform such as Zoom to conduct an interview, but ask the candidate to turn their camera off so the hiring team can make an impartial assessment without worry of unconscious bias. Make sure hiring occurs with a team from all levels of programming. A parent or community member should also be on the hiring team (with understanding of confidentiality).

In an article titled "Advancing Equity in the Early Childhood Workforce" (Byars, Diaz, and Paul, 2020), the authors suggest using standardized interview questions, rubrics for rating candidates, diverse interview teams that include individuals from all levels of an organization, and questions that intentionally ask a candidate's understanding and commitment to elevating equity. Sometimes I am asked, "How do I find diverse applicants?" Diverse applicants are always applying. You don't need to "find" them; they will find you. The MomentPath blog post (2019) suggests some useful approaches to developing your team:

- "Tap into your state's 'Grow Your Own' program." As a home visitor, I was often traveling from outside the community to provide services. Consider providing incentives to people within the community to act as community brokers who are paid to bridge potential cultural gaps between professionals and the communities they serve. For example, fellow professionals assumed that because I was Black I knew the Black community. I did—the *middle-class* Black community. It is important to consider intersectionality when thinking about representation and hiring practices. It would have been helpful to me to have a community broker to help me understand Black families experiencing poverty. Consider incentivizing volunteers, classroom aides, mentees, or interns from the community your program serves to earn credentials and grow into professionals within your organization. Consider reverse mentoring, an approach in which people from the community mentor professionals in the communities your program serves.

- "Partner with local high schools and colleges." To that I add: Partner with other community agencies. I had the pleasure of presenting for an early childhood program in North Dakota that shared space and resources with a retirement home. It was a joy to hear how the programs shared staff such as nurses, therapists, and social workers and how the children and their families helped the elderly and their caregivers in the retirement home and vice versa. Some elderly residents would eat more and smile more just from seeing the children and their families. The families with young children and families with aging family members had similar struggles and much in common. Seeing the circle of life was touching. Equitable funding policies would give incentives for these endeavors.

- "Change your language." Post an equity and inclusion statement on your website. Revisit your mission statement often to evaluate and update for equity. Use a balance of feminine- and masculine-themed words in your job ads.

Get to Know Your Staff's Identities

Before we can get things done, it is important to know about the identities of the staff that we are working with. Over my career, I have completed the Myers-Briggs personality inventory and the HMPI. What is the HMPI? It is the Hershey's Miniatures Personality Indicator. There are four types of Hershey's miniatures in the assortments: milk chocolate, Special Dark, Krackel, and Mr. Goodbar, and based on your preference you are assigned a personality type. I was a Krackel, by the way. When I did this test, they paired us in groups by our personalities. Let me tell you, my group was nice enough, but they were a bit annoying. All the Krackels were perky and giggly and talked all the time telling long-winded stories. Some real Pollyanna, glass-half-full types. We had to travel together and got lost. When we were driving in circles (this was back in the day before GPS), I was really wishing we had at least one Mr. Goodbar or something. As I said, they were pretty annoying peop—oh, what's that? Why are you laughing? Ohhhh, you think that is ironic? Now that you mention it, I guess the Krackel personality does describe me to a T! I have been described as perky on occasion, have been known to giggle, and yes, I started out with the glass half empty and developed a mantra of using my Push Past It tool to make the glass half full. It just shows that being around people just like yourself can be just as difficult as being with polar opposites. The HMPI personality test was a good start, but it just scratched the surface and did not address all aspects of my identity.

I suggest implementing the house exercise, "Who Are You and What Do You Believe?" as we did in the first chapter to help you understand each staff member's complex identity. It would be important to acknowledge that this activity could be triggering. Participants can choose what they share, and programs can adapt the activity to make it work for them. Keep in mind that opting out can be counterproductive and lead to even more exclusion, so adapt the exercise to fit the needs of your program. For example, instead of a house, ask participants to complete a survey or to create a poem or rap about their identity including elements of their own choosing. This activity is a great reflection tool even if it is not shared, and if any aspects are shared it can support collaboration, team building, and equity planning.

Keep in mind the invisible identities of your staff. For example, in a blog post titled "Invisible Identities: Letting Yourself Be Seen," author Paul Emerich France (2014) explains, "Generally, when we discuss diversity, we're apt to refer to more visible identities… race, ethnicity, biological gender, or socioeconomic status." When participating in an activity known as the the Social Identity Wheel, France discovered there are so many types of identities that he describes as "invisible to the naked eye—identities like mental health, sexual orientation, ability, or even the blurred lines of gender identity. They are invisible unless you engage with others, let yourself be seen, and make an effort to help others take down their shields and show themselves for who they are."

Keep in mind that employees might not want to disclose disabilities such as epilepsy, dyslexia, post-traumatic stress disorder, anxiety, or depression. Empower your staff by encouraging them to share often-hidden disabilities and creating a list of reasonable accommodations, such as time for doctor appointments for an employee who has a chronic health condition (Lovejoy, 2023).

Upon hiring, equity training should be required. Survey staff to see if this provokes worries or concerns, and provide emotional supports or referrals to supports. Reflect on your policies yearly. For example, are there various ways employees can accrue sick days? Are all employees entitled to paid family leave? Are tattoos allowed? Long hair or braids on men can have an important cultural significance. Provide space for cultural expression. Ensure policies such as the dress code and grooming are inclusive of all cultures and co-created with feedback from employees at every level of programing.

With these discussions, culture can be a source of conflict. For example, I had an administrator who struggled because she was Hispanic and all the staff were African American. Or educators may struggle when the cultural makeup of a neighborhood changes. And we can't neglect talking about age, job title, language, new teachers versus seasoned teachers, aides versus lead teachers, and educators with degrees and those with experience.

I once participated in a virtual meeting and learned that it was difficult for an educator who needed to read lips. The person felt left out because the closed captions weren't enabled. There have been conflicts over a male teacher in the infant room changing diapers. Another source of conflict occurred when a male teacher was promoted to director after less than a year of employment, but female educators who had been there longer were passed over for the role. Staff may feel resentful over titles, job descriptions, and how they are addressed in the work setting in terms of names or pronouns. Look, I have a peanut allergy that is airborne and have even gotten teed off when someone opened a big bag of nuts without asking if anyone has an allergy. I've gone home with a rash because someone mixed candy bars with nuts and candy bars without. There are too many scenarios to describe.

Gain confidence in elevating equity by being proactive around potential sources of conflict. Consider letting your staff safely share (anonymously, for example in a survey) what aspects of their identity have been assets or have led to experiences that felt challenging. This can help leaders and programs become more responsive, preventative, and productive. It is important for members of your staff community who are part of dominant groups to share the burden with and be inclusive of those who are not part of that group. Is it too hard to have a bowl of candy with nuts and another bowl without or a noncandy option? Does your organization allow employees to choose what religious holidays they want off from work? Does the work calendar include only holidays celebrated by the dominant culture? As we learned earlier, the group we belong to is fluid and changes depending on the situation. We all wear perspectacles, viewing life through our own lenses. Create safe spaces to hear about other viewpoints. It is important to build that foundation of understanding each other and to build respect for others' life views. When walking into work, we need to put on our professional perspectacles so we can elevate equity in the workplace. Use list the of identities and information about their identities you gather from employees and families in your program to consider every school activity from a variety of viewpoints.

> **Inclusion and Exclusion in the Workplace**
>
> Take a moment to list all the ways you have felt included in the workplace.
>
> Next, list any assumptions or judgments that have been made about your age, educational background, race, gender, sexual orientation, ability, religion, socio-economic background, or any other identity I have neglected to mention. How did that experience make you feel?
>
> For example, Laurie Kreg, a colleague of mine with more than thirty years of experience in education, shared assumptions that were made when she adopted her daughter internationally. People asked why she didn't adopt a child from the United States or why she was afraid to adopt a Black child. They made assumptions about her personal decisions as a mother. If they had activated the *U* in *equity*, they would have understood her reasons were due to the ease of the adoption process.

Making Elevating Equity a Practice

After you have hired a diverse staff, there is still more work to elevate equity. Like Laurie, one part of my identity that I found particularly challenging was being a working wife and mother of four children. I have always looked younger than my age, and as a result of my "baby face" and slight stature, I experienced microaggressions in the workplace from people of all ages, races, and genders who assumed, for example, that I was a teen mother. That's not a jab at teen mothers; the challenge I felt had to do with the assumption. I actually had someone at work ask me, "Are you still with all the daddies?" Again, there is nothing wrong with a mother having multiple parenting partners. But there was something wrong with the assumption that this was my experience. From that time on, I have always said, "My husband and I…" to avoid that microaggression. My story is not an isolated one. Leah Georges (2019) explores this type of workplace bias in her TEDx Talk "How Generational Stereotypes Hold Us Back at Work." To navigate a multigenerational workplace, Georges suggests meeting people where they are using an individualized approach. For example, for the "Generation X-er who has four drop-offs, three kids, two hands, and is just trying to keep the wheels on the bus. Sure, maybe she's a little aloof at work. Maybe she's a little independent. Maybe she's exhausted. Or that millennial who asks for a raise after two months because they're 'entitled?' Well, maybe it's because that generation has more debt than any generation before them… and they just need the money to keep going… [W]hen you meet people in their onlyness… we're not talking about a generation anymore."

> What areas around your identity do you feel you must adjust to make others feel comfortable? What do you say or do to avoid microaggressions? What do you say or do when a microaggression occurs? How can early childhood programs and professionals share this burden and become allies?

One way to reduce microaggressions is to normalize a concept that Loretta J. Ross (2021) describes as "calling in." Unlike calling someone out, calling someone in is usually done privately. Before a microaggression occurs, make a spreadsheet with all the ways that each employee would prefer to be called in, should the need arise. Elevate the *T* in *equity* by asking in advance how each staff member would prefer a calling in to occur, for example, by a personal phone call, email, text, or app such as private Slack. Outline action steps of "calling in" another colleague, and also outline steps to take when inequity is putting any employee in physical or emotional danger. When you or a colleague is called in or out for a microaggression or inequitable act, it can be useful to remember to take five:

1. Take a moment to assess your feelings, the comment, or the situation.

2. Take time to listen. If you have committed a microaggression, listen to the person who has experienced it. If someone brings the incident to your attention, listen carefully. Create a space where employees can ask for support if they need to talk with a colleague about a microaggression or get support around microaggressions in the workplace.

3. Take a pause. We learned in chapter 1 that bias is biological, and shame triggers the need for self-protection and inhibits learning. Don't take it out on yourself or colleagues when microaggressions or other biased actions occur. In *Speak Up at School: How to Respond to Everyday Prejudice, Bias, and Stereotypes*, Willoughby (2012) advises, "If changed behavior is what you are after, keep that goal in mind—and let it shape your response. Calling someone a 'racist' may feel satisfying, but it also may reinforce that person's bigotry and be counterproductive." Conversely, no one is "playing the equity card" when they call someone in for a correction. Create specific norms and protocols around these actions.

4. Take time to educate yourself and the staff. Keep in mind a one-and-done training is not enough. Learning requires consistent interactions with a topic over

time. Collect data so your organization can identify patterns and learn when bias is most likely to occur. For example, does it happen during behavior planning? during interviews? during parent-teacher conferences? in performance reviews? It might be tempting to ask the person(s) who experienced a microaggression or inequity to educate everyone else on what to do if they encounter a similar situation. However, just because someone experiences inequity doesn't mean they feel comfortable teaching anyone else about the topic or even feel like an expert. Heck, I am still trying to process the "Are you still with all the daddies?" comment. If someone who has experienced inequity does want to share their experience, it is important provide a space for that. Yes, learning about the experiences of your staff is important, *and* it is important to make sure that one experience or a few experiences do not speak for the experience of an entire group of people. For example, if a colleague or family feels they have experienced inequity in your program, talking with a senior staff member of your organization who originates from the same group is not enough to understand that inequity. That one employee could never speak for an entire culture. This seemingly harmless tactic also does not take into account the intersectionality of that person's identities. Moreover, finding a person from within your organization to educate everyone means they could have an inherent bias as an "insider" within your program. Learning from colleagues does not take the place of doing your homework as an organization. Find an expert whose job it is to teach on this topic of equity and inclusion. A professional trained in teaching others about equity should have a methodology for training that has proven effective within early childhood settings.

5. Take action as an organization to admit that bias and inequity exist. It can be costly to lose talented staff to the stress associated with inequity and bias. Replace stress, silence, frustration, and unawareness with a consistent, conscious effort and honest dialogue. Regularly devote time to teaching and supporting program staff on equity.

Considering Power Differentials

Social events outside of work hours have often presented an awkward challenge for me. I remember being asked to attend a work-related Friday-evening holiday party. At the time, I was a mother of three children under the age of five who was also a graduate student. A holiday party might sound like no big deal, but it was a huge sacrifice after working all week, being up multiple times at night with our children, spending little time with my husband, and still having assignments to complete over the weekend. I already had an hour-and-a-half commute to work each day. The location of the event was even farther than my work location, and due to my lazy eye—one of my invisible identities— you probably don't want me out on the road driving after a long work day, especially at night. But I went. I mean I couldn't *not* go. It was a holiday party after all, and I did not want to be a party pooper or insult my boss.

Another challenge arose at 9 p.m. when I said I had to call it a night. One of the leaders at my job asked me not to go and leave all the "fun." I mean, is it socially acceptable for me to go into graphic detail about our three-year-old's acid reflux, my concerns around our toddlers' poop patterns, and my eight-page paper due Monday? Must I share all of that to convince you that I really couldn't stay? What was intended as a playful remark opened the door for my colleagues to tease me later. Sharing everything that was going on in my life might also send a message that I didn't have the capacity to do my job. What would you do?

I am sure my supervisor was well-intentioned and thought it was light-hearted teasing. She was unaware of what a big "ask" was being requested of me and the anxiety it was provoking. However, there is also an inequitable power dynamic in these types of situations. My supervisor unknowingly could have been experiencing *powerblindness*, something I have been guilty of myself. Professor of sociology Charles Kurzman and colleagues (2014) define elements of *powerblindness* as "failure to notice that one belongs to a privileged group and the belief that all groups are equal in power." In his article "Introducing Powerblindness," Kurzman (2014) contends, "One of the privileges of privilege is obliviousness… but the oppressed always notice."

Now, if the realization that your colleagues might have been fake smiling each time they have been told about another team-building event or impromptu after-school faculty meeting has finally dawned on some of you, think of other instances of potential powerblindness. Even if a leader feels as if an employee is their bestie or calls them "cousin," they must still acknowledge a power differential and the hierarchy in the relationship. Author Cedar Barstow (2015) sheds more light on power, referring to "… those in positions of increased role power as having 'up-power' and those in corresponding positions of lesser power as having 'down-power.' These are simple and directional terms not intended to indicate disrespect, disempowerment, exploitation, manipulation, better, worse, power over, or power under. Instead, these terms are intended to denote role differences in responsibility and vulnerability."

Fast-forward to the present. I am the owner of my own professional-development company. I am grateful to work with an awesome, diverse team of professionals to provide training and consultation. I like my team and hope they like me. However, I know there is a difference between a boss and a BFF. My team needs a compassionate leader who is always on the lookout for potential powerblindness that might leave them vulnerable or excluded. For example, I need to consider the dynamics when I create policies around holiday gifts and events or email protocols when colleagues are out of the office. If I email someone on my team on a Saturday and they reply, could that leave my team feeling pressured to work on weekends? Would they feel vulnerable asking me to stop that practice? The onus is on me to see my position of power and the potential anxiety it could invoke for someone to tell the person who signs their check to stop doing anything. As a result, I am working hard to use a tool in Outlook that notifies me when a team member is not in for work and to schedule the email to arrive when they start their workday.

Yes, it is important to realize all people have personal and spiritual power. *And* in the workplace, there can be a power differential due to professional roles and responsibilities. It is important for those with up-power to create safe spaces with appropriate boundaries. A good leader isn't just an expert at their craft but also an expert at being able to psychologically identify with those they lead, understand their perspectives, and identify any potential challenges.

> Similar to the activity we did in chapter 1, make a list of all the parts of your identity at work that place you in a position of power. What parts of your work identity could lead to potential vulnerability or exclusion? Consider how you are using your power to support those who could potentially be excluded or judged harshly.
>
> Consider how you are elevating equity by searching for any interactions in the workplace that might leave colleagues vulnerable or isolated.

To elevate equity, it is important to remember that *no* is a complete sentence. Back to the holiday party. Did I stay? No. I didn't go into more detail, and I headed home. But this led to my feeling very uncomfortable and fearful as I was the only employee who didn't stay. Needless to say, this had a definite impact on my relationship with my boss and my colleagues going forward.

I get the intention—social events are meant to build team camaraderie and strong working relationships. Yes, these interactions can be great team-building events in many cases. And research by Tracy Dumas and colleagues (2013) shows that these events can also have unintended outcomes that can hinder staff relationships. There is evidence that these types of activities can help colleagues with similar identities form close ties, but activities like this do not have the same benefits for their diverse counterparts.

In the article "Is the Party Over? The Unintended Consequences of Office Social Events," (Knowledge at Wharton Staff, 2013), researcher Nancy Rothbard is quoted as saying, "Going to company picnics and chatting about non-work matters with co-workers at the water cooler—what we refer to as 'integrative activities'—are not as enjoyable, and are in fact can be uncomfortable, for members of diverse teams… [R]ather than bringing people closer together, these activities can underscore our differences." Rothbard adds, "[M]anagers need to be sensitive to what others may be feeling… When companies sponsor social activities for their employees or initiate a diversity training program, they need to ensure they are creating an atmosphere where employees are likely to feel comfortable and have a good experience."

Keeping this in mind, consider the following:

- Choose events that could include the entire family or child care with the understanding that some employees might not want to add more hours in child care for their child(ren).

- Think about the ease in reaching, and the accessibility of, the location. Consider providing transportation to events.

- Survey staff about times, locations, and the types of events they would enjoy. As leaders, we want to make sure our organizations exercise the *T* in *equity* by surveying staff around events so they can be treated as they want to be treated.

- Create norms or policies on the ways all employees, including leaders, can respond if someone declines participation or leaves early.

- Provide activities other than social events to help staff create strong bonds with one another.

- Create affinity groups to let employees who share the same interests or circumstances trade ideas and share experiences. (I would have loved a "Moms at work club," because we all would have left by 9 p.m. Well, if one person did, I think the others might have been more understanding of why they were doing so.)

- Develop relationships through authentic experiences.

- Honor and celebrate successes.

- Create a list of the diverse ways staff wish to develop strong, collaborative work relationships.

Celebrating someone's work accomplishments or sending a card when a family member is ill could create the same relationship-building effect as a social event. Not everything has to involve making potato salad! In fact, I have had many work experiences at which

A WORD ABOUT THAT AWKWARD ICEBREAKER

Give me the look on your face when you see *icebreaker* as the first slide on a professional-development day. Some of your faces might show excitement, others might be full of dread, and still others might look away so they could calculate how much work they could accomplish if they didn't engage in the icebreaker and... wait, who just sneaked out to go to the restroom? When elevating equity, be cautious about icebreakers or activities that reveal personal information about coworkers to other coworkers. Keep in mind that you can engage in an activity like the house exercise in this book without sharing it with the entire group. Icebreakers or similar activities can lead to anxiety for introverts. Rather than sharing, self-reflection can be just as powerful.

Who else has had to play Coworker BINGO at an event? If you haven't had the "joy" of this experience, here's how it works: each participant fills up a card with information they learn about their colleagues. In my experience, the game went nowhere. I found out that someone sews, which was interesting, but we still had a hard time working together. If you choose to have an icebreaker activity, it should have a clear and meaningful connection to how it will support work or collaboration in the professional environment. The activity should have low-risk opportunities that colleagues can choose. (Remember, opting out could lead to more exclusion.) Try to go beyond surface information, and let employees choose something meaningful about themselves they think might help their relationships with their coworkers. (Coworkers might not ever be friends, and that is okay.)

my fellow employees' eating cornbread and collard greens together at a potluck did not translate into positive work collaborations. Listening to colleagues' new ideas and writing a list of how a new idea could be beneficial for the program—instead of ways it could never work—could cultivate very strong working relationships.

Ever hear the saying "Absence makes the heart grow fonder"? Did you ever consider that, after eight hours a day at work, spending time away from your work family and with your actual family, friends, fur-babies, or even by yourself could strengthen work relationships? Be cautious of scheduling multiple social events outside of, or events during, work hours. If attendance is mandatory for a work social event, there should be compensation. According to the U. S. Fair Labor Standards Act of 1938, depending on an individual's employment status, an employee must be paid for that time.

When hosting an event, consider morale and get input from all levels of your organization. Attending a social event should not be tied to achieving an elevated work status, and it should be made clear that nonattendance will not lead to any negative consequences by leadership or colleagues.

Motivating Adults by Knowing Their Why, Who, and What

> Get a piece of paper and write down words or phrases that have negatively affected your motivation as an early childhood educator.

How did you do? Did any of my phrases show up on your list?

- "Do it for the kids!" As if I am selfishly working on lesson plans all weekend for myself.

- "You gotta roll with the punches." I'd like to punch something all right!

- "Well, this is what you signed up for." As if I went into student-loan debt to be called a "B" and get my glasses smacked off my face by a three-year-old.

- "Oh, I do volunteer work too." I am not volunteering. I am an early childhood professional! (I love volunteer work, so not knocking anyone.)

I love an inspirational quote, but sometimes quotes meant to be motivating can invalidate and minimize the experiences of early childhood professionals. In the article "Gaslighting Teachers with 'Inspirational' Memes Needs to Stop," Rachael Moshman (2022) states, "Yes, teachers love those lightbulb moments where they know they're making a difference in the education of a child. However, that doesn't mean they shouldn't expect to get paid a salary… Surgeons do their job for the outcome, too, but they receive fair compensation in addition to the satisfaction of positively impacting lives."

Sayings such as "Work smarter, not harder" without ideas for reducing paperwork, or suggesting self-care without concrete steps to address serious issues such as secondary trauma, safe working environments, lack of resources, and redundant paperwork, are gaslighting. Merriam-Webster (2022) defines *gaslighting* as psychological manipulation that causes a person to question the validity of their own thoughts and perception of reality, leading to, among other outcomes, loss of confidence and self-esteem. These sayings invalidate the concerns of early childhood educators and make them question their motives when they speak up for equity. Gaslighting seems to pop up when conversations about resources, workload, and salaries arise.

Teaching is a female-dominated profession with low salaries, so we must stop and ask ourselves how that correlates to equity. In the article "Is It All about the Money? How a Pay Freeze Affects Motivation" (Costello, 2021), Mioara Cristea, assistant professor in psychology at Heriot-Watt University in Edinburgh, Scotland, reminds us "… when employees are compensated appropriately, they feel valued by their employers as workers but also as human beings. Studies have shown that when employees feel valued, they are more likely to enjoy their work, to perform better, to feel satisfied by their work, and to develop organisational commitment." First of all, don't you just love the British spelling of *organizational*? Employers should be aware there is an imbalance of power between an employer and employee. They should never dismiss the need for proper compensation, especially among groups who have been traditionally marginalized and given unequal pay.

The Why

People in your organization come to work each day to make a difference—that is a given that should never be questioned—and a living. "Teachers do it for the outcome not the income" is nonsense. (Gets on soapbox.) Educators shouldn't be asked to be martyrs. If they aren't paid well, they can't support themselves or their families. According to a study by researchers Elise Dizon-Ross and colleagues (2019), economic stress can affect job performance. The study found that economic stress leads to more negativity about a job, lower attendance, and lower retention. Finally! The answer to why no one comes to work on a Monday or a Friday! Money is a necessity, and unless you are independently wealthy, no one should expect educators to "do it for the kids." It is inequitable to ask this of any person and considered gaslighting when asked to do so when negotiations for salary, supplies, or resources arise.

Nobel Prize–winners Daniel Kahneman and Angus Deaton (2010) found that a higher income leads to people thinking about their quality of life more positively. Another study by Matthew Killingsworth (2021) found well-being rose with income. Along with that, educators are helpers by nature. As a program leader, you really want to know who educators are providing for. You might be surprised; more often than not, the money they earn is not only intended for themselves and their families, but also for children and families in your program.

The Who (No, Not the Rock Band)

Who is your staff providing for? Who would benefit from that raise in salary for your staff? They are working for themselves, but many also give to others: their families and the children in their own program. I think educators are the only professionals who steal from home to give to their workplace. A survey of more than five thousand U.S. pre-K teachers showed they spent an average of 750 dollars of their own money each year on their students (Hruza, 2021). This number has steadily increased each year since the researchers began collecting data in 2015.

Another study by Elizabeth Dunn and colleagues (2008) showed that people who spent money on experiences or to benefit others found happiness. Discourage them from buying materials for their classrooms and instead work to advocate for more materials or using organizations like Donors Choose. A nonprofit organization in the United States, Donors Choose makes it easy for individuals to donate to schools. Find out "who" their income goes to in their lives.

When discussing money, we also need to consider context. As discussed in previous chapters, women are not paid equal salaries to men when doing the same work, and women of color are often paid the lowest. That should always be a part of any salary discussion. Your program should outline your commitment to equal pay. In addition, salary transparency has been shown to have a positive impact on organizational culture. In his article titled "Pay Transparency: What It Is and How to Do It Right," Brian Nordli (2022) outlines some ideas to consider:

- Determine where your company currently falls on the pay-transparency spectrum and where you want to be. (I will never forget a social-worker friend of mine finding out she made the same money as a colleague with fewer credentials and less experience.) Survey the managers to understand what employees want to know about their salaries.

- Develop a pay philosophy that aligns with your talent strategy and culture. What do you value in new hires? Which behaviors do you want to incentivize?

- Clearly define roles and responsibilities, and use market data to set salary ranges. This helps to eliminate bias and create a less subjective pay structure.

- Conduct a payroll audit to identify and resolve salary discrepancies.

- Train managers to have proactive salary conversations with employees.

Money is important, but if you want to motivate your staff for that new mandate or initiative, evidence from a body of research shows employees are also motivated by people they care deeply about. Make your motivation more meaningful. For example, create a folder for each staff member and collect examples of success. When a staff member feels unmotivated or frustrated, pull out something from that folder to remind them of past effectiveness. Literature points to how crucial it is that your staff have a sense that their work is meaningful and purposeful. For instance, researchers Dia Zeglat and Suzi Janbeik (2019) found that meaningful work is associated with organizational outcomes. Framing a new initiative or strategy by how it will help their students and families could be key motivator for educators, if the initiative still allows space for their concerns and ideas. Educators live for the children and the families they work with, and they want to engage in initiatives that make their work easier. Many educators have been burned in the past by failed initiatives and misspending, so it is important to frame conversations that acknowledge the past mistakes, honor their emotions, and express understanding of why they might be hesitant to jump on any new bandwagon.

THREE IMPORTANT REASONS YOUR NEW CURRICULUM INITIATIVE OR STATE MANDATE ISN'T BEING IMPLEMENTED

Why is that new curriculum, which cost your district or your small, privately owned childcare program thousands of dollars, still in its shrink wrap on a shelf collecting dust?

First of all, that fancy new standards-aligned, rigorous, evidence-based curriculum could be giving your staff an identity crisis. Researcher Luca Tateo (2012) explains in the article "What Do You Mean by 'Teacher'? Psychological Research on Teacher Professional Identity": "When teachers are challenged in educational reform processes they may experience a 'loss of self.'" Innovative initiatives force staff and families to change their behavior, and that comes at a psychological cost that is often underestimated. As a result, the delivery of any new curriculum should include not just information about its efficacy with children but also the methodology behind the training and that training's educational psychology component. Tateo goes on to highlight that "teachers experience fear and intimidation when their professional self-understandings are challenged. Only with adequate support by researchers and trainers are they able to reconstruct self-understandings, leading to improvements in student achievement, instructional practices, and positive changes leading to emotions of pride and excitement."

Second, educators may fail to implement new mandates with fidelity because it is normal to overvalue the benefits of what they are already doing over those they haven't seen in action yet. Cognitive dissonance can lead to a disconnect. *Cognitive dissonance* is a term coined by Leon Festinger (1957). It is the mental discomfort that happens when we expect a person to hold two or more contradictory beliefs, ideals, or values as they are experiencing something new. Being negative is normal! Instead of dreading lack of buy-in, expect it as a normal part of the implementation process. A study by Elisabeth McFalls and Deirdre Cobb-Roberts (2001) demonstrated that addressing cognitive dissonance head on and incorporating it into training creates a sense of awareness that can reduce resistance. As a result, the training and coaching should explicitly address cognitive dissonance with evidence-based strategies.

Third, any curriculum implementation or initiative should be transparent about how it is grounded in educational psychology and the phases educators go through as they adjust to new ideas and evidence-based strategies that lead to adult learning. Trainings should specifically and meaningfully address the emotional stress of meeting the needs of multiple mandates and of challenges to teacher/staff identity. In his article "Staying on the Shelf: Why Rigorous New Curricula Aren't Being Used," David Steiner (2019) advises, "one day of professional learning isn't going to change years of teachers' pedagogical practices. If a district adopts a new curriculum, it will take sustained professional learning and principal buy-in and leadership to effectuate fidelity of implementation."

As a leader, I need to be able to explain how a new idea or initiative can inspire more enthusiasm in educators as they come to work each day. What's that? You say an employee should come to work because they're supposed to? That's fair. But I am also supposed to exercise and eat healthy. I don't know about you, but I need constant motivation to do both. If you are determined to hold an attitude that people should hold up their end of the employment bargain, I respect that. I also want you to know that research shows people will come to work, but they may not be as productive or effective without motivation. For example, researchers Idah Naile and Jacob Selesho (2014) found trusting relationships, a shared vision, encouraging creativity, and positivity motivate educators. This wasn't just a one-time finding either; many studies, including one by researcher Jasleen Kour and colleagues (2019), found that optimism and supporting well-being and personal strength at the workplace increase employees' performance and the entire organization's productivity. This is early childhood, and this business is all personal. Just as the body needs food and water to function at its highest levels, we also need to be "fed" by motivation. Inspiration does a body good each and every day!

If you are a leader who feels that you just don't have time for all this touchy-feely stuff, I would ask how you can provide quality care for young children and families *without* the touchy-feely stuff. Caring for young children is by nature an emotional endeavor. Andy Hargreaves' research has demonstrated again and again that emotions are at the epicenter of teaching (Hargreaves, 1994; 1998; 2000; 2001; 2003), and author Sonia Nieto (2003) reminds us in her book *What Keeps Teachers Going?* that it is the emotional stuff that keeps teachers coming to work and families coming to our programs each day.

The What

Each person in a program should identify what inspires them and why they began this career path in the first place. Knowing someone's "what" and "why" is critical. Leaders and colleagues will need to draw on each other's "what" and "why" during times of struggle or conflict. The values of each individual in the program don't have to be identical, but we do need to identify when our own cultural values and the values and vision of the program are not in alignment. That's when compromise is needed to bring both parties into agreement. You might be thinking, "Hey, wait a minute, Angela! I am the leader of this organization. Why should I compromise?" First, you don't have to. But if you do compromise, you might find your relationships with staff and employee retention and attendance improve. Researchers Rebecca Johannsen and Paul Zak (2020) found that when staff have a sense of autonomy, they are more productive. A meta-analysis of forty-three studies showed it is important to be adaptable and provide just enough direction to support learning without being overbearing (Koeslag-Kreunen et al., 2018). An organization that is neither flexible nor adaptable could be a sign of inequity; equity, by definition, involves collaboration.

Equitable Practices at All Levels of Programing

I got into early childhood education because I love babies. What I didn't realize was that, like Beyoncé, babies come with an entourage of adults. For example, I had an experience many years ago as a consultant that I would now describe as a microaggression from a colleague. When I was sharing about that experience, another colleague stated, "Just because she is good with children doesn't mean she is good at working with adults." The quote by Winnicott reminds us that children can only exist within a context that includes adults because young children are not yet self-sufficient. They are always accompanied by adults, such as caregivers, within their community. As a result, if an educator is not good at working with or providing equity for the adults who care for children, they cannot provide equity for children. I don't just mean teachers—I mean any adult who advocates for or provides any in way for the betterment of children. No matter how close or far removed that individual is from providing those services directly with the children themselves, it is important to realize that to provide equity for children, one must be an expert at providing equity for adults.

> "There is no such thing as an infant."
>
> —D. W. Winnicott, *The Maturational Processes and the Facilitating Environment*

Elevate Equity in Your Program

Have a clear statement about your organization's commitment to inclusion and equity. Create an elevating equity leadership (EEL) team that encompasses diverse individuals (gender, race, age, experience, families, culture, and so on) from all levels of the program. Affinity groups are also important spaces. Byars, Diaz, and Paul (2020) define *affinity groups* as "spaces where people of similar identities can come together around particular issues." They write that, for individuals who are often pushed to the margins, affinity groups "can serve as a special place for connection that may not often be found in daily work life as well as being spaces of support and healing." A reflective practice group or community of practice is another way to elevate equity in your program. These meetings can be virtual or in person. Natasha Byers and her colleagues outline some key components to consider:

> "It's all too easy to hire people from diverse backgrounds and then sit back and expect the magic to happen. A passive approach is guaranteed to fail."
>
> —Rocío Lorenzo et al., "How Diverse Leadership Teams Boost Innovation"

- Intentionally create the conditions of trust and safety.

- Create a structure to ensure the "members have the time, space, and resources to work collaboratively."

- Pair staff to mentor each other. These meetings don't have to be long. Meeting each day at the back of the parking lot to walk in together for a five-minute meeting, or having equity minutes at the start of meetings you already have are time efficient (Byars, Diaz, and Paul, 2020).

If you think elevating equity in your program would take too much time, think about it this way: You either spend time dealing with conflicts and challenges, or you devote time to preventing conflicts and challenges. I prefer the latter.

Louise Derman-Sparks and Julie Olsen Edwards (2019) remind us to stop and think about whether we treat all staff, no matter what their role in the program, as "important contributors." Activate the Q in *equity* by asking opinions of all. I remember at one of my equity trainings, a participant asked, "Why am I here? I am the bus driver." "Why?" I replied, "You are the first face families and children see! That is why we need your opinion!" All people from all levels of a program, no matter how close to or far removed from children, are tasked with elevating equity. Derman-Sparks and Olsen also urge early childhood professionals to reflect on whether we treat all staff "respectfully, recognizing and appreciating their cultural styles and belief systems…."

Professional Evaluations

Equitable programs and systems know mistakes are a part of success, and are cherished opportunities for growth. Any evaluative activity in education should be equitable. Evaluative activities could include:

- Employee performance reviews
- Quality rating system reviews for programs/systems
- Feedback on collaborative projects among colleagues

> "Inclusion is not a matter of political correctness. It is the key to growth."
>
> —Rev. Jesse Jackson, civil rights and political activist

For any evaluative activity to be equitable, it must first outline strengths (what I like to call "glows") as well as areas for growth. The term *growth* honors the learning process. Terms such as *weakness*, "area of concern," or "area for improvement," on the other hand, imply a deficit that needs to be corrected or a skill level that is not good enough. Consider that some opportunities for growth or a perceived deficit could actually contribute to strengths, depending on the context of the situation.

For example, a colleague might talk in tangents that are off topic. At a feedback meeting, this could take the meeting away from the agenda. However, talking in tangents could also help your team see connections to the topic they never considered. Instead of trying to stop someone from talking in tangents, add a time to talk about that tangent. Affirm that person's engagement in the learning process by saying something like, "Yes, that is a good topic, and I appreciate you bringing that up. I'm not sure we have the time to give it the space it deserves in this meeting. Can we take a minute from this agenda, write down key ideas about that topic on sticky notes, and put them in the note 'parking lot' for our next meeting?"

What might seem like challenges or concerns could be areas of strength in the workplace and can be invaluable. Consider the following:

Labeling a person in terms of a perceived deficit puts me in a mindset of something to "fix" and provides no information on how to activate the *U* in *equity* to understand an individual. Thinking through a deficit lens can be counterproductive. Equitable feedback

Potential Challenge	Potential Strength
Colleague behaves like a know-it-all	Ask this colleague to share what she knows about a topic for 2 minutes. Lean into her skill, and have her research new ways to accomplish a task.
Colleague keeps talking about the way they did it at their previous job	Ask this colleague to share how something was done at their previous place of practice. We need as many ideas as we can get! Listen and learn more about how they do things at a different work place. It doesn't mean that idea will work for your program, but some elements might. See what you can gain from understanding something new.
Colleague talks in tangents in meetings	Staff will ramble when they are not given time to think and organize their thoughts before speaking. Give everyone a few moments of silence to organize their thoughts and write down their ideas before speaking. Ask this colleague to research ways a topic could connect to other ideas and to share for five minutes at a meeting.
Colleague "sits on the fence" instead of choosing one way over another	Ask this colleague to share the pros and cons of each idea. Consider this person as the "cheerleader" of the group who supports everyone and every idea.
Colleague gossips with or about other colleagues	Ask if this staff member would like to lead an affinity group or reflective-practice group instead. Have this person share announcements of positive things going on with staff members.
Colleague makes negative statements such as, "That will never work"	It is important to know why something might not work, so affirm this skill. Ask this colleague to research all the ways something wouldn't work, then collaborate as a team to tackle each challenge.
Colleague jokes about everything	Give this colleague a certain time to share a joke. Embrace jokes! They are an important way to relax and lighten the mood.
Colleague won't stop talking	Before jumping into a conversation, let this colleague write down what she wants to say for three to five minutes. You *want* this colleague to share her ideas. Give time limits for speaking: "We have five more minutes. What are the three most important ideas you want to share?" Give *unlimited* time for sharing in other formats: "If we don't get to everything, write your ideas down for me—I don't want to miss anything you want to say." Let this colleague start off conversations, and ask her to help you monitor the time and whether everyone has had a turn to speak.

looks at a person's skills, how they can be strengths, and builds on them. I use tools that highlight educators' "glows" (what the teacher is doing well) and "grows" (opportunities for growth). When I offer my feedback, each meeting starts with the teacher reading the observation unfiltered. It includes glows or what they are doing right. Then, we reflect on these glows. The glows always outnumber the grows; having too many grows can overwhelm an educator. When the teacher is ready, we explore the areas for "grows." Grows are always collaborative. I give a maximum of three ideas for growth, and then the educator decides what he thinks are areas for growth. I will only list observations of what I could see and hear without inferences in the growth section.

> **"Good leadership requires you to surround yourself with people of diverse perspectives who can disagree with you without fear of retaliation."**
>
> —Doris Kearns Goodwin, *Leadership in Turbulent Times*

In his article "Guidelines for Effective Use of Feedback," Roger Neugebauer (1983) reminds us that effective feedback "should focus on descriptions, not judgments. In describing an event, a director reports an event to a teacher exactly as it occurred. A judgment of this event, however, refers to an evaluation in terms of good or bad, right or wrong, nice or not nice [and] increases defensiveness." Be aware of the limitations of the sandwich approach—offering praise, then criticism, then more praise. Neugebauer warns, "Often praise arouses defensiveness rather than dispelling it. Parents, teachers, and supervisors so often 'sugarcoat' criticism with praise ("You had a great lesson today, but …") that when we are praised, we automatically get ready for the shock, for the reproof (Farson, 1963)." The article goes on to provide tips that, for me as a supervisor and coach, have changed the game in terms of my own feedback success.

Feedback should be given unfiltered and in small doses. Encourage a team approach to feedback. For example, peer feedback with video can be an effective tool, if you have a standard observation checklist. I don't need to be the only person giving feedback. Also, supervisors should be open to feedback. Why is quality defined only by teacher-child interactions? The leader of the organization sets the tone for a school, and quality coaching and leadership skills should also be evaluated. Equity is always reciprocal. If teachers have classroom observations, coaches and leaders can record their coaching conversations (as I often have) to be evaluated. After each coaching or evaluative session, elevate equity by having the educators fill out a survey on your own effectiveness when giving feedback, training, or coaching. I can't believe I went years without getting feedback on my ability to give feedback.

What happens when you implement all those strategies and nothing seems to work? What do you do if your program always seems to be in conflict or chaos? The last leg of your journey will include how to deal with the inevitable challenges that arise in early childhood programming.

CHAPTER 7

Pushing Past Conflict with Adults

Did you know preschool is the most aggressive time in human development? It was once theorized that the peak of human aggression was the age of eighteen, but research confirms it is actually between the ages of two and five (Tremblay et al., 1996; Tremblay, 2000, 2002; Tremblay, Hartup, and Archer, 2005). If you have ever walked into a two-year-old classroom, you know the first thing the children greet you with is a chorus of "No!" So who better than a former preschool teacher who has been hit, kicked, and bombarded daily with comments such as "You aren't the boss of me!" to help you navigate challenging conversations and flip the script on adult conflict?

If you think perfect harmony is the essential characteristic of healthy relationships, research shows otherwise. A study by Andrew Gianino and Edward Tronick (1988) showed that even the most positive relationships are in perfect harmony 30 percent of the time and spend the other 70 percent of the time navigating conflict. Conflict is an essential part of the human condition. I am not talking about adult aggression, intimidation, or abuse. In those situations, emergency measures should be employed. But if there are equity issues around how to equally divvy up lesson-planning responsibilities or quarrels with families over how much homework is too much, then this chapter is for you and your program! As an early childhood professional, you can capitalize on these opportunities to better understand yourself, your colleagues, and the families you serve. The Push Past It framework provides concrete tools to help you get through conflict so you can elevate equity.

Culture Clash in the Classroom

To start our journey, let's hop on the turnpike and take a trip to the Garden State. I had already been invited to an early childhood program in New Jersey to provide training and consultation for dealing with challenging behaviors exhibited by young children. But this time, the principal wanted advice for a different challenge: dealing with the adults. I started my consultation with a training on adult conflict at the all-staff professional-development day. Then, after eating a six-inch hoagie at the local Wawa convenience store—if you know, you know—I was ready to provide consultation for this early childhood program's most challenging classroom conflicts with adults.

I had many cases to consult on that week, but the following case really speaks to challenges that can arise around equity and inclusion. I first observed this preschool classroom in the morning and had the pleasure of meeting with the newly hired lead teacher after lunch. She described numerous frustrations with her assistant teacher but told me that circle time was the most challenging time of the day. Because they were together for eight hours each day, this "work marriage" was in jeopardy. Imagine the theme music from the your favorite soap opera playing in the background as this teacher told me her story.

The lead teacher (I will call her Maria) said her assistant was rude and negative all day, especially during her circle time. This negativity toward her and the children at the morning meeting seemed to set the tone for the rest of the day and made everyone miserable. I actively listened to every detail of the challenge. I spoke only to ask a clarifying question or offer an occasional comment such as, "That must be hard," or "Tell me more about what that is like for you." I just listened without judgment before offering any ideas or advice. When she was done talking about her challenge, I asked Maria to tell me what she appreciated about her assistant.

> **Maria:** (pause) Okay, I guess we've changed topics. Hmmm… that's a hard one. I can't think of anything.
>
> **Me:** What are her strengths?
>
> **Maria:** Oh, that's easy. Annoying me. (We laugh.)
>
> **Me:** Really think. What do you appreciate about her?
>
> **Maria:** (long pause) Okay, I got something. She comes to work every day.
>
> **Me:** "She comes to work every day." On Mondays *and* Fridays?
>
> **Maria:** (chuckles) Yes, on Mondays and Fridays.
>
> **Me:** You can count on her every day.
>
> **Maria:** (pauses, then smiles) I can count on her every day.

The aha moment that Oprah talks about had happened! The hairs on my arm stood up as Maria's eyes lit up. Maria suddenly realized she had someone she could count on each day. It was hard for sure. Dealing with her assistant was not easy. But she had someone she could count on, and that was a work relationship worth fighting for. This story shows the power of positivity. If you focus on everything that is going wrong, you can't get to making things right. Notice, I didn't bombard her with quotes or sayings. I gave the gift of a reflective question that helped Maria find her own motivation. Maria had finally found the positive mindset she needed to problem solve.

Because Maria was the lead teacher, I shared with her that it was in fact she, *along with* her assistant teacher, who set the emotional tone for each day.

In the article "The Social Brain," Daniel Goleman (2013) describes how "… in groups where there are power differences—in the classroom, at work, in organizations generally—it is the most powerful person who is the emotional sender, setting the emotional state for the rest of the group." Maria didn't know she had any power and was experiencing powerblindness. Goleman goes on to remind us, "There are many studies that show, for example, that if the leader of a team is in a positive mood, that spreads an upbeat mood to the others and that collective positivity enhances the group's performance. If the leader projects a negative mood, that spreads in the same way, and the group's performance suffers." Together, Maria and I developed some prompts for our problem-solving discussion that would occur later that day with her assistant.

Next, I had another meeting with Maria's assistant, whom I will call Mrs. Rodriguez. When I asked her what she would like to be called, she told me to address her by her last name. I was relieved I had activated the Q in *equity*, or I would have started our meeting on the wrong footing and probably never recovered. Mrs. Rodriguez did not begin by discussing any challenges. Again, I am grateful I activated the T in *equity*! I started the meeting where Mrs. Rodriguez wanted to begin. She began by telling me she had almost forty years of experience in early childhood education and that in her country, she had a degree. Her degree was not recognized in the United States, which meant she was an assistant teacher here. Then she exclaimed, "Do you know what they make me do at circle time?! They make me *clean*. I have so many ideas! Circle time was my favorite time of the day when I was a teacher. Here they make me clean off the tables from breakfast and set out the materials for the next activity." At that moment, I knew the reason behind Mrs. Rodriguez's behavior. The challenge was not a lack of positivity; it was a lack of inclusion and the idea that her education and experience were not being valued. It is such a good reminder that negativity is an external expression of an internal struggle. Instead of focusing on making the negativity stop, focus on making safe spaces for it to be understood.

Later, we all met together. Maria started the discussion with our well-designed prompt, a genuine affirmation and a question to elicit dialogue and problem solving: "I appreciate you come to work every day. I appreciate your support. I wonder how I can get more of your support at circle time." Mrs. Rodriguez teared up, paused, and said, "Well, you never say it. Thank you." Aww, I was glad I had some tissues! It just goes to show that a little balance goes a long way, and behind every conflict is someone who doesn't understand what is going right. Finding out what is going right provides the foundation to tackle what is going wrong. The conversation went on, and the end result was Mrs. Rodriguez being included in the planning not only at circle time but throughout the day.

What were the equity lessons learned through this experience?

- Mrs. Rodriguez and Maria were of the same ethnicity, but culture is much more complicated. Remember to exercise the *I* in *equity* and understand that even people who share the same ethnicity will exhibit aspects of their culture to varying degrees in individual ways. Culture also encompasses socio-economic status, immigration status, educational level, and age. Be sure to consider intersectionality when elevating equity.

- It is important to listen to your colleagues without any judgments. Just listen! This is a good first step to making sure everyone's voice is heard, and being heard is an important element in elevating equity. Down the line, when you address conflict in subsequent steps, you might ask a question or provide information to help someone to reflect on their ideas, but that is never a first step. Active listening involves establishing a rapport with the other person, repeating or using reflective statements, and inviting the other person to share their experiences. If you are thinking, "Get real! Angela, I ain't got time for that!" recognize that either way you spend time. Either you are going to spend time implementing ideas that support you and your staff to navigate challenges, or you will spend time hiring new staff.

- No matter what a person's role is in an early childhood program, inclusion is key. Along with inclusion, activate the *Q* in *equity* by asking your colleagues how they wish to be included. For example, what if Mrs. Rodriguez had felt resentful of lesson planning without the title (or pay) of lead teacher. I get questions all the time: "How do I tell my assistant or para what to do in the classroom?" My response is "I understand and admire that you want to collaborate. I am wondering instead of telling, how could you ask?" Freedom of choice is a human right.

- How your discussion about a conflict begins will determine how your conflict will end. I was intentional when I asked Maria to think about what she appreciates about Mrs. Rodriguez. If I had not started with this reflective question to help Maria consider how she felt about her assistant, the conversation would not have been as effective. Reflective questions always come after active listening. If you begin with what is wrong, you can't get to what is right. Research shows that if you begin with a deficit lens, for example with words such as *lack*, *concern*, *challenge*, or *difficult*, there is a great chance the conversation will lead to ineffective outcome. Always start with a strength when you wish to see any type of behavior change, and build on an authentic strength your colleague possesses. Then end on a question that elicits more dialogue for problem solving.

Your Accountability Partner: Give Five Before You Reply

Lessons like those learned with Maria and Mrs. Rodriguez helped me to develop the protocol Give Five Before You Reply (GFBR). When you are dealing with conflicts with families or colleagues, protocols provide an organizational structure for implementation and help offer a consistent response that will elevate equity. In the book *The Power of Protocols: An Educator's Guide to Better Practice* (McDonald, Mohr, Dichter, and McDonald, 2015), the authors describe protocols as tools that define language while "maintaining focus on shared vision and goals." Talking about equity isn't enough; it needs to be carefully planned and scaffolded. Protocols are important tools for confronting issues of diversity. For example, one teacher stated that using "a variety of protocols is one way to hold ourselves accountable to each other" (McDonald, Mohr, Dichter, and McDonald, 2015).

GFBR is on example of an organization-wide protocol. For example, imagine that a colleague asserts a microaggression such as, "I have a hard time approaching you because you're confrontational." Wait. What? I don't have nunchuks in my hand or anything. I just disagree with your idea about the menu for the next staff party. Or imagine that a parent says, "You're one of the good ones." Huh? Is that supposed to be a compliment? *Good* as opposed to what—bad ones? Another type of inequity might occur when workplace hierarchies, such as when senior staff members make decisions without input from the staff members who are directly affected by those decisions. Imagine someone assumes your gender pronouns, repeatedly ignores a colleague's comments at a staff meeting, or shortens a parent's name because it is "too hard to pronounce." Or imagine that a leader imposes an unrealistic deadline to be completed ASAP "or else" or asks the team if we can turn off the closed captions because they are covering up part of the slide deck. Instead of showing them where they can put their slide deck or giving them a piece of your mind, try giving them the gift of a GFBR protocol to elevate equity.

1. **Give space to regulate:** Give yourself space to regulate yourself and breathe, or ask if you can have a moment to step away and come back to this discussion. Make space for a colleague to potentially speak up on your behalf, as well as space for the person who said or behaved in a way that did not elevate equity to notice the reaction and potentially correct their behavior or comment. If you are in conflict because you are trying to prove a point, keep in mind that your point will resonate only within a trusted relationship.

2. **Give the benefit of the doubt:** Why give the benefit of the doubt to rude or insensitive people? I too have been rude and insensitive, and research shows we all can be rude and insensitive or make biased statements at one time or another. It's biology! I don't want to criticize anyone for having the same qualities we all have. Give the person the benefit of the doubt that this is a mistake. We all make mistakes, and each mistake is an opportunity to learn. We can't elevate equity by making people feel bad. If we do make others feel bad, then that action has turned into an elevation of ego instead of equity. However, if you are feeling unsafe or the situation is abusive, seek emergency support.

3. **Give space for open-ended questions:** Ask yourself how that behavior or comment could affect your colleague or a person's identity. Could it send a message that not everyone is included? How would that affect your program's productivity, problem-solving abilities, profits, and possibilities? Reflect on the source of this conflict. For example, if you feel the source of the conflict is never-ending power struggles, I want you to reflect on why you are seeking power. Instead, try to empower colleagues. Elevating equity is all about shared power. "There are two ideas I want to focus on. What are your goals for our meeting?" Conflicts also can arise when different parts of an organization have differing goals. If you feel it is safe to do so, ask open-ended questions. For example, "What is your goal when scheduling an impromptu staff meeting after work?" Or, "I see now that I have made a misstep. How can I repair this situation so we can complete the task at hand?" Think about a question, such as, "I am realizing my comments might be taken the wrong way. Is this a good time to talk about this miscommunication?" Or, if you are the person who is on the other end of an insensitive comment or in equitable action, "Thanks for sharing that deadline. How does imposing a deadline align with our equity protocols for shared decision-making and goal setting?

4. **Give a reflection:** Communication is not just words but also includes tone and nonverbal cues. Take time to observe the tone and nonverbal language of the person you are having a challenging conversation with. Be mindful of your own tone and body language. Keep in mind that how individuals communicate varies by culture. Reflect what the other person in your conversation is saying before you add any of your ideas. Start your reflection with phrases such as, "I hear you saying…" or "Thank you for trusting me enough to share your perspective." Really try to understand before you reply. Remember, you don't add your ideas until you have given someone all five steps.

5. **Give opportunity for connection:** Ask for a time to connect. Is this the right time? The right place? Does either of you need a break? Time to think? If it is the best time to reply, base your response on information you have gathered from the first four steps. If you reply at a later time, keep in mind there is another person on the other side of your point of view. By waiting, you will have even more of an opportunity to reflect on the first four steps so you can give a meaningful reply to support the resolution of your conflict.

Okay, Angela, you said negativity is normal, so let me have a stab at it for a minute here. The real problem is that nowadays everyone is afraid of "hurting someone's feelings" (insert sarcasm here) or offending someone. This is the Voice of Reason, and I approve the content of this message.

Well, thanks, Voice of Reason. I wondered where you went. In light of your concerns, I would like to tell you and any of my readers who feel the same way that, yes, I hear you! *And* it is important for organizations to activate the *E* in *equity* due to evolving laws around workplace discrimination, equity, and inclusion and to protect themselves from litigation due to violations of the Civil Rights Act. In the TEDx Talk "Practical Diversity: Taking Inclusion from Theory to Practice," lawyer Dawn Bennett-Alexander (2015), explains "You get to like anybody you want to… what you don't have the right to do is use those thoughts and translate them into action that gets your employer in trouble and they have to pay for it."

Yes, it is important for you to choose your own level of equity, and it is just as important that the company you work for chooses their own level of equity. It is also important to note the colleague who you give the side eye (and when I say *you*, I mean *me*) has an identity that must be respected in the workplace. If you feel everyone today is a delicate snowflake who is sensitive to everything, I want to honor how uncomfortable this may feel and bring in the framework from my first book *Push Past It! A Positive Approach to Challenging Classroom Behaviors*. The process provides a useful way to navigate intense challenges at any age and offers consistent language for discourse among educators. So far, I have shared many examples of how navigating challenging conversations can be messy. But no need to worry about how to respond to a challenge—you already know all the steps. Cleaning up your act around challenging conversations is almost identical to the steps you use to clean your laundry.

Adult Behavior Laundry List:

1. Sort out your feelings.
2. Repair rips in your relationship.
3. Figure out the care instructions.
4. Put behaviors in the meaning-making machine.
5. Choose a cycle.
6. Be patient during the trying time.

Step 1: Sort Out Your Feelings

The first step to navigating conflict is sorting out your feelings around the conflict, just as you would sort your laundry. I don't know about you, but when I'm going through a conflict, I can always count on my initial feelings to be my most biased ones. Unfortunately, my negativity bias would get me nowhere when dealing with a culture clash. For example, if there was a work conflict, not only did I stop liking that parent or colleague, but I also started recruiting others to not like that parent or colleague. I've also experienced that tactic from the other side. You know that awkward silence you get from a coworker? Guess what. It is not your imagination. Suddenly no one is replying to your emails or giving you the thumbs-up on Google Hangouts because they think you did their work bestie wrong. With the *Push Past It!* framework, instead of looking to blame or punish, I know the way to end conflict and the discomfort that comes with it begins with looking within myself.

> "We don't see things as they are. We see them as we are."
>
> —Anaïs Nin, author (attributed)

To become confident in conflict, the first goal, as the Voice of Reason points out, is to understand that a certain amount of bias and negativity is normal. In fact, managing your emotions is a key component to managing conflicts. According to the article "Understanding and Avoiding Emotional Hijacking" (Magazine, 2013), our emotional brain activity processes information milliseconds faster than the rational brain. Further, researchers completed a systematic review of academic literature concerning emotions and found "… almost everyone remembers negative things more strongly and in more detail. Negative emotions involve more thinking and are processed more thoroughly than positive information" (Baumeister, Bratslavsky, Finkenauer, and Vohs, 2001). To achieve balance when dealing with conflict, all emotions are needed. Being able to accept and talk about these feelings is healthy. If you are like me, I have to get negative before I can get to the positive.

> Take a moment to write down all your negative feelings regarding a conflict. Yes! This is the moment you have been waiting for! This book is like Vegas. What happens here stays here. Whatever you write, know it stays between us without any criticism of whether those feelings are "good" or "bad."
>
> Next, take a moment to reflect. Why do you feel that way?

Push Past It provides an inclusive space where all vibes are accepted. It is not about never being angry or frustrated. Always maintaining a positive emotional state can result in masking emotions and invalidating genuine human experiences. Signs of invalidating negative emotions include criticizing yourself for having strong feelings, hiding painful emotions, dismissing the feelings of others, or ignoring or avoiding conflict.

> "If you can sit with your pain, listen to your pain and respect your pain—in time you will move through your pain."
>
> —Bryant McGill and Jenni Young, *Simple Reminders: Inspiration for Living Your Best Life*

I was talking with a teacher I will call Mrs. Smith about challenges in the workplace. She shared her challenges with her coteacher, and I shared some ideas to support her. She wrote those ideas down eagerly, and together made a plan. Mrs. Smith was smiling, writing down ideas, and responding with phrases such as, "That is a good idea," or "I can do that on Monday." I felt really confident about our plan, but I wanted to check in on how she was feeling, so I said, "Wow, sounds like you are really dedicated to this plan. We've talked about some ideas, but I want to ask how you are feeling." Mrs. Smith paused and looked at me with her bright smile. Suddenly her smile faded, her eyebrows came together, and she broke down and cried. Mrs. Smith is a bright, eager, hard-working teacher who was also masking her feelings about the conflicts at her workplace.

It is important for early childhood programs to make space for strong feelings. I have heard leaders tell me "not to get into a vent session," but from a mental-health standpoint we can't move forward without a venting session. Yes, venting for venting's sake can be counterproductive. However, people need to vent. If strategies are grounded in educational psychology and mental-health research, processing emotional stress is an important part of the learning process. If you only make space for positive feelings, that can cause more stress because your staff can't learn what their triggers are, why those ideas are triggering, and healthy ways to deal with them. Masking conflict on the outside only creates more conflict inside. It is important to process emotions in healthy ways and for those strategies to be promoted and practiced.

Displaying strong emotions can be uncomfortable or even scary. Please keep yourself physically and emotionally safe. Keep in mind that all feelings happen everywhere all the time. Even at the local preschool. When strategies are implemented well, conflict becomes an opportunity for you to learn more about yourself and others. But to gain control over a conflict, you must first gain control over yourself by understanding what you are feeling and why you are feeling that way. Let's not "Letter of the Week" our emotions. You might even feel a variety of emotions at the same time. I know it is hard—even as adults we are still learning how to process our feelings—but look on the bright side: at least we don't have to take gym class anymore.

Now that you have accepted all your emotions and have considered some reasons behind those feelings, keep in mind the importance of moving on from that space. Why? Well, it is kind of like swallowing poison and expecting your nemesis to feel the effects. Letting strong feelings or negative thoughts linger isn't good for your emotional or physical health. Neuroscience shows that when we feel these strong emotions we are accessing the most primitive part of our brains, the lower emotional brain. That part won't be much help in problem solving past a conflict, which requires higher-order thinking skills. What are some other good reasons to tame what you are feeling? If you have a friend who helps fan the flames of conflict or a workplace bestie who stirs the pot instead of supporting you to make the conflict stop, that approach might feel good in the moment (it's almost better than a bubble bath), but it won't help you navigate challenging conversations or support you in avoiding those types of situations in the future.

> **Think of possible reasons to tame those feelings. Make a list.**

I developed a helpful acronym called *Push Past It!* that helps me push myself toward problem solving. Get help from a friend if you need more support thinking of strategies that might support each part of the acronym. A true-blue workplace BFF knows ruminating on negative feelings or having conflictual work relationships are not healthy for you or your program and can negatively affect student learning and relationships with families.

Under each part of the acronym, write down how you might implement that strategy to respond to a conflict.

Next, go back to your list of initial feelings. Look at those feelings without shame or critical judgment, and try to reframe any negative thoughts into useful ideas. Write down your reframed ideas.

Think about Your Approach to Conflict

Often, we develop a pattern for thinking about conflict that we use over and over. We "sing the same old tune."

> **On a piece of paper, write down songs that match the ways you deal with conflict. Then, note why you chose these songs.**

What is in your conflict playlist? Is it "The Big Payback" by James Brown? "Bad Blood" by Kendrick Lamar and Taylor Swift? "Hit Me with Your Best Shot" by Pat Benatar?

It is important to know the soundtrack playing in your head as you go through a conflict. Please don't silence it. Turn it up! Your mental soundtrack is communicating important information about how you perceive a conflict and might even predict how you might react or respond to it. For example, if you are talking to a family who thinks you are being too strict with their child and "Answer to No One" by Colt Ford is playing in the background of your brain, that provides import information about how you feel that family is challenging your authority. Interestingly, did you ever consider that the family might have "What's Going On?" by Marvin Gaye playing in their heads? They might just be confused about the purpose of your rules and how those rules might benefit their child. If the song

P Pick out positives.	**U** Understand everyone's perspective.	**S** Seek neutral support.	**H** Home in on everyone's intentions.

P Pay attention to your own behavior.	**A** Ask questions.	**S** Step back.	**T** Take care of yourself.

I **T**

"9 to 5" by Dolly Parton is the melody at the heart of your headache at work, could your boss have the song "Do Something" by Matthew West on their mind? Don't you wish all areas of your life had background music so you could make sense of what is happening?

> Take some time now to think about what tune could be playing for the other person on the other side of your conflict. How do you know? Could they have a mixtape full of feelings?

Psychologist John Gottman (1993, 1994a, 1994b) identifies four reactions you might want to remove from your conflicts: criticism, contempt, defensiveness, and the silent treatment.

- **Criticism:**

    "If you would just do what I ask, we wouldn't be going through this."

    "If you stopped emailing me, I could get some work done. You never think of anyone but yourself."

- **Contempt:**

    "You're frustrated? Give me a break! I'm the one who should be frustrated by your lack of compliance."

    "Really? I care more about your child than you do."

- **Defensiveness:**

    "Why are you blaming me for this?"

    "You do the same thing all the time."

- **The Silent Treatment:**

    "I refuse to respond to this madness."

    Stop responding to emails and phone calls, avoid eye contact, address everyone in a message thread except that *one* person, give monosyllabic, lackluster replies in a discussion.

Recognize any familiar go-to moves? According to Gottman (2022), how you start your response can determine your outcome. His research revealed that 96 percent of the time you can predict the outcome of a fifteen-minute conversation based on the first three minutes of the interaction. Instead of these negative strategies, here are some replacement moves that can lead to connection.

- **Instead of criticism:**

    I am feeling stress around this protocol.

    What is getting in the way of following this protocol?

    How can I help?

    Is there something we should change about the protocol?

- **Instead of contempt:**

    Work hard to become solutions focused; there is a person behind the point of view.

    Work toward dealing with conflict head on without sarcasm or personal judgments about someone's character.

    Start with a meaningful strength, and think about how to apply that strength to the challenge at hand, for example: "I appreciate your work around the past project on lesson planning. I'm wondering how we can use similar strategies with this protocol."

- **Instead of defensiveness:**

    Instead of spinning the conflict around to a colleague. Try to be solution driven. Take a break from defending your idea to listen to someone else's ideas.

    Ask them questions about their perspective. Try to create dialogue with open-ended questions.

- **Instead of silence:**

    It's okay to take a break if you communicate that clearly. Yes, breaks are good for us. And try not to take too long a break or give up on working toward a solution. "I am going to take a break for a couple of days. After some rest, I feel I can come back to tackle this challenge after I calm down."

> Think about how you tend to respond when presented with a conflict at work. What are your go-to moves? Are those moves helping or hurting your interactions? Do you do take over the dance floor during a conflict, making yourself the center of attention? Do you do a two-step and collaborate? Do you bring other colleagues into the conflict and have a dance-off? Are you able to follow your work partner's lead? Do you make like Michael Jackson and moonwalk yourself away from confrontation to avoid conflict at all costs?
>
> How did you learn these moves? Who taught you these moves? What is your history around conflict? Are the moves you use a pattern? Are they generational?

Elevating Equity in the Teachers' Lounge

Yep, we are still in the sorting phase! The first phase does take the longest—because how you begin plays a big part in how your conflict will end. For my book *Push Past It!* I created the Teachers' Lounge: Bias Filter Worksheet. You can find it at https://www.gryphonhouse.com/our-authors/author-detail/angela-searcy-edd

For this book, I wanted to create a more inclusive tool that goes beyond teachers. What is the bias in the breakroom in your program?

> "Pay attention to your patterns. The ways you learned to survive may not be the ways you want to continue to live. Heal and shift."
>
> —Dr. Thema Bryant-Davis, psychologist

> Take time now to write down any breakroom banter related to conflict.

To elevate equity, programs must deal with conflicts that arise in our spaces. The breakroom is not a place—it is a mindset. It is a sacred space that allows educators to vent frustrations, share ideas, and build camaraderie. Your "breakroom" is anywhere colleagues connect and congregate. While these spaces hold value, they can also hold bias. Before you actively engage in a conversation, you need to address any potential feelings of bias. Keep in mind this is not an attack on your moral character. Everyone has an unconscious tendency toward bias, called *implicit bias*, which typically runs counter to a person's own belief system.

Your brain is biologically wired for bias. Bias is not a personal flaw but a human adaptation that simplifies information and helps your brain make quick, automatic associations and decisions. The human brain is not inherently neutral, but research has shown that presenting new narratives that run counter to stereotypes can reduce implicit bias (Nosek et al., 2014). The following tool can help professionals look out for potential bias, ask filtering questions, consider opposing ideas, and respond with more neutral actions. Think of this next activity as fabric softener that helps protect our interactions against the static that comes from implicit bias. No one should ever feel guilt or be shamed for whatever is said or shared. It is important to have safe space to process.

> **"We cannot grow when we are in shame, and we can't use shame to change ourselves or others."**
>
> **—Brené Brown, *I Thought It Was Just Me***

As mentioned earlier, the problem that often arises with elevating equity is the lack of places to process and practice conflicts around equity and inclusion. It is important for programs to go beyond saying equity slogans to using concrete guides that professionals can use to analyze conversations that are often heard only in the in the breakroom. Use the tool below as a self-reflective guide that will help anyone make these conversations work for them by filtering out potential bias and offering suggestions for neutral discussions and decisions.

We all have an ongoing internal monologue. Mine has the actor Morgan Freeman narrating it. The goal is not for that monologue to be neutral—that's impossible. The goal is to recognize when our internal speech might cause us to make mental shortcuts. Then we can filter this internal speech and respond with neutrality. Use this tool to help you step out of your own values and walk in someone else's shoes.

> Look at the comments you wrote down from the staff breakroom. Use the following questions to filter those comments and consider elevating equity and neutral decision making. This tool does not have to be used in a linear manner. You can use the parts most relevant to the statements you jotted down.

Potential Bias	Why Might This Signal Potential Bias?	Elevating Equity Actions and Neutral Decision Making
List any statements that label or measure whether a behavior is "right" or "wrong."	Ethnocentricity involves imposing a value judgment on the actions of others based on the standards of your own culture. Whether a behavior is "right" or "wrong" can vary within and between cultures. It does not mean a behavior is never wrong. However, to avoid bias, educators should engage in meaning making. Interpreting the actions of others without meaning renders those interpretations meaningless.	- List potential origins of a behavior. - List potential meanings behind a behavior. - List potential functions behind a behavior. *Remember: Actions don't always match values, and it can be easy to fall into the idea that someone doesn't care about or value something. Time, capacity, skill level, and other factors affect action.
List any statements that suggest there is only one way to accomplish a goal.	Ethnocentricity involves thinking your way of living is the only correct way. When you think you know everything about something, it puts a ceiling on your knowledge that prevents you from knowing everything there is to know about something. Healthy conversations seek understanding rather than agreement.	List a variety of ways to accomplish a goal.
List any statements that assign blame.	Blame shifts thoughts and conversation away from the difficult task of our own self-reflection to reflecting on what we perceive as the shortcomings of others. Blaming could be a mechanism that helps us cope with uncomfortable feelings associated with a challenge.	- List ways you or your team could be contributing to a problem. - List ways you could contribute to a solution.
List any statements that put the perspectives, feelings, or needs of the professional above those of children and families.	Yes, the perspectives, feelings, and needs of educators are important and should not be neglected or overlooked. However, centering involves putting focus only on the values, norms, perspectives, needs and feelings of professionals over the families and children they serve, especially when that professional is working with a group whose needs are pushed to the margins.	- List the perspectives, feelings, and needs of children and families. - List norms and values of families. - Instead of saying *we, we all*, or "the human race," consider that an issue or challenge is specific to a particular group.

Potential Bias	Why Might This Signal Potential Bias?	Elevating Equity Actions and Neutral Decision Making
List any negative statements.	The brain has a natural negativity bias. If you look only at what is wrong, you won't be able to get to what is right. Viewing people or situations through a deficit lens can stagnate problem solving and productivity.	Using a strengths-based lens, write down all the strengths of the: • Child • Family • Coworker • School
List any statements that suggest excluding professionals from work events or communication such as emails.	Even though we all have our work besties, and work cliques are common, this could undermine equity and inclusion.	List new ways to cope with conflict besides exclusion. Make sure staff have access to mental-health supports, both for those who exclude and for those who are excluded.
List any assumptions not verified by the individual and not based on factual evidence.	Because the brain often looks for shortcuts, educators must constantly question whether they are viewing a person or situation in an overly simplistic way based on limited information and preconceived ideas. Keep in mind, individuals exhibit their culture to varying degrees in their own individual ways.	Intersectionality involves viewing an individual or group through many aspects of their identity, such as race, class, gender, language, and so on. Examine the assumptions and list ways the assumption may not apply to the person or situation, along with supporting evidence. Remember: Individuals always self-identify.
List any statements that call into question someone's lived experience.	Gaslighting is an attempt to make another person question their perception or lived experience. People are always the experts on their own lived experiences.	Believe someone's lived experience as they describe it. If you are unclear about someone's perception, before questioning their reality, ask questions to understand that lived experience.
List any statements that make comparisons.	A false equivalency results from flawed reasoning that assumes two different situations are the same because they share some of the same characteristics while ignoring important differences.	• List similarities between the situations. • List differences between the situations. Make sure you know all the differences and similarities. Also note the degree or magnitude of a difference or similarity and how that may affect the situation.

Potential Bias	Why Might This Signal Potential Bias?	Elevating Equity Actions and Neutral Decision Making
List any statements that corroborate your own views.	An echo chamber is a place where someone only encounters ideas or opinions that correspond with their own existing views. These views are reinforced, and alternative ideas are rebuffed.	• List opposing ideas and consider how they might be true. • List common word(s) that link seemingly opposing ideas.
List any statements that put the needs of one professional above the needs of another professional.	Yes, the perspectives, feelings, and needs of educators are important and should never be neglected or overlooked. However, centering involves putting focus only on the values, norms, perspectives, needs and feelings of one person over the needs of colleagues who should be treated equally.	List perspectives and needs of colleagues. Instead of saying *we, we all*, or "the human race," consider that an issue or challenge is specific to a particular group or person.
List any statements that dismiss potential protective or risk factors for a person or group.	The term *powerblind* refers to the failure to notice one's protective factors, the belief that all groups are equal in power, an emphasis on one's own risk factors, and the belief that the present-day hierarchy is merited or inevitable.	We all have protective factors that could increase the probability of positive outcomes and risk factors that could potentially reduce the likelihood of a positive outcome. • List your protective factors and potential risk factors. • List the potential protective and risk factors of children, families, and colleagues.

Step 2: Repair Rips in Your Relationship

Have you ever found a tiny hole in your favorite pair of jeans? If you don't take the time to immediately repair that rip, it can get worse. Relationships are the fabric of our early childhood programs and businesses. As James P. Comer, professor of child psychiatry at the Yale Child Study Center, said, "No significant learning can occur without a significant relationship." Neuroscience research provides a scientific explanation of how emotional climates are integral for optimal all learning communities, colleges, and companies.

To flip the script on conflict, you must be excellent at repairing those inevitable rips that occur in relationships. Psychologist John Gottman (2022) describes a repair attempt as "any statement or action—silly or otherwise—that prevents negativity from escalating out of control." In the article "Family Conflict Is Normal; It's the Repair That Matters," Diana Divecha (2020), developmental psychologist and assistant clinical professor at the Yale Child Study Center and Yale Center for Emotional Intelligence, writes, "Life is a series of mismatches, miscommunications, and misattunements that are quickly repaired." She continues, "… a bid for a repair is one of the most… important kinds of communication that humans offer to each other." Create a culture within your program or company that values repair with these tips from Divecha:

- Watch for tiny rips that need repair. Divecha (2020) points out that we may have "so much on our minds that we miss the look, gesture, or expression that shows that what they really want is to reconnect."

- She recommends, "We need to be able to let others know when the relationship has been harmed," by using requests such as, "I need a repair," or "Can we have a redo?"

- Further, she writes, "If you think you might have stepped on someone's toes, circle back to check. Catching a misstep early can help."

Step 3: Figure Out the Care Instructions

Before you clean your clothes, you must check the label for the care instructions. Otherwise, your shirt shrinks or your pants turn a different color. Similarly, relationships need care instructions, or you might experience unintended outcomes. The identities of the children, families, and staff at your program provide clues on how to care for them.

When you are navigating a challenging conversation, context tells you what to do next. What is the backstory for this person or group? What is their knowledge about the topic in question? Just like knowing the makeup of a garment, how you move forward in your response to a conflict depends on the makeup of that person's personal story or background. For example, have they been ignored or excluded in the past? Are they part of a group whose voices and experiences historically have been pushed to the margins? Activate the *I* in *equity* by understanding the degree to which they express their culture in their own unique way.

For example, children with disabilities have historically been excluded. Therefore, you might handle talking with a parent of a child with a disability more delicately than talking with a parent of a child without a disability. But the strategy on how that discussion will go will depend heavily on individual needs. If that parent of a child with a disability is a person of color or is a member of several groups that have been underrepresented by the dominant society, then that circumstance will add more layers of complexity to the fabric of the conversation.

Considering care instructions in a staff meeting might involve being extra sensitive to a staff member who is bilingual by asking them how you could support them in the meeting. Those strategies will depend on that person's specific needs and interests. If that staff member is part of any groups who have not always been welcomed in the work environment, such as mothers who were and often still are discouraged from working outside the home, then that background, too, will add more to consider in the conversation.

Whataboutisms

What are whataboutisms? According to Randy Haupt and Amy Shockley (2020) in their article "Whataboutery [Ethically Speaking]," whataboutism "refers to responding to a hard question or accusation by making a different accusation or changing the subject. The name is derived from a typical response to an accusation: 'What about when you…?' or 'What about that person…?'" Whataboutisms are abso-freaking-lutely awesome! Personally, whenever someone in my family tries to point out some imperfection in my *perfect* personality (snickers to self) or to pin some responsibility on me with something like, "Hey, you didn't do the dishes like you said you would." I bounce back with a whataboutism: "What about when you said you would go shopping last week? Let's talk about that! (insert glaring and hand on hip with a neck roll) Huh! I didn't think so." It is a tactic that takes the attention off me and points conversation back where it should be: on someone else's flaws and imperfections. I will pull it out occasionally. After all, I can't overdo this type of thing in the comfort of my home with people who are bound to me through marriage or by blood.

But seriously, in a work environment, whatabouts are a not a good way to go. The approach can derail conversations about individuals who are part of groups whose needs are often pushed to the margins. For example, a sign in front a toy store announced, "Proudly ASD Friendly," meaning they welcomed young children with autism and their families. The store staff was responsive to the needs of people with ASD, such as turning down lights or music if asked. On social media, someone posted, "I love this, but I wish it said 'human friendly.'" This got me thinking. Isn't it already implied that the store is human friendly? What was the intention? Was it to welcome a group that is often ignored or whose needs are not recognized?

If you ever find yourself in a "whatabout" conversation, Haupt and Shockley (2020) offer these tips:

- "Recognize whataboutism and approach it analytically." To do this, you will need to pause before responding.

- "Isolate and resolve whataboutery by recognizing a person, phrase, or subject that acts as a trigger." Think about what is triggering your defenses in this situation.

- "Strip away the emotion, and evaluate the simple facts of the scenario to give an appropriate response." Consider what might be driving the person to criticize or second-guess. Is it ignorance? Do they know someone who has ASD?

- "A defensive response can be countered with curiosity." Ask a question, such as "What do you know about autism?"

Considering the Context

In the early childhood profession, we often value messy play such as mud play. In earlier chapters, we learned that families in poverty are often judged more harshly for their children's appearance. Additionally, Black families are often referred to foster care and child protective services at disproportionately high rates (Child Welfare Information Gateway, 2021). Those characteristics concerning identity are going to affect how a family should be cared for and whether a conversation around messy play might be a delicate one. To elevate equity, both perspectives should be prioritized *equally* without judgment. Yes, it is valuable to have messy play. Also yes, messy play can be a serious concern and even have consequences for some families. The professional should validate and give care around both perspectives and realities. Asking a parent to bring "messy" clothes might put undue stress on a family experiencing poverty. Making this request only meets the needs of the professional in the conflict. Including mud play while also offering to wash the students' clothes after that play might be a good compromise. Or putting messy mud in a sealed ziplock bag might be a way to offer this sensory play and honor the families' wishes and values.

Consider further: many cultures might not value play. Is this really even a conflict? Elevating equity is not about changing someone's culture. As a professional, I don't feel the need to convince families of the value of play, because when I ask them, I tend to find that people from all cultures value learning. As the professional, the onus is on me to explain how play fits within what they already value and to communicate how my work fits within their belief system. For example, if a family has a strong belief in academic learning and their child engages in block play, they may not connect that block play with their goals for academic learning. When I talk to that family, I might say their child is engaged in "math content learning" and omit the word *play* from my description. As early childhood professionals, we know that blocks support understanding of shapes, colors, and spatial awareness, along with cognitive, fine motor, and language skill development. The word *play* has a pedagogical value in our profession that a lay person, such as a parent, might not understand. Water-table play might be better understood by families as "science content learning" in which children explore cause and effect and conduct experiments. I am using the language that fits within the values of a family, but by no means am I compromising play in my classroom.

Feedback and Constructive Criticism

Have you ever been to a staff meeting during which someone shares a new term for an old practice? Take for example, "data-driven decision making." Isn't that just making objective observations to guide our decisions? It's just a fancy new term for what many good educators have been doing since the beginning of education. New research doesn't always provide new ideas, but sometimes it validates which old ideas are the best to continue or increase. It is important for professionals to find commonality instead of conflict in a conversation. Stop arguing over ideas you agree on.

To do this, take into account the texture of any criticism in your conversation (Booher, 1999).

In previous chapters, we address how criticism can crush your efforts to elevate equity. As a leader and coach, it has been a challenge for me to balance being constructive and offering criticism. Often, my workplace feedback didn't lead to better performance but did lead to someone giving me the side eye. The article "Constructive Criticism: Creating Positive Behaviour at Work Places" (Tripathy, 2021), reminds us, "The emotional state, perception of the receiver, and the texture of the message are [a] few key elements that matter... These elements assist in either developing or deteriorating the communication process." Further, if a "message conveyed in the communication is based on personal biases… the receiver may not reciprocate positively." Marcus Buckingham and Ashley Goodhall (2019) write, "Telling people what we think of their performance doesn't help them thrive and excel, and telling people how we think they should improve actually hinders learning." It is critical for staff to understand themselves and their own work identity. Yes, quality performance ratings by outside professionals can be helpful and are required. The same can be true for self-performance ratings—the key is to have a balance of both independent and self-evaluations. Include opportunities to ask, "How do you think you did?" If a colleague says, "Great!" when it clearly *wasn't*, it is probably because they had no objective standard of measurement to make their assessment. When possible, use a checklist for them to measure their own performance. Buckingham and Goodhall make the point, "Learning rests on our grasp of what we're doing well, not on what we're doing poorly, and certainly not on someone else's sense of what we're doing poorly. And second, that we learn most when someone else pays attention to what's working within us and asks us to cultivate it intelligently." In her article "Communicate with Confidence and Give Constructive Criticism without Crippling Others," Dianna Booher (1999) gives us some ideas to consider: "Identify your motive before you speak… [and] include your commitment to and concern for another person and a sense of responsibility to do things correctly…"

Consider these ideas on offering feedback:

- When starting a professional relationship with staff or with a family member, ask the person how they would like to receive feedback. Dianna Booher gives examples such as, Would you prefer direct feedback or a softer, less direct approach? Would you prefer to wait until the end of the day or to talk early in the morning? Would you prefer to talk on site or away from our facility? Having a feedback preferences questionnaire activates the Q and the T in *equity* by asking how a person would like to be treated.

- Make sure you have all the information needed to give meaningful advice or feedback. Ever get feedback telling you to do something that you are already doing? Or get advice that doesn't fit your goals? I used to get that all the time from the in-laws! Booher reminds us to gather information, facts, and circumstances before stumbling into the "hornet's nest." She warns, "Otherwise, you'll come away from the discussion with a sting…"

- Consider that when you are in a conflict, there is a person and sometimes an entire family and culture behind their point. What are your ultimate goals for this professional relationship? How can you learn from this interaction?

- Avoid surprises and provide an opportunity to create a shared agenda. Before a meeting, send over a timed agenda and intended outcomes and allow staff to add to the agenda. Prepare what you will share based on what you know about a colleague or family. Booher (1999) points out that "truth" is often subjective, and frankness may be a code for insult.

- Your emotional state sets the tone. Gain confidence with preparation. Pick a time that you both agree is a good one for feedback—and not, say, right after a person has gotten bad results from a biopsy at the doctor's office. "You want to maximize the chance of catching the other person at a peak of emotional strength, so she has the self-confidence, control, and motivation necessary to accept your comments."

- Keep your comments objective. For example, saying, "I am frustrated by your lack of input," is vague. But saying, "You submitted lesson plans on time three days this week. What can we do to increase that to four times?" is a specific, time-bound goal that can be measured. Change, "Your child had a hard time this week," which is subjective, to "Your child cried for two hours to get to sleep. Is this typical? Tell me about your routine at home."

How a situation improves will depend on how the professional supports the confidence of the listener. Elevating equity is all about preserving someone's dignity and self-esteem while problem solving through a conflict and considering how the solution prioritizes the needs of all involved.

Wash away the need for control and compliance. If I had to describe myself in one word, it would be "not good at following directions." (Yes, I know that's more than one word.) Keep in mind that equity is embedded in the choice to do things your own unique way. None of your colleagues signed away their rights to free will when they signed their W-9 forms. As Mister Rogers (1995) wrote, "There's a world of difference between insisting on someone's doing something and establishing an atmosphere in which that person can grow into wanting to do it." In the article "Your Meeting is NOT Mandatory," Eryc Eyl (2014) points out, "If you've led or managed an organization… odds are you've sent at least one meeting request… labeled *mandatory*… I know *you* think it's mandatory… but it isn't. Behind that word, *mandatory*, there is an implicit 'or else.'… I suggest you leave it out."

Instead of compliance, consider choice: If you come to this meeting, you are going to get the most updated information on our new initiative and how it will affect your work. If you can't attend in person, join us virtually on your phone or listen to the recording of the meeting later. Conflict can arise from control. I know this intellectually, but I still sometimes forget to ask instead of tell. Leaders and educators don't have to solve challenges for families. If there is a safety issue, some mandatory might be involved. But sometimes I have to pause and poll families and colleagues on what they think might work, and sometimes they come up with an idea that I never would have considered. We cross a boundary when we as educators try to control the decisions of others. Give a reflection instead of a direction. Provide spaces that help educators connect to the voice and needs of families and colleagues over compliance. For example, when the source of conflict is the control of someone's expression of their culture, such as dress codes and hair styles, rethink the need for compliance.

You might be thinking, "Okay, Angela, is this going to be *Lord of the Flies*?" Of course not, Voice of Reason. Figure out the care instructions first. Instead of *telling* families and colleagues about rules such as dress codes, ask for their input in developing those rules to prevent conflict.

Step 4: Put Behaviors in the Meaning-Making Machine

Now that we have sorted out our feelings, repaired the rips in our relationships, and figured out the care instructions, it is time to put the challenges in the meaning-making machine. This tool began as a way to support educators as they navigate challenges with young children. It wasn't until an educator asked if I had one for adults that I created the adult version. Filling out this tool can help someone find meaning to navigate a conflict.

I was called to a program for a child with an intense challenging behavior. I was triggered as soon as I walked in and saw a little Black boy sitting with a security guard at the entrance of the school. I let myself sit in my frustration for a few minutes. In my head, I named what I was experiencing: "I am tired of every 'intense behavior' case being a Black boy!" I explained it: "I feel this way because I see all the Black men in my life, whom I love dearly, represented." I tamed it: "I can't help this child if I am angry." I pushed past my anger. I thought: "This program called me out here because they care, and we have

Adult Meaning-Making Machine

Name: _____ Support Team/Person: _____ Date: _____ Time: _____

Skill/Task for Implementation:

What does the adult feel about the skill or task?

- ☐ Excited
- ☐ Overwhelmed
- ☐ Confident
- ☐ Confused
- ☐ Disrespected
- ☐ Frustrated
- ☐ Anxious
- ☐ Fearful
- ☐ Angry
- ☐ Undervalued
- ☐ Other:

What does the person/team know about the skill or task?

On a scale of

1 2 3 4 5 6 7 8 9 10

circle the number that represents how confident the adult feels about implementing skill. What supports need to be in place to increase this number?

Example of how adult has used skill before:

How often? ____/week
How long? ____/week
Accuracy: 1 2 3 4 5
Past success with the skill or task:

Past challenges with the skill or task:

What are strengths of the adult?

What have supervisors/support team done to support implementation?

- ☐ Told to implement skill
- ☐ Modeled skill
- ☐ Sent staff to outside training
- ☐ Used peers to teach skill
- ☐ Shown video of implementation
- ☐ Shown video at your site of implementation
- ☐ Talked to staff about barriers to implementation
- ☐ Provided materials
- ☐ Made materials
- ☐ Gave encouragement
- ☐ Extended deadline
- ☐ Did periodic check ins
- ☐ Given visuals or flow chart of steps
- ☐ Simplified directions

How did the person/team respond?

Note Any Barriers to Implementation:

- ☐ Absence of person
- ☐ Recent illness (family member illness)
- ☐ Lack of team collaboration
- ☐ Change in routine
- ☐ Lack of materials
- ☐ In school/working long hours
- ☐ Absence of sleep
- ☐ Lack of planning time
- ☐ Family challenges
- ☐ Multi-tasking many tasks
- ☐ Goals are too vague
- ☐ Goals not time bound
- ☐ Failure to see the need for skill
- ☐ Anxiety/fear of change
- ☐ Other (specify):

the same goals." I reframed it: "How can you say you want to help children without helping the staff and teachers who care for them? Children and adults are like cookies and milk—they go together."

I did my observation in the classroom with the child present, and then I met with the lead teacher. I shared her glows and some ideas for potential growth that would support working through the intense challenges in the classroom with this child. I read her body language. If I hadn't known any better, I would've thought she was about to square up. My mental-health training told me the teacher might have shifted to the fight-or-flight path, and she looked as if she had chosen the fight route. She looked at me with her arms crossed and her hands balled up into fists, as if she dared me to cross an invisible line at the table where we were seated. Her posture felt angry, but in my heart, I know anger is a protector of pain. Thinking of this teacher as "behaving badly," "resistant" or "unprofessional" would put me in the mindset to be angry or to provide a consequence or an ultimatum. That would only reinforce what she was already feeling. Instead, I reminded myself of my meaning-making machine.

I thought about the barriers to implementation and, stepping out on a limb, I said, "This must be a lot with everything else you're going through." That was all she needed; her body slumped, and she began to cry. I began to cry, too, as I got this teacher some tissues. She didn't speak, but we cried together, and when she grabbed the tissue we held hands. She shared, "My aunt is sick. I drove for hours to see her… and now I am here." She didn't have to say another word. This new understanding led me to my next statement. "I am so grateful for you… your sacrifice. I know you can't try three new ideas with this child, but how about one?" She nodded and agreed: "Yes, I can. I can try one new idea." Teachers can reflect and problem solve only when they feel safe and supported.

> "Administrators want teachers to be sensitive to the home life of kids. [A]dministrators need to be sensitive to the home life of their teachers… They need compassion too."
>
> —Danny Steele, EdD, principal

The teacher's statement forever changed how I coach. How can I sit across from that teacher and say, "All behavior is communication," and not try to understand her communication? How can I say I dislike negativity and then be negative? I am only promoting what I don't like. If I alter my behavior because of someone else's behavior, I will become like a leaf being blown in the wind, controlled by emotions that have nothing to do with

Chapter 7: Pushing Past Conflict with Adults | 233

me. To ask anyone to leave their problems at the door doesn't understand that problems permeate your spirit and soul. There shouldn't be anything "unprofessional" about naming barriers to implementation. Equity isn't a bunch of sayings, it involves a bunch of doing. Every. Single. Day. When done right, you should feel tired! I was elevating equity all day! Dance like no one is watching, but implement equity as if everyone is watching. Ask yourself, "How would someone else see this? Am I on the right side of equity?"

Meaning making should also be done with families. I remember a parent saying, "You don't have rules until you're twelve." My first thought was, "If you don't have rules until you're twelve, somebody's going to jail." (I warned you my first thought was always my most biased.) Luckily, I had a water bottle in my reach and took a long sip to make meaning before responding. Maybe rules were abuse to this parent as a child. Maybe they had trauma. Let me listen and meet in the middle. "Thanks for trusting me enough to share something so personal with me. I see you don't have rules, and that is okay (my eyeballs itched a bit here, but I kept going). I do have rules in my classroom. I noticed you mentioned you read to your child before bed (at one in the morning!). What if I send home a book about my rules to read to your child each night?" The parent agreed when I showed her the book full of pictures of her child posing—not following the rules, just posing as the other children followed the rules. (I will take what I can get.) Goes to show you if your eyeballs don't itch at least once a day, honey, you are not elevating equity as much as you could be.

Step 5: Choose a Cycle

When doing your laundry, you must choose a cycle. Elevating equity is always about choice. Is this situation delicate? Is this a heavy load? My worst enemy is a blank sheet of paper. Where do I begin? The suggestions in the following chart are there to get you started. The most balanced plans use a suggestion from each cycle, but ultimately you get to choose what works best for you.

Worksheet Warfare

Surprisingly, some of my most successful outcomes have come from changing myself. Travel with me to the Midwest, where I had worked with an early childhood program as a consultant for three years. I noticed that each year I had informed one of the teachers

Change You, Change the Adult, Change the Consequences

Change You

Check or describe all you will apply:

- ☐ Use positive language—Tell adult what you want them to do
- ☐ Let adult choose the sequence of activities or the order in which they would accomplish a goal or task
- ☐ Show adult visual examples of each stage of a goal with real life examples
- ☐ Add adult interest to activity or ask adult where they feel comfortable starting a goal—Assess readiness for goal

- ☐ Instead of "telling" adult, ask adult about how they think they should carry out tasks
- ☐ Give more detailed feedback
- ☐ Set time bound goals
- ☐ Set fewer goals—They may be overwhelming
- ☐ Start feedback with strengths then move to areas of growth

- ☐ Give more immediate feedback
- ☐ Explain expectations in multisensory way (visuals, charts, graphs, etc.) to enhance comprehension
- ☐ Demonstrate or model goal for adult

Materials needed:

Change the Adult with Skill Building

Check or describe all you will apply:

- ☐ Teach adult to "*Push Past It!*"
- ☐ Teach adult self-care strategies
- ☐ Teach adult new skill with examples from teaching books/videos or pictures
- ☐ Teach adult by modeling
- ☐ Teach adult problem solving and support decision making
- ☐ Other:

Materials needed:

Change Consequences/Responses

Check or describe all you will apply:

- ☐ Give attention to adult using "shout outs" and "brag boards" after doing right thing
- ☐ Provide encouragement
- ☐ Let adult choose a positive reinforcement
- ☐ Effort is encouraged even if adult doesn't accomplish task or goal

- ☐ Reward system used to track new skills
- ☐ Adult is shown tally of all the right things they are doing
- ☐ Adult reminded what to do with words and visuals

Materials needed:

that it was against the program's quality rating standards to use worksheets. I had done this twice, and the teacher would nod and smile. But, doggone it, if I didn't come back a third year and see—you guessed it—worksheets!

By then, I had grown children, and if you are a parent you know for a fact you can't tell an adult anything. So, this year I decided to change my behavior and elevate equity with collaboration instead of control. You cross a boundary when you try to control the decision of others. So this year, after I shared the glows, I asked matter-of-factly about the worksheets she had used that day. I saw her eyes sparkle, and even though I started breaking out in hives, I commented on her eyes. "You really like worksheets, don't you?" She replied, "Yes!" and went on to share what the children learned and shared about past students who were successful in kindergarten. My body was on fire with itchiness as I listened. I was thinking with every fiber of my being, "Worksheets are NOT developmentally appropriate for young children!" I held it together to listen without judgment. I didn't have to be neutral—thank goodness—I just had to respond with neutrality. Not fake neutrality. I was genuinely trying to listen and to understand her. Then I came to it! This woman wasn't evil. She loved children and loved seeing them learn, and so did I! I listened and then said, "I really enjoyed listening to you and how you genuinely helped and supported young children over the years with great success." I truly did believe her. And then I asked her if she minded if I shared my ideas that have been successful. And she said she didn't mind. After our conversation, she made immediate changes in her room for the first time in three years. Listening begets listening.

Here are more tips for collaborations that elevate equity instead of ego.

- Any attempt, no matter how big or small, to help a child or family should be acknowledged and celebrated.

- Put things in proper perspective. This teacher was a standout. The "worksheet warfare," as it came to be called, was really the only area for growth I could identify for this teacher. Does it make sense to die on that hill? Which do I value more: being right or being supportive? ~~Being right!~~ Being supportive. Of course, there is no other answer. Being supportive.

- Share ideas. Unless an idea will physically harm a child or family, give space for all ideas. An equity conversation is not a lecture. No one dominates the conversation or the collaboration.

- Listen for positivity, and center your ideas within the ideas of the other person's interests. I mean really listen. This teacher deserved to be listened to. It is a human right to be heard and treated with dignity. Listen for love. Listen for strengths. I mean, you really have to love children for your eyes to light up when you talk about their learning. We have that in common. We love seeing children learn; we just differed on how that should be done.

- Give families and colleagues time to process new ideas. Come on, it wasn't like I'd never ever used a worksheet over the course of my career. Keep in mind, I had years of opportunities to integrate my ideas on how young children should learn over time, and so should this teacher.

Step 6: Be Patient during the Trying Time

You're ready for the last step! You've tried setting boundaries, giving reflections, and asking open-ended questions. These attempts are getting you nowhere! The conflicts are giving you hives and wreaking havoc in your program. I get it. My sister, Lisa, is a social worker and has seen my workshops on *Push Past It!* I was venting on the phone one day about a program, and she said, "Look for the positives…" I hung up. I thought, "Why are you on their side!" She was like *Push Past It!* I had created that tool, and intellectually I know it works, but I am in the same boat as everyone else when it comes to implementing these ideas consistently. Just like exercise or eating healthy. Some days I nail it. Other days I struggle to navigate it.

> "One doesn't have to operate with great malice to do great harm. The absence of empathy and understanding are sufficient."
>
> —Charles M. Blow, *Fire Shut Up in My Bones*

Epic Equity Fail

I was working with a teacher on an intense challenging behavior. We had been working together a short while, maybe a few months. She called me one day, and even though I had a meeting in twenty minutes, I took the call. Big mistake. We started talking about the child's behavior and how strategies we had talked about a week ago weren't working. If you notice on my meaning-making machine for use with children, there are two warnings:

- All strategies should be given 4–6 weeks to work before applying a new strategy.
- Behavior can get worse before it gets better.

Why didn't I take my own advice? I looked at the clock and realized I now had five minutes before my meeting. The music you hear in a horror movie started playing in my head. Then the words just fell out of my mouth: "Strategies don't work. You need to work." Let's just say I failed at pushing past it. I didn't elevate equity in that moment. I tried repair and kept working with the program, but I know that exchange affected our professional relationship. To this day, if she sees me she is very polite, but she doesn't turn her camera on when I lead a Zoom call.

What did I learn from that equity fail? That equity is hard and pushing past it is not a one-and-done endeavor. It is a process. And, like deodorant, you need to apply it every day. Just like eating healthy or exercising or sleep, you can't always "catch up" on equity. It is a continuous cycle of responding, reflecting, and trying again. Your skills are constantly evolving and growing over time, so embrace the process.

> "The most important spiritual growth doesn't happen when you're meditating or on a yoga mat. It happens in the midst of conflict… when you're frustrated, angry, or scared and you're doing the same old thing, and then you suddenly realize that you have a choice to do it differently."
>
> —Tiny Buddha

References and Recommended Reading

29 U.S.C. § 203. Fair Labor Standards Act of 1938. https://www.dol.gov/agencies/whd/flsa

Aboud, Frances E., and Shelagh Skerry. 1984. "The Development of Ethnic Attitudes: A Critical Review." *Journal of Cross-Cultural Psychology* 15(1): 3–34.

Acho, Emmanuel. 2021. *Uncomfortable Conversations with a Black Boy*. New York: Roaring Book Press.

Adichie, Chimamanda N. 2009. "The Danger of a Single Story." TED Conferences. https://www.ted.com/talks/chimamanda_ngozi_adichie_the_danger_of_a_single_story?language=en

Administration for Children and Families. 2017. "Trauma." Administration for Children and Families. https://www.acf.hhs.gov/trauma-toolkit/trauma-concept

Agustin, Mubiar, Henry Djoehaeni, and Asep Gustiana. 2021. "Stereotypes and Prejudices in Young Children." In *Proceedings of the 5th International Conference on Early Childhood Education* (ICECE 2020). Zhenzhou, China: Atlantis Press.

Aknin Lara B., J. Kiley Hamlin, and Elizabeth W. Dunn. 2012. "Giving Leads to Happiness in Young Children." *PLOS ONE* 7(6): e39211.

Albert, Alexa A., and Judith Porter. 1983. "Age Patterns in the Development of Children's Gender-Role Stereotypes." *Sex Roles* 9(1): 59–67.

Alessandra, Tony, and Michael O'Connor. 1995. *The Platinum Rule*. New York: Grand Central Publishing.

Alexander, Gerianne M., and Janet Saenz. 2012. "Early Androgens, Activity Levels, and Toy Choices of Children in the Second Year of Life." *Hormones and Behavior* 62(4): 500–504.

Allen, Rosemarie, Dorothy L. Shapland, Jen Neitzel, and Iheoma U. Iruka. 2021. "Viewpoint. Creating Anti-Racist Early Childhood Spaces." *Young Children* 76(2). https://www.naeyc.org/resources/pubs/yc/summer2021/viewpoint-anti-racist-spaces

Ambady, Nalini, Margaret Shih, Amy Kim, and Todd L. Pittinsky. 2001. "Stereotype Susceptibility in Children: Effects of Identity Activation on Quantitative Performance." *Psychological Science* 12(5): 385–390.

Anderson, Riana Elyse, Farzana T. Saleem, and James P. Huguley. 2019. "Choosing to See the Racial Stress That Afflicts Our Black Students." *Phi Delta Kappan* 101(3): 20–25.

Andrews, Erin E., et al. 2019. "#SaytheWord: A Disability Culture Commentary on the Erasure of 'Disability.'" *Rehabilitation Psychology* 64(2): 111–118.

Augsburger, David. 1982. *Caring Enough to Hear and Be Heard: How to Hear and How to be Heard in Equal Communication*. Grand Rapids, MI: Baker Publishing.

Bal, Vanessa Hus, et al. 2020. "The Adapted ADOS: A New Module Set for the Assessment of Minimally Verbal Adolescents and Adults." *Journal of Autism and Developmental Disorders* 50(3): 719–729.

Baron, Andrew S., and Mahzarin Banaji. 2006. "The Development of Implicit Attitudes: Evidence of Race Evaluations from Ages 6 and 10 and Adulthood." *Psychological Science* 17(1): 53–58.

Baron, Jonathan. 2006. *Thinking and Deciding*. 4th edition. New York: Cambridge University Press.

Barrera, Isaura, and Lucinda Kramer. 2009. *Using Skilled Dialogue to Transform Challenging Interactions: Honoring Identity, Voice, and Connection*. Baltimore, MD: Paul H. Brookes Publishing.

Barstow, Cedar. 2015. "The Power Differential and Why It Matters So Much in Therapy." *Good Therapy*. https://www.goodtherapy.org/blog/power-differential-why-it-matters-so-much-in-therapy-1009154#:~:text=The%20power%20differential%20is%20the,the%20core%20of%20ethical%20awareness

Bascandziev, Igor, and Paul Harris. 2014. "In Beauty We Trust: Children Prefer Information from More Attractive Informants." *British Journal of Developmental Psychology* 32(1): 94–99.

Batson, C. Daniel, et al. 1997. "Empathy and Attitudes: Can Feeling for a Member of a Stigmatized Group Improve Feelings toward the Group?" *Journal of Personality and Social Psychology* 72(1): 105–118.

Baumard, Nicolas, Olivier Mascaro, and Coralie Chevallier. 2012. "Preschoolers Are Able to Take Merit into Account when Distributing Goods." *Developmental Psychology* 48(2): 492–498.

BBC. 2022. "Left-Handers Day: Amazing Facts about Lefties." BBC. https://www.bbc.co.uk/newsround/53739189#:~:text=Research%20suggests%20that%20between%20ten,a%20lefty%20is%20pretty%20cool

Baumeister, Roy F., Ellen Bratslavsky, Catrin Finkenauer, and Kathleen D. Vohs. 2001. "Bad Is Stronger Than Good." *Review of General Psychology* 5(4): 323–370.

Begus, Katarina, Teodora Gliga, and Victoria Southgate. 2016. "Infants' Preferences for Native Speakers Are Associated with an Expectation of Information." *Proceedings of the National Academy of Sciences* 113(44): 12397–12402.

Bennett, Mark, and Fabio Sani, eds. 2004. *The Development of the Social Self*. New York: Psychology Press.

Bennett-Alexander, Dawn. 2015. "Practical Diversity: Taking Inclusion from Theory to Practice." TEDxUGA. https://www.youtube.com/watch?v=ExcDNly1Dbl

Bezo, Brent, and Stefania Maggi. 2015. "Living in 'Survival Mode': Intergenerational Transmission of Trauma from the Holodomor Genocide of 1932–1933 in Ukraine." *Social Science and Medicine*, 134: 87–94.

Bigler, Rebecca S., and Lynn Liben. 1993. "A Cognitive-Developmental Approach to Racial Stereotyping and Reconstructive Memory in Euro-American Children." *Child Development* 64(5): 1507–1518.

Biklen, Douglas, and Jamie Burke. 2006. "Presuming Competence." *Equity and Excellence in Education* 39(2): 166–175.

Bishop, Rudine S. 1990. "Mirrors, Windows, and Sliding Glass Doors." *Collected Perspectives: Choosing and Using Books for the Classroom*. Norwood, MA: Christopher-Gordon Publishers.

Blake, Peter R., et al. 2015. "The Ontogeny of Fairness in Seven Societies." *Nature* 528(7581): 258–261.

Blake, Peter R., and Katherine McAuliffe. 2011. "'I had so much it didn't seem fair': Eight-Year-Olds Reject Two Forms of Inequity." *Cognition* 120(2): 215–224.

Blake, Peter R., Katherine McAuliffe, and Felix Warneken. 2014. "The Developmental Origins of Fairness: The Knowledge-Behavior Gap." *Trends in Cognitive Sciences* 18(11): 559–561.

Blow, Charles M. 2015. *Fire Shut Up in My Bones*. Boston, MA: Mariner Books.

Boe, Josh L., and Rebecca J. Woods. 2018. "Parents' Influence on Infants' Gender-Typed Toy Preferences." *Sex Roles* 79(5–6): 358–373.

Bombay, Amy, Kimberly Matheson, and Hymie Anisman. 2014. "The Intergenerational Effects of Indian Residential Schools: Implications for the Concept of Historical Trauma." *Transcultural Psychiatry* 51(3): 320–338.

Booher, Dianna. 1999. "Communicate with Confidence and Give Constructive Criticism without Crippling Others." *Women in Business* 51(5): 44.

Brand, Bethany. 2022. "Mini Trauma Activity." *TeachTrauma*. https://teachtrauma.com/educational-tools/classroom-activities/

Brave Heart, Maria Y. H. 1999. "Gender Differences in the Historical Trauma Response among the Lakota." *Journal of Health and Social Policy* 10(4): 1–21.

Bronfenbrenner, Urie. 1979. *The Ecology of Human Development: Experiments by Nature and Design*. Cambridge, MA: Harvard University Press.

Bronson, Po, and Ashley Merryman. 2009. *NurtureShock: New Thinking about Children*. New York: Twelve.

Brown, Brené. 2007. *I Thought It Was Just Me (but It Isn't): Making the Journey from "What Will People Think?" to "I Am Enough."* New York: Avery.

Brown, Brené. 2014. "Brené Brown on Empathy." YouTube. https://www.youtube.com/watch?v=1Evwgu369Jw

Brown, Monica. 2011. *Marisol McDonald Doesn't Match/Marisol McDonald no combina*. New York: Children's Book Press.

Buckingham, Marcus, and Ashley Goodall. 2019. "The Feedback Fallacy." *Harvard Business Review*. https://hbr.org/2019/03/the-feedback-fallacy

Buffett, Jimmy, Will Jennings, and Michael Utley. 1984. "Burn That Bridge." *Riddles in the Sand*. Universal City, CA: MCA Records.

Butler-Sweet, Colleen. 2011. "'Race Isn't What Defines Me': Exploring Identity Choices in Transracial, Biracial, and Monoracial Families." *Social Identities* 17(6): 747–769.

Byars, Natasha, Raquel Munarriz Diaz, and Sandipan Paul. 2020. "Advancing Equity in the Early Childhood Workforce." *Zero to Three* 40(5): 28–35.

Cameron, Daryl, et al. 2019. "Empathy Is Hard Work: People Choose to Avoid Empathy Because of Its Cognitive Costs." *Journal of Experimental Psychology: General* 148(6): 962–976.

Campbell, Anne, Shirley Louisa, Charles Heywood, and Charles Crook. 2000. "Infants' Visual Preference for Sex-Congruent Babies, Children, Toys, and Activities: A Longitudinal Study." *British Journal of Developmental Psychology* 18(4): 479–498.

Carlson, Vivian J., Xin Feng, and Robin L. Harwood. 2004. "The 'Ideal Baby': A Look at the Intersection of Temperament and Culture." *Zero to Three* 24(4): 22–28.

Carlson, Vivian J., and Robin L. Harwood. 2000. "Understanding and Negotiating Cultural Differences Concerning Early Developmental Competence: The Six-Raisin Solution." *Zero to Three* 20(3): 19–24.

Carter, Craig R., Lutz Kaufmann, and Alex Michel. 2007. "Behavioral Supply Management: A Taxonomy of Judgment and Decision-Making Biases." *International Journal of Physical Distribution and Logistics Management* 37(8): 631–669.

Celano, Marianne, Marietta Collins, and Ann Hazzard. 2018. *Something Happened in Our Town: A Child's Story about Racial Injustice*. Washington, DC: Magination Press.

Charafeddine, Rawan, et al. 2016. "Children's Allocation of Resources in Social Dominance Situations." *Developmental Psychology* 52(11): 1843–1857.

Chávez, Vivian. 2012. Cultural Humility: People, Principles, and Practices. Video. https://www.youtube.com/watch?v=SaSHLbS1V4w

Chavous, Tabbye M., et al. 2008. "Gender Matters, Too: The Influences of School Racial Discrimination and Racial Identity on Academic Engagement Outcomes among African American Adolescents." *Developmental Psychology* 44(3): 637–654.

Chiao, Joan Y., and Vani Mathur. 2010. "Intergroup Empathy: How Does Race Affect Empathic Neural Responses?" *Current Biology* 20(11): R478–R480.

Child Welfare Information Gateway. 2018. Leaving Your Child Home Alone. Washington, DC: U.S. Department of Health and Human Services, Children's Bureau. https://www.childwelfare.gov/pubpdfs/homealone.pdf

Child Welfare Information Gateway. 2021. "Child Welfare Practice to Address Racial Disproportionality and Disparity." https://www.childwelfare.gov/pubpdfs/racial_disproportionality.pdf

Cho, Hyonsuk, and X. Christine Wang. 2020. "Fluid Identity Play: A Case Study of a Bilingual Child's Ethnic Identity Construction across Multiple Contexts." *Journal of Early Childhood Research* 18(2): 200–213.

Choi, Yangsook. 2003. *The Name Jar*. New York: Dragonfly Books.

Christ, Oliver, et al. 2014. "Contextual Effect of Positive Intergroup Contact on Outgroup Prejudice." *Proceedings of the National Academy of Sciences* 111(11): 3996–4000.

Cimpian, Andrei, Yan Mu, and Lucy Erickson. 2012. "Who Is Good at This Game? Linking an Activity to a Social Category Undermines Children's Achievement." *Psychological Science* 23(5): 533–541.

Clark, Kenneth B., and Mamie K. Clark. 1939. "The Development of Consciousness of Self and the Emergence of Racial Identification in Negro Preschool Children." *Journal of Social Psychology* 10(4): 591–599.

Clements, Andrew. 1997. *Big Al*. New York: Aladdin.

Cooper, Marianne. 2018. "Too Many Women in Corporate America Are Still the Only Woman in the Room." *Slate*. https://slate.com/human-interest/2018/10/women-corporate-america-diversity.html

Cooperative Children's Book Center. 2019. "The Numbers Are In: 2019 CCBC Diversity Statistics." Cooperative Children's Book Center, School of Education, University of Wisconsin–Madison. https://ccbc.education.wisc.edu/the-numbers-are-in-2019-ccbc-diversity-statistics/

Cooperative Children's Book Center. 2022. "Books by and/or about Black, Indigenous, and People of Color (All Years)." Cooperative Children's Book Center, School of Education, University of Wisconsin–Madison. https://ccbc.education.wisc.edu/literature-resources/ccbc-diversity-statistics/books-by-about-poc-fnn/

Corbit, John, et al. 2017. "Children's Collaboration Induces Fairness Rather Than Generosity." *Cognition* 168: 344–356.

Costello, Rose. 2021. "Is It All about the Money? How a Pay Freeze Affects Motivation." *Welcome to the Jungle*. https://www.welcometothejungle.com/fr/articles/pay-freeze-affect-on-motivation

Cramer, Phebe, and Tiffany Steinwert. 1998. "Thin Is Good, Fat Is Bad: How Early Does It Begin?" *Journal of Applied Developmental Psychology* 19(3): 429–451.

Danieli, Yael, Fran H. Norris, and Brian E. Engdahl. 2017. "A Question of Who, Not If: Psychological Disorders in Holocaust Survivors' Children." *Psychological Trauma: Theory, Research, Practice, and Policy* 9(S1), 98.

Davies, Kristin, et al. 2011. "Cross-Group Friendships and Intergroup Attitudes: A Meta-Analytic Review." *Personality and Social Psychology Review* 15(4): 332–551.

Day, Jennifer C., and Danielle Taylor. 2019. "In Most Occupations, Workers with or without Disabilities Earn about the Same." United States Census Bureau. https://www.census.gov/library/stories/2019/03/do-people-with-disabilities-earn-equal-pay.html

Dean, Ruth G. 2001. "The Myth of Cross-Cultural Competence." *Families in Society* 82(6): 623–630.

DeGruy, Joy. 2017. *Post Traumatic Slave Syndrome: America's Legacy of Enduring Injury and Healing*. 2nd edition. Portland, OR: Joy DeGruy Publications.

de Lange, Floris P., Micha Heilbron, and Peter Kok. 2018. "How Do Expectations Shape Perception?" *Trends in Cognitive Sciences* 22(9): 764–779.

Demetriou, Kyriakos. 2020. "Do You Want to Play with Me? Acceptance and Preference Dilemmas in Choosing Playmates with Physical Disability." *Early Child Development and Care* 192(6): 1–17.

Derman-Sparks, Louise, and Patricia G, Ramsey. 2006. *What If All the Kids Are White? Anti-Bias Multicultural Education with Young Children and Families*. New York: Teachers College Press.

Derman-Sparks, Louise. 2016a. "Guide for Selecting Anti-Bias Children's Books." Social Justice Books. https://socialjusticebooks.org/guide-for-selecting-anti-bias-childrens-books/

Derman-Sparks, Louise. 2016b. "What I Learned from the Ypsilanti Perry Preschool Project: A Teacher's Reflections." *Journal of Pedagogy* 7(1): 93–105.

Derman-Sparks, Louise, and Julie O. Edwards. 2019. "Understanding Anti-Bias Education: Bringing the Four Core Goals to Every Facet of Your Curriculum." *Young Children* 74(5). https://www.naeyc.org/resources/pubs/yc/nov2019/understanding-anti-bias#:~:text=Teachers%20will%20nurture%20each%20child's,pride%2C%20and%20positive%20social%20identities

Derman-Sparks, Louise, and Julie O. Edwards. 2021. "Teaching about Identity, Racism, and Fairness: Engaging Young Children in Anti-Bias Education." *American Educator* 44(4): 35–40.

Derman-Sparks, Louise, Julie O. Edwards, and Catherine Goins. 2020. *Anti-Bias Education for Young Children and Ourselves*. 2nd edition. Washington, DC: NAEYC.

Deschene, Lori (@tinybuddha). 2021. "The most important spiritual growth." Twitter, April 26, 2021, 3:45 p.m. https://twitter.com/tinybuddha/status/1386768322293899271?lang=en

Deschene, Lori. 2022. "The Quote Archive." Tiny Buddha. https://tinybuddha.com/wisdom-quotes/three-solutions-every-problem-accept-change-leave-cant-accept-change-cant-change-leave/

DesJarlait, Maria "White Cedar Woman." 2021. *I'm Not a Costume!* Self-published.

deVries, Marten W., and M. Rachel deVries. 1977. "Cultural Relativity of Toilet Training Readiness: A Perspective from East Africa." *Pediatrics* 60(2): 170–177.

Dewar, Gwen. 2020. "Stress in Babies: How to Keep Babies Calm, Happy, and Emotionally Healthy." Parenting Science. https://parentingscience.com/stress-in-babies/

DiAngelo, Robin. 2018. *White Fragility: Why It's So Hard for White People to Talk about Racism*. Boston, MA: Beacon Press.

Divecha, Diane. 2020. "Family Conflict Is Normal; It's the Repair That Matters." Greater Good Magazine. https://greatergood.berkeley.edu/article/item/family_conflict_is_normal_its_the_repair_that_matters?fbclid=IwAR3437TIMsVcLcP_PUvSMx4_JsmYyo6M7OC5_ZE7i6En-2z_8ErOlOScvDE

Dizon-Ross, Elise, Susanna Loeb, Emily Penner, and Jane Rochmes. 2019. "Stress in Boom Times: Understanding Teachers' Economic Anxiety in a High-Cost Urban District." AERA Open. https://doi.org/10.1177/2332858419879439

Donnellan, Anne M. 1984. "The Criterion of the Least Dangerous Assumption." *Behavioral Disorders* 9(2): 141–150.

Dotterer, Aryn M., Susan M. McHale, and Ann C. Crouter. 2009. "Sociocultural Factors and School Engagement among African American Youth: The Roles of Racial Discrimination, Racial Socialization, and Ethnic Identity." *Applied Developmental Science* 13(2): 51–73.

Doucet, Fabienne, and Jennifer K. Adair. 2013. "Addressing Race and Inequity in the Classroom." *Young Children* 68(5): 88–97.

Dumas, Tracy L., Katherine W. Phillips, and Nancy P. Rothbard. 2013. "Getting Closer at the Company Party: Integration Experiences, Racial Dissimilarity, and Workplace Relationships." *Organization Science* 24(5): 1377–1401.

Dunn, Elizabeth W., Lara B. Aknin, and Michael I. Norton. 2008. "Spending Money on Others Promotes Happiness." *Science* 319(5870): 1687–1688.

Duong, Thi Hoa, Ulla-Britt Jansson, and Anna-Lena Hellström. 2013. "Vietnamese Mothers' Experiences with Potty Training Procedure for Children from Birth to 2 Years of Age." *Journal of Pediatric Urology* 9(6): 808–814.

Eisenberg, Nancy, Natalie Eggum, and Laura Di Giunta. 2010. "Empathy-Related Responding: Associations with Prosocial Behavior, Aggression, and Intergroup Relations." *Social Issues and Policy Review* 4(1): 143–180.

Essler, Samuel, Anja Lepach, Franz Petermann, and Markus Paulus. 2020. "Equality, Equity, or Inequality Duplication? How Preschoolers Distribute Necessary and Luxury Resources between Rich and Poor Others." *Social Development* 29(1): 110–125.

Eyl, Eryc. 2014. "Your Meeting Is NOT Mandatory." LinkedIn Pulse. https://www.linkedin.com/pulse/20140623215939-4647240-your-meeting-is-not-mandatory/

Fabes, Richard A., Carol Martin, and Laura Hanish. 2003. Young Children's Play Qualities in Same-, Other-, and Mixed-Sex Peer Groups." *Child Development* 74(3): 921–932.

Fadiman, Anne. 1997. *The Spirit Catches You and You Fall Down: A Hmong Child, Her American Doctors, and the Collision of Two Cultures*. New York: Farrar, Straus, and Giroux.

Farson, Richard E. 1963. "Praise Reappraised." *Harvard Business Review*. https://hbr.org/1963/09/praise-reappraised

Farver, Jo Ann, and Yoolim Lee-Shin. 2000. "Acculturation and Korean-American Children's Social and Play Behavior." *Social Development* 9(3): 316–336.

Feeley, Sarah, director. 2016. *Raising Ryland*. CNN Films. 37 mins.

Fenaughty, John, and Niki Harré. 2003. "Life on the Seesaw: A Qualitative Study of Suicide Resiliency Factors for Young Gay Men." *Journal of Homosexuality* 45(1): 1–22.

Fernández, Madeline. 2006. "Bilingual Preschoolers: Implications for the Development of Identity and Self-Concept." *Journal of Early Childhood and Infant Psychology* 2: 5–16.

Festinger, Leon. 1957. *A Theory of Cognitive Dissonance*. Stanford, CA: Stanford University Press.

Figley, Charles, ed. 1995. *Compassion Fatigue: Coping with Secondary Traumatic Stress Disorder in Those Who Treat the Traumatized*. New York: Routledge.

Flippin, Royce. 2022. "Hyperfocus: The ADHD Phenomenon of Intense Fixation." *ADDitude*. https://www.additudemag.com/understanding-adhd-hyperfocus/

France, Paul Emerich. 2014. "Invisible Identities: Letting Yourself Be Seen." July 30, Blog. https://www.paulemerich.com/blog/2014/07/30/invisible-identities-letting-yourself-be-seen

Gaither, Sarah, Samantha Fan, and Katherine Kinzler. 2020. "Thinking about Multiple Identities Boosts Children's Flexible Thinking." *Developmental Science* 23(1): e0012871.

Galinsky, Adam D., et al. 2013. "The Reappropriation of Stigmatizing Labels: The Reciprocal Relationship between Power and Self-Labeling." *Psychological Science* 24(10): 2020–2029.

Galinsky, Ellen. 1987. *The Six Stages of Parenthood*. Reading, MA: Perseus Books.

Gallagher, Peggy A., Janice Fialka, Cheryl Rhodes, and Cindy Arceneaux. 2002. "Working with Families: Rethinking Denial." *Young Exceptional Children* 5(2): 11–17.

Garrett, R. Kelly, and Brian E. Weeks. 2013. "The Promise and Peril of Real-Time Corrections to Political Misperceptions." In *Proceedings of the 2013 Conference on Computer-Supported Cooperative Work Companion*. New York: Association for Computing Machinery.

Georges, Leah. 2019. "How Generational Stereotypes Hold Us Back at Work." TEDxCreightonU. https://www.ted.com/talks/leah_georges_how_generational_stereotypes_hold_us_back_at_work/transcript?language=en

Gianino, Andrew, and Edward Tronick. 1988. "The Mutual Regulation Model: The Infant's Self and Interactive Regulation and Coping and Defensive Capacities." In *Stress and Coping Across Development*. Hillsdale, NJ: Lawrence Erlbaum Assoc.

Glazier, Jocelyn. 2003. "Moving Closer to Speaking the Unspeakable: White Teachers Talking about Race." *Teacher Education Quarterly* 30(1): 73–94.

Glazier, Jocelyn, et al. 2000. "Teacher Learning in Response to Autobiographical Literature." In *Reader Response in Secondary and College Classrooms*. 2nd edition. Mahwah, NJ: Lawrence Erlbaum Associates.

Goleman, Daniel. 2013. "The Social Brain." LinkedIn. https://www.linkedin.com/pulse/20130201162026-117825785-the-social-brain/

Goodman, Bryan. 2020. "Children Notice Race Several Years before Adults Want to Talk about It." American Psychological Association. https://www.apa.org/news/press/releases/2020/08/children-notice-race

Goodman, Diane. 2000. "Motivating People from Privileged Groups to Support Social Justice." *Teachers College Record* 102(6): 1061–1085.

Goodwin, Doris Kearns. 2018. *Leadership in Turbulent Times*. New York: Simon and Schuster.

Goodwyn, Susan W., and Linda P. Acredolo. 1993. "Symbolic Gesture versus Word: Is There a Modality Advantage for Onset of Symbol Use?" *Child Development* 64(3): 688–701.

Goodwyn, Susan W., Linda P. Acredolo, and Catherine A. Brown. 2000. "Impact of Symbolic Gesturing on Early Language Development." *Journal of Nonverbal Behavior* 24(2): 81–103.

Gordon, Patrice. 2022. *Reverse Mentoring: Removing Barriers and Building Belonging in the Workplace*. New York: Hachette Go.

Gorman, Amanda. 2021. *The Hill We Climb: An Inaugural Poem for the Country*. New York: Viking.

Gottman, John M. 1993. "A Theory of Marital Dissolution and Stability." *Journal of Family Psychology* 7(1): 57–75.

Gottman, John M. 1994a. *What Predicts Divorce? The Relationship between Marital Processes and Marital Outcomes*. Hillsdale, NJ: Lawrence Erlbaum Assoc.

Gottman, John M. 1994b. *Why Marriages Succeed or Fail: And How You Can Make Yours Last*. New York: Fireside.

Gottman, John M. 2022. "The 6 Things That Predict Divorce." The Gottman Institute. https://www.gottman.com/blog/the-6-things-that-predict-divorce/

Grabot, Laetitia, and Christoph Kayser. 2020. "Alpha Activity Reflects the Magnitude of an Individual Bias in Human Perception." *Journal of Neuroscience* 40(17): 3443–3454.

Grady, Constance. 2020. "Why the Term 'BIPOC' Is So Complicated, Explained by Linguists." Vox. https://www.vox.com/2020/6/30/21300294/bipoc-what-does-it-mean-critical-race-linguistics-jonathan-rosa-deandra-miles-hercules

Green, Sara E. 2003. "'What Do You Mean, "What's Wrong with Her?"': Stigma and the Lives of Families of Children with Disabilities." *Social Science and Medicine* 57(8): 1361–1374.

Grisham, Dana L., and Paul Molinelli. 1995. *Cooperative Learning: Professional's Guide*. Westminster, CA: Teacher Created Materials.

Gülgöz, Selin, Eric M. Gomez, Madeleine DeMeules, and Kristina R. Olson. 2018. "Children's Evaluation and Categorization of Transgender Children." *Journal of Cognition and Development* 19(4): 325–344.

Hargreaves, Andy. 1994. *Changing Teachers, Changing Times: Teachers' Work and Culture in the Postmodern Age*. London, UK: Cassell.

Hargreaves, Andy. 1998. "The Emotional Practice of Teaching." *Teaching and Teacher Education* 14(8): 835–854.

Hargreaves, Andy. 2000. "Mixed Emotions: Teachers' Perceptions of Their Interactions with Students." *Teaching and Teacher Education* 16(8): 811–826.

Hargreaves, Andy. 2001. "Emotional Geographies of Teaching." *Teachers College Record* 103(6): 1056–1080.

Hargreaves, Andy. 2003. *Teaching in the Knowledge Society: Education in the Age of Insecurity*. New York: Teachers College Press.

Harriger, Jennifer A., Rachel M. Calogero, David C. Witherington, and Jane E. Smith. 2010. "Body Size Stereotyping and Internalization of the Thin Ideal in Preschool Girls." *Sex Roles* 63: 609–620.

Harris, Nadine B. 2018. *The Deepest Well: Healing the Long-Term Effects of Childhood Trauma and Adversity*. Boston, MA: Houghton Mifflin Harcourt.

Hatt, Beth. 2007. "Street Smarts vs. Book Smarts: The Figured World of Smartness in the Lives of Marginalized, Urban Youth." *The Urban Review* 39(2): 145–166.

Hatzenbuehler, Mark. 2011. "The Social Environment and Suicide Attempts in Lesbian, Gay, and Bisexual Youth." *Pediatrics* 127(5): 896–903.

Haupt, Randy L., and Amy J. Shockley. 2020. "Whataboutery [Ethically Speaking]." *IEEE Antennas and Propagation Magazine* 62(3): 118–119.

Heiphetz, Larisa, Elizabeth Spelke, and Mahzarin Banaji. 2013. "Patterns of Implicit and Explicit Attitudes in Children and Adults: Tests in the Domain of Religion." *Journal of Experimental Psychology: General* 142(3): 864–879.

Higa, Darryl, et al. 2014. "Negative and Positive Factors Associated With the Well-Being of Lesbian, Gay, Bisexual, Transgender, Queer, and Questioning (LGBTQ) Youth." *Youth and Society* 46(5): 663–687.

Hildebrand, Verna P., Lillian A. Phenice, Mary M. Gray, and Rebecca P. Hines. 2007. *Knowing and Serving Diverse Families*. 3rd edition. New York: Pearson.

Hirschfeld, Lawrence A. 2008. "Children's Developing Conceptions of Race." In *Handbook of Race, Racism, and the Developing Child*. Hoboken, NJ: John Wiley and Sons.

Hobson, Mellody. 2014. "Color Blind or Color Brave?" TEDx Talk. https://www.ted.com/talks/mellody_hobson_color_blind_or_color_brave/transcript?language=en

Hollett, Karen B. 2019. "Anti-Bias Education in Action: One Center's Journey to Learn and Teach an Anti-Bias Curriculum." Blog. NAEYC. https://www.naeyc.org/resources/blog/anti-bias-education-in-action

Holub, Shayla C. 2008. "Individual Differences in the Anti-Fat Attitudes of Preschool Children: The Importance of Perceived Body Size." *Body Image* 5(3): 317–321.

Hruza, Melissa. 2021. "2021 Teacher Spending Survey." Adopt a Classroom.org. https://www.adoptaclassroom.org/2021/07/29/how-much-do-teachers-spend-on-supplies/

Hudgens, Laura. 2022. "10 Ways to Rethink the Family Tree Project—And Be More Inclusive to All Students!" Bored Teachers. https://www.boredteachers.com/post/family-tree-alternatives

Hughes, Diane, et al. 2006. "Parents' Ethnic-Racial Socialization Practices: A Review of Research and Directions for Future Study." Developmental Psychology 42(5): 747–770.

Hung, Elena (@ElenaHung202). 2022. "She can't get inside the building because of her wheelchair." Twitter, October 4, 2022, 4:48 p.m. https://twitter.com/elenahung202/status/1577400344329719809?lang=en

Hunt, Vivian, Lareina Yee, Sara Prince, and Sundiatu Dixon-Fyle. 2018. "Delivering through Diversity." McKinsey and Company. https://www.mckinsey.com/business-functions/people-and-organizational-performance/our-insights/delivering-through-diversity

International Trade Union Confederation. n.d. *ITUC Economic and Social Policy Brief: The Gender Wage Gap*. https://www.ituc-csi.org/IMG/pdf/the_gender_wage_gap_en.pdf

Jackson, Peter, dir. 2012. *The Hobbit: An Unexpected Journey*. Beverly Hills, CA: Metro-Goldwyn-Mayer.

Jernigan, Maryam M., and Jessica H. Daniel. 2011. "Racial Trauma in the Lives of Black Children and Adolescents: Challenges and Clinical Implications." *Journal of Child and Adolescent Trauma* 4(2): 123–141.

Johannsen, Rebecca, and Paul J. Zak. 2020. "Autonomy Raises Productivity: An Experiment Measuring Neurophysiology." *Frontiers in Psychology* 11: 963.

Kahneman, Daniel, and Angus Deaton. 2010. "High Income Improves Evaluation of Life but Not Emotional Well-Being." *Proceedings of the National Academy of Sciences* 107(38): 16489–16493.

Kao, James. 1996. *Jamming: The Art and Discipline of Business Creativity*. New York: HarperCollins.

Katch, Jane. 2001. *Under Deadman's Skin: Discovering the Meaning of Children's Violent Play*. Boston, MA: Beacon Press.

Kelly, David J., et al. 2005. "Three-Month-Olds, but Not Newborns, Prefer Own-Race Faces." *Developmental Science* 8(6): F31–F36.

Kenedy, Robert A. n.d. "Why Being Wrong Is Good for You." York University. https://rkenedy.info.yorku.ca/online-links/critical-skills-for-students/why-is-it-great-to-be-able-to-make-mistakes/

Kenward, Ben, and Matilda Dahl. 2011. "Preschoolers Distribute Scarce Resources According to the Moral Valence of Recipients' Previous Actions." *Developmental Psychology* 47(4): 1054–1064.

Khalil, Aya. 2020. *The Arabic Quilt: An Immigrant Story*. Thomaston, ME: Tilbury House.

Killingsworth, Matthew A. 2021. "Experienced Well-Being Rises with Income, Even Above $75,000 per Year." *Proceedings of the National Academy of Sciences* 118(4): e2016976118.

King, Bernice A. 2020. "Dr. Bernice A. King Calls Out People Twisting Her Dad Martin Luther King Jr.'s Words." The Tonight Show with Jimmy Fallon. YouTube. https://www.youtube.com/watch?v=U2vYhF0PmjU

King, Martin L., Jr. 1963. *Strength to Love*. New York: Harper and Row.

Kircher, Mary, and Lita Furby. 1971. "Racial Preferences in Young Children." *Child Development* 42(6): 2076–2078.

Kluger, Jeffrey. 2014. "Your Baby Is a Racist—Why You Can Live with That." Time. https://time.com/67092/baby-racists-survival-strategy/

Knobloch-Westerwick, Silvia, and Jingbo Meng. 2009. "Looking the Other Way: Selective Exposure to Attitude-Consistent and Counterattitudinal Political Information." *Communication Research* 36(3): 426–448.

Knowledge at Wharton Staff. 2013. "Is the Party Over? The Unintended Consequences of Office Social Events." Knowledge at Wharton. https://knowledge.wharton.upenn.edu/article/is-the-party-over-the-unintended-consequences-of-office-social-events/

Koeslag-Kreunen, Mieke, et al. 2018. "When Leadership Powers Team Learning: A Meta-Analysis." *Small Group Research* 49(4): 475–513.

Kotler, Jennifer, Tanya Haider, and Michael H. Levine. 2019. *Identity Matters: Parents' and Educators' Perceptions of Children's Social Identity Development*. New York: Sesame Workshop.

Kour, Jasleen, Jamal El-Den, and Narumon Sriratanaviriyakul. 2019. "The Role of Positive Psychology in Improving Employees' Performance and Organizational Productivity: An Experimental Study." *Procedia Computer Science* 161: 226–232.

Kurzman, Charles. 2014. "Introducing Powerblindness." The University of North Carolina at Chapel Hill. https://kurzman.unc.edu/powerblindness/

Kurzman, Charles, et al. 2014. "Powerblindness." *Sociology Compass* 8(6): 718–730.

La Cour, Michael J., and Donald P. Green. 2014. "When Contact Changes Minds: An Experiment on Transmission of Support for Gay Equality." *Science* 346(6215): 1366–1369.

La Freniere, Peter, F. F. Strayer, and Roger Gauthier. 1984. "The Emergence of Same-Sex Affiliative Preferences among Preschool Peers: A Developmental/Ethological Perspective." *Child Development* 55(5): 1958–1965.

Lamminmäki Annamarja, et al. 2012. "Testosterone Measured in Infancy Predicts Subsequent Sex-Typed Behavior in Boys and in Girls." *Hormones and Behavior* 61(4): 611–616.

Lanius, Ulrich F., Sandra L. Paulsen, and Frank M. Corrigan, eds. 2014. *Neurobiology and Treatment of Traumatic Dissociation: Toward an Embodied Self*. New York: Springer.

Lavoie, Alaina. 2021. "Why We Need Diverse Books Is No Longer Using the Term #OwnVoices." WNDB. https://diversebooks.org/why-we-need-diverse-books-is-no-longer-using-the-term-ownvoices/

LeanIn.org and McKinsey and Company. 2018. Women in the Workplace. LeanIn and McKinsey and Company. https://womenintheworkplace.com/

Lee, Bruce. 1971. "Interview with Bruce Lee." The Pierre Berton Show. September 12. https://www.youtube.com/watch?v=fEDfznOP820

Lee, Grace Y., and Barbara Kisilevsky. 2014. "Fetuses Respond to Father's Voice but Prefer Mother's Voice after Birth." *Developmental Psychobiology* 56(1): 1–11.

Levison-Johnson, Jody. 2021. "Poverty and Neglect Are Not the Same—It's Time to Realign Our Response." American Public Human Services Association. https://aphsa.org/APHSABlog/mhhspp/poverty-and-neglect-are-not-the-same.aspx

Liebkind, Karmela. 1995. "Bilingual Identity." *European Education* 27(3): 80–87.

LoBue, Vanessa, et al. 2011. "When Getting Something Good Is Bad: Even Three-Year-Olds React to Inequality." *Social Development* 20(1): 154–170.

Long, Chelsea. 2022. "How the Parasympathetic Nervous System Can Lower Stress." Hospital for Special Surgery. https://www.hss.edu/article_parasympathetic-nervous-system.asp#:~:text=The%20parasympathetic%20nervous%20system%20is,%22rest%20and%20digest%22%20state

Lorenzo, Rocío, et al. 2018. "How Diverse Leadership Teams Boost Innovation." Boston Consulting Group. https://www.bcg.com/publications/2018/how-diverse-leadership-teams-boost-innovation

Lovejoy, Sandy. 2023. "What Is Reasonable Accommodation?" Monster. https://www.monster.com/career-advice/article/whats-reasonable-accommodation

Lummis, Max, and Harold W. Stevenson. 1990. "Gender Differences in Beliefs and Achievement: A Cross-Cultural Study." *Developmental Psychology* 26(2): 254–263.

Magazine, Anuj. 2013. "Understanding and Avoiding Emotional Hijacking." TechWell Insights. https://www.techwell.com/techwell-insights/2013/08/understanding-and-avoiding-emotional-hijacking

Mahdawi, Arwa. 2016. "The Surprising Solution to Workplace Diversity." TEDxHamburg. https://www.youtube.com/watch?v=mtUlRYXJOvI

Manushkin, Fran. 2018. *Happy in Our Skin*. Somerville, MA: Candlewick Press.

Marcelo, Ana K., and Tuppett M. Yates. 2019. "Young Children's Ethnic-Racial Identity Moderates the Impact of Early Discrimination Experiences on Child Behavior Problems." *Cultural Diversity and Ethnic Minority Psychology* 25(2): 253–265.

Marron, Dylan. 2018. "Empathy Is Not Endorsement." TED. https://www.ted.com/talks/dylan_marron_empathy_is_not_endorsement/transcript

Martin, Carol L. 1990. "Attitudes and Expectations about Children with Nontraditional and Traditional Gender Roles." *Sex Roles: A Journal of Research* 22(3–4): 151–165.

Martin, Dierdre, and Jane Stuart-Smith. 1998. "Exploring Bilingual Children's Perceptions of Being Bilingual and Biliterate: Implications for Education Provision." *British Journal of Sociology of Education* 19(2): 237–254.

McDonald, Allison. 2018. "How to Use Funds of Knowledge in Your Classroom and Create Better Connections." Blog. No Time for Flash Cards. https://www.notimeforflashcards.com/2018/02/funds-of-knowledge.html#:~:text=Funds%20of%20Knowledge%20can%20include,baby%2C%20or%20prepare%20a%20Seder

McDonald, Joseph P., Nancy Mohr, Alan Dichter, and Elizabeth C. McDonald. 2015. *The Power of Protocols: An Educator's Guide to Better Practice*. New York: Teachers College Press.

McFalls, Elisabeth, and Deirdre Cobb-Roberts. 2001. "Reducing Resistance to Diversity through Cognitive Dissonance Instruction: Implications for Teacher Education." *Journal of Teacher Education* 52(2): 164–172.

Magee, Joe C., and Adam D. Galinsky. 2008. "Social Hierarchy: The Self-Reinforcing Nature of Power and Status." *Academy of Management Annals* 2(1): 351–398.

McGill, Bryant, and Jenni Young. 2018. *Simple Reminders: Inspiration for Living Your Best Life*. Green Bay, WI: Simple Reminders.

McIntosh, P. 1989. "White Privilege: Unpacking the Invisible Knapsack." *Peace and Freedom* 1989(July/August): 10–12.

Merchant, Nilofer. 2019. "How Power Powers Ideas." TEDxUniversityofNevada. https://www.ted.com/talks/nilofer_merchant_how_power_powers_ideas/transcript?language=en

Merriam-Webster.com Dictionary. 2022. "Gaslighting." https://www.merriam-webster.com/dictionary/gaslighting

Metzger, Isha W., Riana Elyse Anderson, Funlola Are, and Tiarney Ritchwood. 2021. "Healing Interpersonal and Racial Trauma: Integrating Racial Socialization into Trauma-Focused Cognitive Behavioral Therapy for African American Youth." *Child Maltreatment* 26(1): 17–27.

Milken Institute the School of Public Health, The George Washington University. 2020. "Equity vs. Equality: What's the Difference?" GW Online Public Health. https://onlinepublichealth.gwu.edu/resources/equity-vs-equality/

Miller, Jonas G., Sarah Kahle, Natalie Troxel, and Paul Hastings. 2020. "The Development of Generosity from 4 to 6 Years: Examining Stability and the Biopsychosocial Contributions of Children's Vagal Flexibility and Mothers' Compassion." *Frontiers in Psychology* 11: 590384. https://doi.org/10.3389/fpsyg.2020.590384

Mitchell, Colter, et al. 2014. "Social Disadvantage, Genetic Sensitivity, and Children's Telomere Length." *Proceedings of the National Academy of Sciences* 111(16): 5944–5949.

Moll, Luis C., Cathy Amanti, Deborah Neff, and Norma Gonzalez. 1992. "Funds of Knowledge for Teaching: Using a Qualitative Approach to Connect Homes and Classrooms." *Theory into Practice* 31(2): 132–141.

MomentPath. 2019. "Equality Matters: How to Hire Diverse ECE Staff for Your Preschool." MomentPath. https://www.momentpath.com/blog/owners-directors-equality-matters-how-to-hire-diverse-ece-staff-for-your-preschool

Moore, Carla. 2021. "I wasn't meant to be a special needs mom…" August 5. Facebook. https://www.facebook.com/permalink.php?story_fbid=pfbid0rimoSNmVmLtwnaHDwC-dekdTye8aQxmwmZagTqby2RnW8kSXCwWbYCu4eUjhieNWml&id=100009466209216

Morrison, Toni. 1992. *Playing in the Dark: Whiteness and the Literary Imagination*. Cambridge, MA: Harvard University Press.

Moshman, Rachael. 2022. "Gaslighting Teachers with "Inspirational" Memes Needs to Stop." Bored Teachers. https://www.boredteachers.com/post/gaslighting-teachers

Mother Bridge of Love. 2007. *Motherbridge of Love*. Cambridge, MA: Barefoot Books.

Naile, Idah, and Jacob M. Selesho. 2014. "The Role of Leadership in Employee Motivation." *Mediterranean Journal of Social Sciences* 5(3): 175–182.

National Association for the Education of Young Children. 2011. Code of Ethical Conduct and Statement of Commitment. Position statement. https://www.naeyc.org/sites/default/files/globally-shared/downloads/PDFs/resources/position-statements/Ethics%20Position%20Statement2011_09202013update.pdf

National Black Child Development Institute. 2014. *Being Black Is Not a Risk Factor*. Silver Spring, MD: NBCDI. https://www.nbcdi.org/node/665

National Child Traumatic Stress Network. n.d. "Secondary Traumatic Stress." NCTSN. https://www.nctsn.org/trauma-informed-care/secondary-traumatic-stress

National Child Traumatic Stress Network. 2017. *Addressing Race and Trauma in the Classroom: A Resource for Educators*. NCTSN. https://www.nctsn.org/sites/default/files/resources//addressing_race_and_trauma_in_the_classroom_educators.pdf

National Partnership for Women and Families. 2022. *Black Women and the Wage Gap. Fact Sheet*. https://www.nationalpartnership.org/our-work/resources/economic-justice/fair-pay/african-american-women-wage-gap.pdf

Neugebauer, Roger. 1983. "Guidelines for Effective Use of Feedback." *Child Care Information Exchange* 5(3): 34. https://www.childcareexchange.com/library/5003201.pdf

Newheiser, Anna-Kaisa, et al. 2014. "Preference for High Status Predicts Implicit Outgroup Bias Among Children from Low-Status Groups." *Developmental Psychology* 50(4): 1081–1090.

Newhouse, Kara. 2020. "Diversifying Your Classroom Book Collections? Avoid These 7 Pitfalls." KQED. https://www.kqed.org/mindshift/57026/diversifying-your-classroom-book-collections-avoid-these-7-pitfalls?fbclid=IwAR0VMp6vuhcumHE7lNYdL_ZWJaGj8ZclTN-wk0Wp4yWd_F93ApwSzwSbS_0

Niaura, Dominykas. 2018. "Teacher Uses Band-Aids to Explain Difference between Equality vs. Equity, 8-Year-Olds Understand It Better Than Adults." BoredPanda. https://www.boredpanda.com/equality-equity-band-aid-student-lesson/?utm_source=google&utm_medium=organic&utm_campaign=organic

Nieto, Sonia. 2003. *What Keeps Teachers Going?* New York: Teachers College Press.

Nordli, Brian. 2022. "Pay Transparency: What It Is and How to Do It Right." Built In. https://builtin.com/people-management/pay-transparency

Nosek, Brian A., et al. 2014. "Understanding and Using the Brief Implicit Association Test: Recommended Scoring Procedures." *PLOS One* 9(12): e110938.

Nottingham Spirk. 2021. "Your Not-to-Do List: More Phrases that Stifle Innovation." Nottingham Spirk. https://www.nottinghamspirk.com/musings/your-not-to-do-list

Nyhan, Brendan, Ethan Porter, Jason Reifler, and Thomas J. Wood. 2020. "Taking Fact-Checks Literally but Not Seriously? The Effects of Journalistic Fact-Checking on Factual Beliefs and Candidate Favorability." *Political Behavior* 42(3): 939–960.

Nyong'o, Lupita. 2019. *Sulwe*. New York: Simon and Schuster Books for Young Readers.

Nyhan, Brendan, Jason Reifler, Sean Richey, and Gary L. Freed. 2014. "Effective Messages in Vaccine Promotion: A Randomized Trial." *Pediatrics* 133(4): e835–e842.

O'Brien, Marion, and Aletha C. Huston. 1985. "Development of Sex-Typed Play Behavior in Toddlers." *Developmental Psychology* 21(5): 866–871.

Okanda, Mako, and Shoji Itakura. 2008. "Children in Asian Cultures Say Yes to Yes-No Questions: Common and Cultural Differences between Vietnamese and Japanese Children." *International Journal of Behavioral Development* 32(8): 131–136.

Olson, Kristina R., and Elizabeth Spelke. 2008. "Foundations of Cooperation in Young Children." *Cognition* 108(1): 222–231.

Orellana, Marjorie F. 1994. "Appropriating the Voice of the Superheroes: Three Preschoolers' Bilingual Language Uses in Play." *Early Childhood Research Quarterly* 9(2): 171–193.

PACEs Connection. 2022. "A Conversation with Bruce Perry on *What Happened to You?*" YouTube. https://www.youtube.com/watch?v=YxI1OVVBGSw

Patton, Stacey. 2017. *Spare the Kids: Why Whupping Children Won't Save Black America*. Boston, MA: Beacon Press.

Paulus, Marcus, and Bibiana Rosal-Grifoll. 2017. "Helping and Sharing in Preschool Children with Autism." *Experimental Brain Research* 235(7): 2081–2088.

Paulus, Marcus, and Samuel Essler. 2020. "Why Do Preschoolers Perpetuate Inequalities? Theoretical Perspectives on Inequity Preferences in the Face of Emerging Concerns for Equality." *Developmental Review* 58: 100933.

Perry, Brea, Kathi Harp, and Carrie Oser. 2013. "Racial and Gender Discrimination in the Stress Process: Implications for African American Women's Health and Well-Being." *Sociological Perspectives* 56(1): 25–48.

Perry, Bruce D., and Oprah Winfrey. 2021. *What Happened to You? Conversations of Trauma, Resilience, and Healing*. New York: Flatiron Books.

Perry, Bruce D., et al. 1995. "Childhood Trauma, the Neurobiology of Adaptation, and "Use-Dependent" Development of the Brain: How 'States' Become 'Traits.'" *Infant Mental Health Journal* 16(4): 271–291.

Pettigrew, Thomas F., and Linda R. Tropp. 2006. "A Meta-Analytic Test of Intergroup Contact Theory." *Journal of Personality and Social Psychology* 90(5): 751–783.

Pettigrew, Thomas F., and Linda R. Tropp. 2008. "How Does Intergroup Contact Reduce Prejudice? Meta-Analytic Tests of Three Mediators." *European Journal of Social Psychology* 38(6): 922–934.

Piaget, Jean. 1952. *The Origins of Intelligence in Children*. Margaret Cook, translator. New York: International Universities Press.

Pohl, Rüdiger F. 2017. "What Are Cognitive Illusions?" In *Cognitive Illusions: Intriguing Phenomena in Thinking, Judgment, and Memory*. 3rd edition. New York: Routledge.

Pope, Alexander. 1711. *An Essay on Criticism*. London, UK: W. Lewis.

Powlishta, Kimberly K. 1995. "Intergroup Processes in Childhood: Social Categorization and Sex Role Development." *Developmental Psychology* 31(5): 781–788.

Pryce, Jessica. 2018. "To Transform Welfare, Take Race out of the Equation." TEDx Talk. https://www.ted.com/talks/jessica_pryce_to_transform_child_welfare_take_race_out_of_the_equation/ transcript?language=en

Quizlet. 2023. "16 Elements of Grammar." Quizlet. https://quizlet.com/68266062/16-elements-of-grammar-flash-cards/#:~:text=Adjectives%20Definition%3A%20a%20word%20or,to%20modify%20or%20describe%20it.

Raabe, Tobias, and Andreas Beelmann. 2011. "Development of Ethnic, Racial, and National Prejudice in Childhood and Adolescence: A Multinational Meta-Analysis of Age Differences." *Child Development* 82(6): 1715–1737.

Rakoczy, Hannes, Marlen Kaufmann, and Karoline Lohse. 2016. "Young Children Understand the Normative Force of Standards of Equal Resource Distribution." *Journal of Experimental Child Psychology* 150: 396–403.

Reis, Harry T., and Stephanie Wright. 1982. "Knowledge of Sex-Role Stereotypes in Children Aged 3 to 5." *Sex Roles* 8(10): 1049–1056

Renno, Maggie P., and Kristin Shutts. 2015. "Children's Social Category-Based Giving and Its Correlates: Expectations and Preferences." *Developmental Psychology* 51(4): 533–543.

Rivas-Drake, Deborah, et al. 2014. "Ethnic and Racial Identity in Adolescence: Implications for Psychosocial, Academic, and Health Outcomes." *Child Development* 85(1): 40–57.

Rizzo, Michael, and Melanie Killen. 2016. "Children's Understanding of Equity in the Context of Inequality." *British Journal of Developmental Psychology* 34(4): 569–581.

Rogers, Fred. 1995. *You Are Special: Neighborly Words of Wisdom from Mister Rogers*. New York: Penguin.

Rogoff, Barbara. 2003. *The Cultural Nature of Human Development*. New York: Oxford University Press.

Ross, Loretta J. 2021. "Don't Call People Out—Call Them In." TEDx Talk. https://www.ted.com/talks/loretta_j_ross_don_t_call_people_out_call_them_in?language=en

Ryder, Gina, and Tanesha White. 2022. "How Intergenerational Trauma Impacts Families." *PsychCentral*. https://psychcentral.com/lib/how-intergenerational-trauma-impacts-families#how-its-passed-down

Sanchez, Kiara L., David A. Kalkstein, and Gregory M. Walton. 2021. "A Threatening Opportunity: The Prospect of Conversations about Race-Related Experiences between Black and White Friends." *Journal of Personality and Social Psychology* 122(5): 853–872.

Schäfer, Sarina J. 2020. "Understanding the Effects of Positive and Negative Intergroup Contact." Diss. FernUniversität in Hagen. https://ub-deposit.fernuni-hagen.de/servlets/MCRFileNodeServlet/mir_derivate_00001939/Diss_Schaefer_Intergroup_Contact_2020.pdf

Schäfer, Sarina J., et al. 2021. "Does Negative Contact Undermine Attempts to Improve Intergroup Relations? Deepening the Understanding of Negative Contact and Its Consequences for Intergroup Contact Research and Interventions." *Journal of Social Issues* 77(1): 197–216.

Schmidt, Marco F. H., and Jessica A. Sommerville. 2011. "Fairness Expectations and Altruistic Sharing in 15-Month-Old Human Infants." *PLOS ONE* 6(10): e23223.

Schmidt, Marco F. H., Margarita Svetlova, Jana Johe, and Michael Tomasello. 2016. "Children's Developing Understanding of Legitimate Reasons for Allocating Resources Unequally." *Cognitive Development* 37(2016): 42–52.

Schum, Timothy R., et al. 2002. "Sequential Acquisition of Toilet-Training Skills: A Descriptive Study of Gender and Age Differences in Normal Children." *Pediatrics* 109(3): E48. http://www.pediatrics.org/cgi/content/full/109/3/e48

Schumann, Karina. 2014. "An Affirmed Self and a Better Apology: The Effect of Self-Affirmation on Transgressors' Responses to Victims." *Journal of Experimental Social Psychology* 54: 89–96.

Searcy, Angela. 2019. *Push Past It! A Positive Approach to Challenging Classroom Behaviors*. Lewisville, NC: Gryphon House.

Searing, Linda. 2019. "The Big Number: Lefties Make Up about 10 Percent of the World." *The Washington Post*. https://www.washingtonpost.com/health/the-big-number-lefties-make-up-about-10-percent-of-the-world/2019/08/09/69978100-b9e2-11e9-bad6-609f75bfd97f_story.html

Seaton, Eleanor K., et al. 2011. "The Moderating Capacity of Racial Identity between Perceived Discrimination and Psychological Well-Being over Time among African American Youth." *Child Development* 82(6): 1850–1867.

Segal, Laura A., Jack Rayburn, and Stacey E. Beck. 2017. *The State Of Childhood Obesity: Better Policies for a Healthier America*. Washington, DC: Trust for America's Health.

Serrano-Villar, Maria, and Esther J. Calzada. 2016. "Ethnic Identity: Evidence of Protective Effects for Young Latino Children." *Journal of Applied Developmental Psychology* 42: 21–30. https://doi.org/10.1016/j.appdev.2015.11.002

Seuss, Dr. 1961. "Too Many Daves." *The Sneetches and Other Stories*. New York: Random House Books for Young Readers.

Shonkoff, Jack P., and Andrew S. Garner. 2012. "The Lifelong Effects of Early Childhood Adversity and Toxic Stress." *Pediatrics* 129(1): e232–e246.

Shutts, Kristin, Caroline Pemberton Roben, and Elizabeth Spelke. 2013. "Children's Use of Social Categories in Thinking About People and Social Relationships." *Journal of Cognition and Development* 14(1): 35–62.

Singarajah, Anantha, et al. 2017. "Infant Attention to Same- and Other-Race Faces." *Cognition* 159: 76–84.

Skočajić, Milica, et al. 2020. "Boys Just Don't! Gender Stereotyping and Sanctioning of Counter-Stereotypical Behavior in Preschoolers." *Sex Roles* 82(5–6): 163–172.

Slater, Alan, et al. 1998. "Newborn Infants Prefer Attractive Faces." *Infant Behavior and Development* 21(2): 345–354.

Smith, Craig, and Felix Warneken. 2016. "Children's Reasoning about Distributive and Retributive Justice across Development." *Developmental Psychology* 52(4): 613–628.

Sohn, Hansem, Devika Narain, Nicolas Meirhaeghe, and Mehrdad Jazayeri. 2019. "Bayesian Computation through Cortical Latent Dynamics." *Neuron*. 103(5): 934–947.e5.

Sol. 2021. "There Are More Children's Books about Animals Than People of Colour." An Injustice! https://aninjusticemag.com/there-are-more-childrens-books-about-animals-than-people-of-colour-efdea63d1ef0

Sotero, Michelle M. 2006. "A Conceptual Model of Historical Trauma: Implications for Public Health Practice and Research." *Journal of Health Disparities Research and Practice* (1)1: 93–108.

Spencer, Margaret B. 2006. "Phenomenology and Ecological Systems Theory: Development of Diverse Groups." *Handbook of Child Psychology: Theoretical Models of Human Development*. Vol. 1. New York: Wiley and Sons.

Spencer, Margaret B., Davido Dupree, and Tracey Hartmann. 1997. "A Phenomenological Variant of Ecological Systems Theory (PVEST): A Self-Organization Perspective in Context." *Development and Psychopathology* 9(4): 817–833.

Stanovich, Keith E. 2009. "Distinguishing the Reflective, Algorithmic, and Autonomous Minds: Is It Time for a Tri-Process Theory?" In *In Two Minds: Dual Processes and Beyond*. Oxford, UK: Oxford University Press.

Steele, Danny (@SteeleThoughts). 2021. "Administrators want teachers to be sensitive." Twitter. https://twitter.com/steelethoughts/status/1381369450167943168?lang=en

Steele, Jennifer R., Meghan George, Amanda Williams, and Elaine Tay. 2018. "A Cross-Cultural Investigation of Children's Implicit Attitudes toward White and Black Racial Outgroups." *Developmental Science* 21(6): e12673.

Steiner, David. 2019. "Staying On The Shelf: Why Rigorous New Curricula Aren't Being Used." Thomas B. Fordham Institute. https://fordhaminstitute.org/national/commentary/staying-shelf-why-rigorous-new-curricula-arent-being-used

Stevens-Watkins, Danielle, et al. 2014. "Examining the Associations of Racism, Sexism, and Stressful Life Events on Psychological Distress among African-American Women." *Cultural Diversity and Ethnic Minority Psychology* 20(4): 561–569.

Study.com. 2022. "Humility: Definitions, Forms, and Examples." Study.com. https://study.com/academy/lesson/humility-definition-forms-examples.html

Substance Abuse and Mental Health Services Administration. n.d. Tips for Disaster Responders: Understanding Historical Trauma when Responding to an Event in Indian Country. SAMHSA. https://store.samhsa.gov/sites/default/files/d7/priv/sma14-4866.pdf

Sullivan, Jessica, Leigh Wilton, and Evan P. Apfelbaum. 2021. "Adults Delay Conversations about Race Because They Underestimate Children's Processing of Race." *Journal of Experimental Psychology: General* 150(2): 395–400.

Svetlova, Margarita. 2013. "Development of Fairness Understanding in Preschoolers." PhD diss. Pittsburgh, PA: University of Pittsburgh.

Szuster, Anna, and Maria Jarymowicz. 2020. "Human Empathy of Automatic vs. Reflective Origin: Diverse Attributes and Regulative Consequences." *New Ideas in Psychology* 56: 100748.

Talbot, Donna M. 2008. "Exploring the Experiences and Self-Labeling of Mixed-Race Individuals with Two Minority Parents." *New Directions for Student Services* 2008(123): 23–31.

Tateo, Luca. 2012. "What Do You Mean by 'Teacher'? Psychological Research on Teacher Professional Identity." *Psicologia y Sociedade* 24(2): 344–353.

Tervalon, Melanie, and Jann Murray-Garcia. 1998. "Cultural Humility versus Cultural Competence: A Critical Distinction in Defining Physician Training Outcomes in Multicultural Education." *Journal of Health Care for the Poor and Underserved* 9(2): 117–125.

Thompson, Rachel H., et al. 2007. "Enhancing Early Communication through Infant Sign Training." *Journal of Applied Behavior Analysis* 40(1): 15–23.

Tremblay, Richard E. 2000. "The Development of Aggressive Behaviour During Childhood: What Have We Learned in The Past Century?" *International Journal of Behavioral Development* 24(2): 129–141.

Tremblay, Richard E. 2002. Prevention of Injury by Early Socialization of Aggressive Behavior." *Injury Prevention* 8(Suppl. IV): 17–21.

Tremblay, Richard E., et al. 1996. "Do Children in Canada Become More Aggressive as They Approach Adolescence?" In *Growing Up in Canada*. Ottawa, ON: Statistics Canada.

Tremblay, Richard E., Willard W. Hartup, and John Archer, eds. 2005. *Developmental Origins of Aggression*. New York, NY: Guilford Press.

Tripathy, Mitashree. 2021. "Constructive Criticism: Creating Positive Behaviour at Work Places." *Journal of Management and Technology* 21(4): 76–92.

Todd, Brenda K., John A. Barry, and Sara A. O. Thommessen. 2016. "Preferences for 'Gender-Typed' Toys in Boys and Girls Aged 9 to 32 Months." *Infant and Child Development* 26(3): e1986.

Toldson, Ivory A. 2019. "Why It's Wrong to Label Students 'At-Risk.'" The Conversation. https://theconversation.com/why-its-wrong-to-label-students-at-risk-109621

Tronick, Ed, and Marjorie Beeghly. 2011. "Infants' Meaning-Making and the Development of Mental Health Problems." *American Psychologist* 66(2): 107–119.

Ülger, Zuhal, Dorothea Dette-Hagenmeyer, Barbara Reichle, and Samuel L. Gaertner. 2018. "Improving Outgroup Attitudes in Schools: A Meta-Analytic Review." *Journal of School Psychology* 67: 88–103.

United Nations Population Fund. 2017. "The State of World Population 2017." United Nations Population Fund. https://www.unfpa.org/press/state-world-population-2017

University of California, San Francisco. 2023. "Unconscious Bias Training." Office of Diversity and Outreach, University of California, San Francisco. https://diversity.ucsf.edu/programs-resources/training/unconscious-bias-training#:~:text=Bias%20is%20a%20prejudice%20in,have%20negative%20or%20positive%20consequences

University of Toronto. 2017. "Infants Show Racial Bias toward Members of Own Ethnicity, against Those of Others." ScienceDaily https://www.sciencedaily.com/releases/2017/04/170411130810.htm

Urban Dictionary. 2023. "Surface Dweller." Urban Dictionary. https://www.urbandictionary.com/define.php?term=surface%20dweller

U.S. Census Bureau. 2012. "Nearly 1 in 5 People Have a Disability in the U.S., Census Bureau Reports." Press release. https://www.census.gov/newsroom/releases/archives/miscellaneous/cb12-134.html#:~:text=Adults%20age%2021%20to%2064,for%20those%20with%20no%20disability

U.S. Census Bureau. 2017. Disability Data Tables. https://www.census.gov/topics/health/disability/data/tables.2017.html

U.S. Census Bureau. 2021. "Current Population Survey, Annual Social and Economic Supplement: Table PINC-05: Work Experience in 2020—People 15 Years Old and Over by Total Money Earnings in 2020, Age, Race, Hispanic Origin, Sex, and Disability Status." https://www.census.gov/data/tables/time-series/demo/income-poverty/cps-pinc/pinc-05.html

Van Ausdale, Debra, and Joe R. Feagin. 2001. *The First R: How Children Learn Race and Racism*. New York: Rowman and Littlefield.

Vouloumanos, Athena. 2018. "Voulez-vous jouer avec moi? Twelve-Month-Olds Understand That Foreign Languages Can Communicate." *Cognition* 173: 87–92.

Walker-Moffat, Wendy. 1995. *The Other Side of the Asian American Success Story*. San Francisco, CA: Jossey-Bass.

Wallace, Kelly. 2015. "When Your Young Daughter Says, 'I'm a Boy.'" CNN. https://www.cnn.com/2015/03/18/living/feat-transgender-child-raising-ryland/index.html

Wang, Ming-Te, and James P. Huguley. 2012. "Parental Racial Socialization as a Moderator of the Effects of Racial Discrimination on Educational Success among African American Adolescents." *Child Development* 83(5): 1716–1731.

Weinraub, Marsha, et al. 1984. "The Development of Sex Role Stereotypes in the Third Year: Relationships to Gender Labeling, Gender Identity, Sex-Typed Toy Preference, and Family Characteristics." *Child Development* 55(4): 1493–1503.

Weisz, Erika, Desmond Ong, Ryan Carlson, and Jamil Zaki. 2020. "Building Empathy through Motivation-Based Interventions." *Emotion* 21(5): 990–999.

West Virginia Center for Children's Justice. n.d. "Handle with Care." West Virginia Center for Children's Justice. http://www.handlewithcarewv.org/handle-with-care.php

Whittington, Hillary. 2015. *Raising Ryland: Our Story of Parenting a Transgender Child with No Strings Attached*. New York: William Morrow.

Williams, Monnica T., Destiny Printz Pereira, and Ryan DeLapp. 2018. "Assessing Racial Trauma with the Trauma Symptoms of Discrimination Scale." *Psychology of Violence* 8(6): 735.

Willoughby, Brian. 2012. *Speak Up at School: How to Respond to Everyday Prejudice, Bias, and Stereotypes*. Montgomery, AL: Southern Poverty Law Center.

Winkler, Erin N. 2009. "Children Are Not Color Blind: How Young Children Learn Race." *PACE* 3(3): 1–8. https://inclusions.org/wp-content/uploads/2017/11/Children-are-Not-Colorblind.pdf

Wise, Cat. 2017. "Making the Grade: Anti-Bias Lessons Help Preschoolers Hold Up a Mirror to Diversity." PBS NewsHour. November 7. https://www.pbs.org/newshour/show/anti-bias-lessons-help-preschoolers-hold-up-a-mirror-to-diversity

Wong, Carol A., Jacquelynne Eccles, and Arnold Sameroff. 2003. "The Influence of Ethnic Discrimination and Ethnic Identification on African American Adolescents' School and Socioemotional Adjustment." *Journal of Personality* 71(6): 1197–1232.

Wörle, Monika, and Marcus Paulus. 2018. "Normative Expectations about Fairness: The Development of a Charity Norm in Preschoolers." *Journal of Experimental Child Psychology* 165: 66–84.

Xiao, Naiqi G., et al. 2017. "Infants Rely More on Gaze Cues from Own-Race than Other-Race Adults for Learning under Uncertainty." *Child Development* 89(3):e229–e244.

Xiao, Naiqi G., et al. 2018. "Older but Not Younger Infants Associate Own-Race Faces with Happy Music and Other-Race Faces with Sad Music." *Developmental Science* 21(2). DOI: 10.1111/desc.12537

Xiao, Sonya X., Rachel Cook, Carol Martin, and Matthew Nielson. 2019. "Characteristics of Preschool Gender Enforcers and Peers Who Associate with Them." *Sex Roles* 81(11): 671–685.

Yehuda, Rachel, and Amy Lehrner. 2018. "Intergenerational Transmission of Trauma Effects: Putative Role of Epigenetic Mechanisms." *World Psychiatry* 17(3): 243–257.

Yehuda, Rachel, Amanda Bell, Linda Bierer, and James Schmeidler. 2008. "Maternal, Not Paternal, PTSD Is Related to Increased Risk for PTSD in Offspring of Holocaust Survivors." *Journal of Psychiatric Research* 42(13): 1104–1111.

Zeglat, Dia, and Suzi Janbeik. 2019. "Meaningful Work and Organizational Outcomes: The Mediating Role of Individual Work Performance." *Management Research Review* 42(7): 859–878.

Zhou, Haotian, Elizabeth A. Majka, and Nicholas Epley. 2017. "Inferring Perspective versus Getting Perspective: Underestimating the Value of Being in Another Person's Shoes." *Psychological Science* 28(4): 482–493.

Index

A

Access to equity, 20–26

Activities in equity
- early elementary children, 91–93
- infants, toddlers, and two-year-olds, 66–68
- preschoolers, 76–77

Adult behavior laundry list, 213, 224–238

"Adult Meaning-Making Machine," 151

Affinity groups, 199–200

Anger, 159, 172

"At-risk" students, 19–20, 120

Attention-deficit hyperactivity disorder (ADHD), 142

Autism spectrum disorder, 48

Autonomy, 198–199

B

Being an "only," 177–178

Bias, 7, 26–29

Biliberating, 75–76

Bilingual children, 75–76

Buddy bench, 91

C

Call-out culture, 3–4, 187

Challenging behaviors, 1, 59–60, 213, 231–234

"Change You, Change the Adult, Change the Consequences" worksheet, 235

Change your language, 141, 183

Child development goals/milestones, 43–44, 114–121, 127–129

Children's books
- for early elementary children, 98–105
- for infants, toddlers, and two-year-olds, 61–64, 69–71
- for preschoolers, 79–90
- reassessing classics, 111

Choosing a cycle, 213, 234–237

Chronic exhaustion, 172

Classroom environment
- infants, toddlers, and two-year-olds, 61–62
- preschoolers, 73–75

Code switching, 86

Cognitive biases, 28–29

Cognitive dissonance, 197

"Colorblindedness," 7–10, 58

Compensation, 194–198

Conflict playlist, 216–218

Conflict resolution, 4, 205–239

Considering context, 227–228

Considering power differentials, 188–192

constructive criticism, 228–231

Contempt, 218–219

"Cooling Down Strategy for Teachers," 150

Coregulation, 162–163

Criticism, 218–219

Cultural brokers, 130

Cultural humility, 2–4, 30

Cultural responsiveness, 177

Culture clash, 206–209

D

Defensiveness, 218–219, 227

Deficit lens, 13, 201–202

Deficit model, 145–146

Dialogue, 31, 206–209

Differences
- what infants, toddlers, and two-year-olds know about, 37–41
- what kindergarteners through third-graders know about, 53–55
- what preschoolers know about, 44–47

"Difficult" topics, 2–4, 60

Disabilities, 18

Disenfranchised grief, 157

"Disrespect," 159

Diversity, 108, 180–183

Diversity Informed Mental Health Tenets, 161

E

Early childhood educators, 59–60, 105–112, 175–239

Early elementary children
- activities and activism in equity, 97
- books on equity, 98–105
- 4 Cs Framework, 104
- interpretive stage, 124–125
- learning about equity, 94–97
- listening for equity, 93–94

looking inward and outward for equity, 91–93

what they know about differences, 53–55

what they know about equity, 55–58

Ecological Systems Theory, 20

Egocentric behaviors, 21–22

Elevating equity leadership (EEL), team, 199–200

Empathy, 1, 7, 31–36

Equality, 47–48, 95, 170

Equitable practices at all levels of programming, 199–204

Equity, 4, 13–14

books about, 62, 64

creating access for others, 25–26

defined, 34–35

effect of the parasympathetic nervous system, 48–49

elevating with your staff, 175–204

empowering with, 13–14

family tree project, 17

in the teachers' lounge, 220–224

listening for, 64, 75–76, 93–94

modeling, 95

potential biases, 222–224

shame doesn't work, 30–36

teaching infants, toddlers, and two-year-olds about, 60–68

training, 184–185

vs. equality, 47–48, 95, 170

what educators know, 60

what infants, toddlers, and two-year-olds know about, 41–44

what kindergarteners through third-graders know about, 55–58

what preschoolers know about, 47–56

Ethnocentrism, 116–117

Evaluating conversations, 13–14

Evaluating ideas, 179

Exclusionary discipline, 1

Explain, Acknowledge, and Teach (EAT) tool, 65, 76, 94

Explanatory fictions, 151

Eye contact, 60–61

F

Families

children behave differently at school, 146–149

common questions, 139–140

equity and, 113–114

equity understanding of child development milestones, 127–129

family development, 122

five years old to adolescence, 124–125

get to know their identities, 173–174

Handle With Care (HWC) model, 149–152

help that hurts, 125–126

infancy/toddler, 123–124

learners' bill of rights, 143–145

potty training, 121–122

pregnancy, 122–123

setting aside your own perspective, 129–141

two- to five-year-olds, 124

viewing children through a strengths-based lens, 141–143

viewing through a strengths-based lens, 145–146

why it always depends, 114–121

"Family tree" project, 17, 162, 170

Feedback, 201–204, 228–231

Figuring out the care instructions, 213, 225–231

The 4 Cs Framework, 104

Funds of knowledge, 117–119

G

Gaslighting, 194–195

Gender-role stereotypes, 44–47

Give Five Before You Reply (GFBR), 210–213

Golden Rule, 35

"Grow Your Own" programs, 182–183

Guilt, 172

H

Hershey's Miniatures Personality Indicator (HMPI), 183–184

Hiring practices, 180–183

Historical trauma, 4, 153–155

dismissing 154–158

effects on the body, 154

getting to know family identities, 173–174

impact by age, 162–167

making sense of the senseless, 158–162

secondary trauma, 171–173

understanding your own, 167–171

Hopelessness, 172

Hypervigilance, 172

I

Identity

educators uncomfortable talking about, 60

getting to know your staff's, 183–186

language and formation, 46

power differentials and, 190

risk and protective factors, 24–26

setting goals, 108

supporting, 22–25

understanding families', 173–174

Implicit bias, 1, 29, 220–224

Inclusion, 180–183, 186, 209

Indian residential schools, 155–156, 180

Infants

activities in equity, 66–68

books on equity, 62–64, 69–71

impact of historical trauma, 162–165

learning about equity, 65

listening for equity, 64

nurturing stage, 123–124

responding to historical trauma, 164–165

symptoms of historical trauma, 163

teaching about equity, 60–62

what they know about differences, 39–41

what they know about equity, 41–44

In-group bias, 40–42

J

Jim Crow, 160, 165

Justice goal, 109

K

Kindergarteners

interpretive stage, 124–125

what they know about differences, 53–55

what they know about equity, 55–58

Knowledge-behavior gap, 50

L

Labeling, 7, 18–19

disabilities, 18

families, 124–125

in feedback, 201–202

language to evaluate, 20

self, 18

Language

changing, 183

identity formation and, 46

skills, 61

talking about grades, 141–143

to evaluate labels, 20

Leading activities in equity

early elementary students, 97

infants, toddlers, and two-year-olds, 66–68

preschoolers, 76–77

Learners' Bill of Rights, 143–145

Listening, 209, 236–237

Listening for equity

early elementary children, 93–94

infants, toddlers, and two-year-olds, 64

preschoolers, 75–76

M

Microaggressions, 186–188, 199

Mindfulness, 1, 78

Minimizing, 172

Motivating adults, 193–199

Multigenerational trauma. *See* historical trauma

Multigenerational workplaces, 186–188

Multisensory learning, 144

Myths. *See also* Stereotypes

model minorities, 120

special needs children, 120

tiger mom, 120

N

Negative emotions, 213–216

Nervous system, 48–49, 78

Neutral decision making, 222–224

O

Onlyness, 35

P

Pair mentoring, 200

Patience, 213, 237–238

Peer buddies, 77–78

People of Color (POC)
- families referred to foster care and CPS at higher rates, 227
- historical trauma, 160
- impact of race and neighborhood on home visits, 134
- negative views of, 117
- self-created label, 19
- wage discrepancies, 196

Phenomenological Variant of Ecological Systems Theory (PVEST), 20–21

Play, 145, 228

Potty training, 120–122

Poverty, 227

Power, 2–4, 177–178, 188–193

Powerblindness, 189, 205–209

Preschoolers
- activities in equity, 76–77
- authority stage, 124
- books on equity, 77–90
- gender-role stereotypes, 44–47
- impact of historical trauma, 165
- listening for equity, 75–76
- responding to historical trauma, 166–167
- symptoms of historical trauma, 165–166
- teaching about equity, 72–75, 76–77
- what they know about differences, 44–47
- what they know about equity, 47–56

Professional evaluations, 201–204

PUSH PAST IT approach to problem solving, 216–217

Q

Questions
- about families, 139–140
- filtering, 221
- space for, 211

R

Recognizing individuality, 34–35

Reflecting, 211

Reframe Game, 96

Repairing relationships, 224–225

Resistance, 159, 197

Respect, 2–4, 200

S

Safety, 143

Scaffolding, 210

Secondary trauma, 171–173

Self-labeling, 18

Self-protection triggers, 187

Self-reflection, 2–4, 15–19, 184

Shame, 30–36

Silent treatment, 218–219

Social constructs, 20–26

Social Identity Wheel, 184

Sorting out your feelings, 213–224

Spanking, 160

Stages of parenthood, 122–125

Stereotypes, 80, 91, 96

Strengths-based lens, 141–143, 145–146

Stress, 59–60

Supporting identity, 22–26

Surface dwelling, 161

T

Talking in tangents, 201–202

Toddlers
- activities in equity, 66–68
- books on equity, 62–64, 69–71
- impact of historical trauma, 162–165
- learning about equity, 65
- listening for equity, 64
- nurturing stage, 123–124
- responding to historical trauma, 164–165
- symptoms of historical trauma, 163
- teaching about equity, 60–62
- what they know about differences, 39–41
- what they know about equity, 41–44

Tokenism, 74–75, 111

Transparency, 197

Trauma Symptoms of Discrimination Scale, 155

Triggers, 15–16, 187, 227

Trust, 198, 200

Two-year-olds
- activities in equity, 66–68
- authority stage, 124
- books on equity, 62–64, 69–71
- impact of historical trauma, 162–165
- learning about equity, 65
- listening for equity, 64
- peak of human aggression, 205–206
- responding to historical trauma, 164–165
- symptoms of historical trauma, 163
- teaching about equity, 60–62
- what they know about differences, 39–41
- what they know about equity, 41–44

U

Understanding behavior meanings, 213, 231–234

V

Value judgments vs. observations, 127–129

Violent play, 165–167

W

Wage gap, 23–25

Whataboutisms, 226–227

White privilege, 18–19